FACING THE FIRE, TAKING THE STAGE

FACING THE FIRE, TAKING THE STAGE

Ritual, Performance, and Belonging in Buryat Communities of Siberia

Joseph J. Long

INDIANA UNIVERSITY PRESS

This book is a publication of

Indiana University Press
Office of Scholarly Publishing
Herman B Wells Library 350
1320 East 10th Street
Bloomington, Indiana 47405 USA

iupress.org

© 2025 by Joseph J. Long

All rights reserved
No part of this book may be reproduced or utilized in any form or by any means, electronic or mechanical, including photocopying and recording, or by any information storage and retrieval system, without permission in writing from the publisher. The paper used in this publication meets the minimum requirements of the American National Standard for Information Sciences—Permanence of Paper for Printed Library Materials, ANSI Z39.48-1992.

Manufactured in the United States of America

First Printing 2024

Cataloging information is available from the Library of Congress.

ISBN 978-0-253-07118-7 (hardback)
ISBN 978-0-253-07119-4 (paperback)
ISBN 978-0-253-07121-7 (epub)
ISBN 978-0-253-07120-0 (web PDF)

For Jenny, Elodie, and Orla, who define belonging for me

CONTENTS

Acknowledgments   ix

Notes on Transliteration, Terminology, and Style   xv

Acronyms and Abbreviations, Groups and Associations   xvii

Introduction   *1*

Mankhai, October 2005   *35*

1. Western Buryats in Context   *37*
2. Hospitality, Reciprocity, and Everyday Ritual   *67*
3. Kinship, Ritual, and Belonging in Western Buryat Communities   *85*
4. Constructing Culture, Framing Performance   *116*
5. Territorial Unification and National Cultural Autonomy in Cisbaikalia   *151*
6. Buryat Dance and the Aesthetics of Belonging   *170*
7. Institutionalized Shamanism and Ritual Change   *192*
8. Mankhai Revisited: Placemaking and Precedence after Territorial Autonomy   *222*

Conclusions, Returns, and Reflections   *238*

Bibliography   255

Index   271

ACKNOWLEDGMENTS

THERE ARE MANY PEOPLE TO thank for supporting the work that went into this book—practically, professionally, and personally. Any acknowledgments for a book of this kind, made in the political context of 2024, should start with the caveat that while this work is the product of many people sharing their experiences, knowledge, and worldviews with me, the conclusions are mine alone. I heard a diverse range of political views in Cisbaikalia. Those documented in this book cannot be attributed to any individual appearing in the text.

The research on which this book was based was made possible by support from the University of Aberdeen's College of Arts and Social Sciences from 2004 to 2008. The fieldwork was generously funded by the Canadian Social Science and Humanities Research Council's Baikal Archaeology Project, and the same project helped enormously in the last year of writing, as did a Radcliffe-Brown Trust award from the Royal Anthropological Institute. From 2003 to 2004, I enjoyed a year as an English-speaking union fellow in the Central Eurasian Studies department at Indiana University Bloomington. There I gained an invaluable grounding in the history and languages of the region, and I am grateful to the English-Speaking Union of Indianapolis and Indiana University's Office of International Services for that opportunity. Many of the ideas in this book were refined during return visits to the field during a research fellowship in the Siberian Studies Centre at the Max Planck Institute for Social Anthropology (2010–2013), for which I am very grateful. Having stepped away from this work for several years, I was immensely fortunate to receive a writing grant from the European Research Council's Arctic Domus project (Grant No. 295458) in 2018 in order to revisit some of the material on ritual and sacrifice presented here. I am also grateful to my current employers at Scottish Autism for facilitating a secondment to the University of Aberdeen to undertake that work.

I would like to set down my thanks to all at Indiana University Press who have helped see this book into production. Jennika Baines's enthusiasm for the project has been matched by great support from Bethany Mowry and Sophia Hebert in shepherding the book into production. Two anonymous peer reviewers gave very generous and helpful comments for revising the text. I am grateful to all of the production team for seeing this through to fruition.

Elements of the ethnography presented here in chapters 2 and 3 were previously published in the report "Libations and Ritual Offerings in Ekhirit Buriat Shamanism" in *Sibirica*. I also described some of the hospitality practices in "The Paradox of Alcohol in Western Buriat Communities: Vodka and Ritualised Commensality in Ekhirit Bulagat Raion" in *The Healing Landscapes of Central and Southeastern Siberia*, edited by David G. Anderson. Some of the observations on territorial unification in chapter 5 were reported in "The Dissolution of the Buryat Autonomous Okrugs in Siberia: Notes from the Field," co-written with Kathryn Graber and published in *Inner Asia*. Much of chapter 8 was also included in "Shamanist Topography and Administrative Territories in Cisbaikalia, Southern Siberia" in *Nomadic and Indigenous Spaces: Productions and Cognitions*, edited by Judith Miggelbrink,

Joachim Otto Habeck, Nuccio Mazzullo, and Peter Koch. I am grateful to Berghahn, the University of Alberta Press, Brill, and Routledge respectively for permission to reproduce this work. I am especially thankful to the Leibnitz Institute for Regional Geography in Leipzig for permission to reproduce Silke Dutzman's wonderful maps, originally created for *Nomadic and Indigenous Spaces*.

In Ust-Orda Okrug I owe the largest debt of gratitude to a small group of people. Without Gena and Sesegmaa Ankheev, Vasia Azhunov, Petr Azhunov, Erzhen Khamaganova, Aleksandr Khantuev, and Bato Petrunin, this work would not have been possible. I will remain forever grateful for the hospitality, care, and practical support they all gave me. I must also acknowledge the help and support of Anatolii Tarshinaev and Semien Bubaev, who both left us far too soon.

In Khuty and Novonikolaevsk, many people have shown me hospitality and kindness: these relatives, neighbors, friends, ensemble members, school and *dom kul'tura* staff are too numerous to mention individually, but I am grateful to them all. In Ust'-Orda, I extend my thanks to all of the *Stepniki* who indulged my curiosity, especially the ensemble director at that time, Valentina Zhambalova. The staff of the *dom kul'tura* in Ust'-Orda also gave me much of their time and made me very welcome at numerous cultural events. In Irkutsk, the staff and volunteers at the Center for Buryat Culture were always welcoming. Alexander and Alexandra Amagzaev and Roza Haltueva deserve special mention for their kindness and the time and practical assistance they gave me on many occasions. Members of the *Ayanga* and *Ulaalzai* ensembles at the center bore my many questions on dance with patience.

Through much of my research, I was a visiting researcher at Irkutsk State Technical University. Artur Kharinskii and his colleagues in the Laboratory of Ancient Technology gave me a warm welcome and were consistently supportive of my work.

Zhargalmaa Muraeva in the Faculty of Oriental Studies gave her precious time to help me with my elementary Buryat language skills.

During my research in Ulan-Ude, I was a visiting scholar at Buryat State University, where Tsymzhit Bazarova provided excellent tuition in Buryat language. Dora Matveeva provided a great deal of support and did much to help me feel at home in the city.

I count myself fortunate to have been part of an energetic and collegial community of anthropologists at the University of Aberdeen. Peter Loovers, Masha Shaw, Volodia Davydov, Vika Simonova, Donatas Brandisauskus, Amber Lincoln, Hiroko Ikuta, Rachel Harkness, and Caroline Gatt, among others, shared fieldwork experiences, friendship, and a melting pot of ideas. Elena Glavatskaya and Tanya Argounova-Low also gave helpful comments on my work. During postdoctoral research at the Siberian Studies Centre of the Max Planck Institute for Social Anthropology, I enjoyed valuable debates and discussions with Eleanor Peers, Ludek Broz, Stephan Dudeck, Ina Shroeder, Artem Rabogoshvilli, Kirill Istomin, Sayana Namsaraeva, and Jaraslava Haliganda, all under the caring leadership of Otto Habeck. I have also been part of a wider network of Mongolists and Siberianists who have shared ideas and comradeship on many occasions. They include Mette High, Kate Graber, Justine Buck Quijada, Tristra Newyear Yeager, Nikolai Tsyrempilov, Jargal Bagadarov, Stefan Krist, Istvan Santha, Tania Safonova, Craig Campbell, Katherine Metzo, and Margarita Khandagurova.

I was immensely fortunate in having Tim Ingold and Caroline Humphrey as mentors. Their generous engagement with this work has helped me develop my research into a book. I am also grateful to Caroline Humphrey for encouragement and input at several junctures since then, including the opportunity to present some of the ideas herein at the Mongolia and Inner Asia Studies Unit in Cambridge, where I received useful feedback. A kind invitation from Virginie Vaté to visit the Centre for Mongolian and Siberian Studies in Paris led to memorable discussions with Roberte Hamayon, who shared many valuable insights.

I have been lucky enough to have had some inspirational university teachers. Though I am not sure this is quite what he had in mind when suggesting postgraduate study, I would like to thank Michael Walton for encouraging my interest in Russian theatre as an undergraduate in drama at the University of Hull. Christopher Atwood at Indiana University gave me a thorough grounding in Mongolian studies during my year there, all undertaken with infectious enthusiasm and accompanied by great personal kindness and support. At Aberdeen, I benefitted greatly from the critical eye of Alex King, particularly in relation to performance theory and the drive to become a better writer. I would especially wish to acknowledge David Anderson as an exemplary mentor. He often went well beyond the call of duty to support me by providing close and incisive readings of my work and ensuring that I had funding for fieldwork, conferences, and writing. He remains a valued mentor to this day.

On a more personal note, I have to thank members of my family: Corin Long, who helped enormously in preparing the images for this book, and Anna-May Long, James Baker, and Simali Shah for their enduring support. My in-laws, Mihoko Narita and Angela Peachey, provided a great deal of practical help with childcare as I prepared this work for publication. It is impossible to overstate the myriad forms of love and support shown by my parents, Jess and Martyn Long, through many years of postgraduate study and long absences overseas. For this, and much else, I will be forever thankful. In the final, stressful months of PhD study, I was stabilized by the appearance of Jenny Peachey in my life whose love and care got me through to the finishing line. In the years between completing that thesis and writing this book, we have married and our lives have been enriched by the arrival of our daughters, Elodie and Orla. It is to the three of them that I dedicate this book.

NOTES ON TRANSLITERATION, TERMINOLOGY, AND STYLE

THROUGHOUT THE TEXT I USE the simplified version of the Library of Congress's system of Cyrillic Russian transliteration for Russian words, place names, and personal names. For Buryat words I use the more phonetic transliteration scheme used in wider Mongolian studies literature and systematized by C. P. Atwood for the Tibetan and Himalayan Library. The latter renders Buryat words more readable for a nonspecialist audience. For example *yokhor* is a clearer phonetic rendering of the Buryat circle dance than *ëkhor* for English speakers For uniquely Buryat letters in the Cyrillic script, Ө/ө appears as Ö/ö, һ/һ as H/h, and Ү/ү as Ü/ü. Where it may not be clear from the context whether a word is transliterated from Russian or Buryat, I indicate the origin with the abbreviation *Rus.* or *Bur.*

For Russian words and names that have common English spellings (e.g., Russia, Yeltsin, Soviet), I use those spellings. The same goes for common spellings of ethnonyms (e.g., Buryat), conventional spellings of place names (e.g., Yakutsk, Kyakhta), and the endings of place names (e.g., Buryatia rather than *Buriatiia*).

I refer to Russian territorial units such as oblast, okrug, and raion by their Russian terms rather than translate them as province, region, county, or district. I do so firstly because they have been so variously translated into English as to create confusion and secondly because the complex nature of Russian federalism requires specific discussion in the text. These terms appear in the *Oxford English Dictionary* so I do not use italics or mark soft signs when using them. I drop the Russian adjectival endings when referring to place names, so *Irkutskaia Oblast'*, for example, becomes Irkutsk Oblast here.

The geographical term Cisbaikalia refers to the area adjacent to the west coast of Lake Baikal (sometimes rendered as *Cis-Baikal*). The direct equivalent in Russian is *Predbaikal'e*, which is used in scholarly literature on the region. The region became increasingly referred to in official discourse during my time there as *Pribaikal'e* (more literally "next to Baikal") to assert an identity for the newly unified territory of Irkutsk Oblast and Ust'-Orda Buryat Autonomous Okrug. (See chap. 5.) The use of *Cisbaikalia* therefore ensures consistency over time and across changing territorial divisions and avoids confusion with the Pribaikal Raion of Buryatia on the eastern shore of the lake. Where I refer in the text to the Baikal region, I am not referring to an administrative territory but rather the wider geographical area around the lake.

In order to maintain consistency with both Russian and English-language literature on the region, I use ethnonyms and clan names based on transliteration from Russian.

Some scholars translate the Russian terms *natsional'nost* and *natsional'noi* respectively as *ethnicity* and *ethnic*. I prefer to render them in English as *nationality* and *national* as this is closer to the vernacular use and Soviet policy discourse. Moreover the Russian concept of *etnos* has a specific and distinct history, which is discussed in chapter 5.

Finally, I should note that in referring to the "2000s" in this text, I am denoting the decade rather than the century, though I hope that context generally makes this clear.

Except for public figures and those whose comments and activities are already on public record, pseudonyms are used for my interlocutors in this work.

ACRONYMS AND ABBREVIATIONS, GROUPS AND ASSOCIATIONS

ACRONYMS AND ABBREVIATIONS

ASSR	Autonomous Soviet Socialist Republic
BAO	Buryat Autonomous Okrug
BMASSR	Buryat-Mongolian Autonomous Soviet Socialist Republic
BMNP	Buryat-Mongolian People's Party (*Buryat Mongol'skaia Narodnaia Partiia*)
RSFSR	Russian Soviet Federative Socialist Republic
TsSRBE	Centre for the Preservation and Development of the Buryat Ethnos (*Tsentr Sokhraneniia i Razvitiia Buryatskogo Etnosa*)
USSR	Union of Soviet Socialist Republics
VARK	All-Buryat Association for the Development of Culture (*VseBuryatskaia Assosiatsiia Razvitiia Kul'tury*)

GROUPS AND ASSOCIATIONS

Ayanga	Buryat folklore ensemble in Irkutsk

Baikal ensemble	Professional state ensemble of the Republic of Buryatia
Bayan Tala	Buryat folklore ensemble in Novonikolaevsk village
Böö Murgel	An association of Buryat shamans based in Ulan-Ude
Burnatskom	Buryat National Committee in the years of the revolution
Edinaia Rossia	Political party in Russia supportive of the president
Khudain Gol	Buryat folklore ensemble in Ust'-Orda
Komsomol	Communist Youth League in Soviet times
Magtaal	Western Buryat folklore ensemble based in Ulan-Ude
Muskom	Committee representing Muslims in early Bolshevik governments
Negedel	The movement for national unity in the Republic of Buryatia
Sakhilgaan	Association of shamans in the Ust'Orda Buryat Autonomous Orkug
Stepnye Napevy	Steppe Melodies, the professional state ensemble of Ust'-Orda Buryat Autonomous Okrug
Tengeri	An association of modern shamans based in Ulan-Ude
Tsentr Buryatskoi Kul'tury	Centre for Buryat Culture (Irkutsk)
Ulaalzai	Buryat youth ensemble in Irkutsk
Yabloko	Opposition political party in Russia

FACING THE FIRE, TAKING THE STAGE

INTRODUCTION

THE ERDEM THEATER STANDS ON Lenin Street. It is one of a cluster of brick buildings in the center of Ust'-Orda settlement, some seventy kilometers north of Irkutsk in Cisbaikalia, the area to the west of Lake Baikal in southeastern Siberia. The settlement center features all the usual characteristics of Soviet infrastructure: the government administration buildings, a house of culture, a secondary school, a Lenin statue in the middle of a broad square, a war memorial, and half a dozen low-rise apartment buildings. Nestled among these Soviet archetypes are more recent additions: a small shopping complex and a modern hotel. Next to the hotel, a sculpture of a Buryat Mongol horseman in traditional clothing tells of the renaissance of indigenous cultural identity in post-Soviet Siberia. The settlement was the administrative center of the former Ust'-Orda Buryat Autonomous Okrug, a designated national territory for the Buryat people. Beyond the asphalt and brick of the settlement center stand rows of traditional wooden houses with their painted shutters, high fences, and gated yards. The surrounding grasslands of the southern-Siberian steppe are visible from throughout within the settlement.

Erdem is a Buryat word denoting knowledge and education. The theater bearing this title is home to *Stepnye Napevy* (Rus.

"Steppe Melodies"), Ust'-Orda's state song-and-dance ensemble who specialize in performing Buryat national culture. On a freezing January morning in 2006, Misha, a senior artist of the ensemble, greeted me with a bear hug and took me on a tour of the building. In the main auditorium, a pianist sat with the ensemble's chief soloist, an Honored Artist of the Soviet Union, while younger members of the group went through a series of voice exercises. In the dance studio upstairs, we sat in on a rehearsal for a forthcoming concert. Misha talked me through the Buryat myths that the dance was based on before the choreographer took some time out to explain unique features of Buryat national dance and the way that the dancers' gestures evoked the nature and topography of the steppe. Junior ensemble members seemed a little bemused by the interest from a British ethnographer, but the team agreed that I could return over the coming months to sit in on rehearsals and interview ensemble members about their work. Before I departed that day, a trip to the canteen across the street and a round of vodka with several of the ensemble's musicians sealed my friendship with Misha. As each person took up their glass, they poured a little onto the table for "the spirits," as is customary among Buryats in this region. Before catching my bus back to the city, Misha left me with some advice: "If you *really* want to understand Buryat culture, you need to come to a *tailgan* ceremony. You need to be here in the middle of June."

I boarded the bus with a spring in my step. I had to come to Siberia to investigate the relationships between the performing arts and shamanist culture, but I had begun to wonder whether I really could invoke a link between the shamanist rituals that I had read about in historical literature and the colorful displays of Buryat culture I had seen in the Erdem theater and at public events. I was excited by the idea of attending a *tailgan* ceremony, a clan offering rite dedicated to the spirits that dwell in the landscape. Misha's point both heartened and intrigued me: here was an artist steeped in the "official" version of Buryat culture articulating a link with shamanist practice. At the same time, the hint that the "real" culture was to be found out there on the steppe left me wondering just how the relationship between shamanism and public culture was understood locally. This relationship was one I was to see played out in a number of ways over the coming years.

The performing arts had brought me to both Russia and the discipline of anthropology. A visit to Moscow on a youth theater exchange in 1992 began a deep interest in a country undergoing momentous change. This interest led me to travel across Siberia some years later and learn about the indigenous cultures of the region. As an undergraduate in drama, I had studied the classics of Russian theater, but I had also been engaged by performance theorists such as Erving Goffman, who found elements of theatricality and performance in everyday life, director Richard Schechner, and anthropologist Victor Turner, who drew parallels between the theatre of Europe and the ritual traditions of non-European cultures.[1] Anthropology therefore seemed a natural discipline in which to continue my academic career—a subject area that brought all of these interests and ideas together and allowed me to undertake the research presented here. The anthropology of performance and ritual has evolved considerably since those early pioneers, yet I hope to demonstrate that ideas first put forward by Goffman, Turner, and others remain pertinent for understanding the ways that people draw attention to activities that express who they are, where they belong, and to whom they belong.

ABOUT THIS BOOK

This book explores relationships between shamanist ritual practices and institutionalized performing arts in Buryat communities living to the west of Lake Baikal in Siberia. It does so at a revealing moment in the region's history. In the mid-2000s the Russian government sought to merge a number of autonomous indigenous territories into surrounding federal regions. This included the unification of Ust-Orda Buryat Autonomous Okrug with the much larger territory of Irkutsk Oblast. As part of this process, Buryat performing arts were mobilized by state institutions to make a public show of support for Buryat culture, while local politicians argued for the dissolution of Ust'-Orda okrug. Meanwhile Buryat shamanist rituals that were once banned under Soviet communism gained an increasing visibility, often articulating a deep-rooted relationship to the land. Both performing arts and ritual were therefore central to raising questions of Buryat belonging in a public sphere that had little space for balanced political debate.

The context I describe here is a quintessentially post-Soviet one and parallels the experiences of other Siberian peoples and national minorities across the Soviet Union. The creation of an official national culture during the Soviet era, the persecution of the national intelligentsia and religious practices under high Stalinism, and a revival of national consciousness and religious practice in the 1980s and 1990s is common to many peoples in northern Eurasia.[2] However the dissolution of Ust-Orda Buryat Autonomous Okrug and policy of *National Cultural Autonomy* espoused by the Russian state, offer new insights into the legacies of Soviet federalism and the experiences of a national minority navigating cultural preservation outside of a titular territory. In this regard Buryat experience resonates with that of indigenous peoples around the world whose relationships to place and other people are constituted through cosmologies and practices that differ markedly from the official regimes that regulate culture, territory, and autonomy in post-imperial states.

What follows is essentially an investigation into form and the ways that ritual and dance reflect and constitute various kinds of social assemblage—kin groups, civic communities, and nationalities—through the different formal conventions that they employ. This inquiry takes the experience of participation in collective ritual and dance as seriously as the symbolic elements found within those forms in seeking to understand the means through which my Buryat interlocutors related to people and place.

While theorists of performance have often made comparisons between the role of ritual processes and theatrical presentation of performing arts across cultures, my aim here is to look at the interrelationship of these mediums in a particular context. In trying to make sense of the mixed meanings and messages of ostensibly distinct cultural forms, I look at the ways that local shamanist practice and official Buryat culture have evolved in relation to one another over the past century. I took to heart Misha's assertion that to understand Buryat public culture you have to understand the rituals and ethics of shamanism. This book investigates the ways that sensibilities and aesthetics underpinning forms of public culture are informed by ritual practice. I also suggest that the reverse is true and illustrate how the presentational conventions of institutionalized Buryat culture increasingly influenced the framing of ritual practice in Siberia in the 2000s. Throughout the book I employ anthropological categories of ritual and performance to examine these practices as both comparable and differentiated types of activity.

Here I explore what happens when shamanist ritual practices historically associated with closed, kin-based communion rites are reshaped as performing arts and public symbols of national identity. This is a move that occurred under the nation-building projects of the early Soviet era, when dance and song were removed from their ritual context to create an official Buryat national culture. While shamanist practices were outlawed under Soviet communism, this institutionalized Buryat culture flourished and persists to this day.

Despite the Soviet assault on religion in the twentieth century, elements of shamanist practice persisted during the Soviet era. Since the end of communism, kin-based offering rites and large clan rituals have been reinvigorated among Buryats. In recent years some shamans have drawn on the presentational conventions of official culture to make local practices visible in the public domain. In considering these activities together, I argue that understanding formal qualities of ritual can elucidate the aesthetics of Buryat dance. I also highlight where tensions exist in transforming rituals of bounded kin groups into public events. Through detailed ethnography I reveal different orientations toward place and space implicit in these forms of practice, orientations that were brought into sharp contrast as Buryat territorial autonomy in Cisbaikalia was dissolved in the late 2000s.

In this ethnography I make a broad differentiation between what I refer to as *inward-facing* and *outward-facing* forms. I use the terms heuristically in order, first, to evoke the spatial configuration of different rituals and performing arts and, second, to draw attention to the fundamentally different ways that kin-focused and public events constitute senses of belonging to people and place. This difference lies in participation and communion on the one hand and the presentation of skilled performers and cultural specialists on the other. The comparison between ritual practices focused on kin and clan hearths and public performances on the stages of civic theaters give the book its title. If this distinction appears too simple a dichotomy, I should assure the reader that in what follows I illustrate the ways that everyday acts are made performative, and formerly closed ritual forms are turned outward. Echoing a metaphor used by the anthropologist Caroline Humphrey, I suggest that such acts take on a "Janus-like" quality—facing inward and outward at the same time—as kin-based rituals are publicized, scaled up, and given visibility in the public domain.[3] In employing this metaphor, I do not imply hypocrisy or deceit. Rather, I wish to suggest that forms can simultaneously hold experiences and meanings that are salient to participants and messages intended for the public domain. Moreover, my choice of terminology rests on the fact that I do not wish to make a simple cleavage between *performances* and *rituals* as types of bounded events; instead, I look at ritual and performance as modes of action found within a multitude of practices and coexisting in everything from everyday offerings of tea to collective events and public occasions.

WESTERN BURYATS

Buryats are one of the largest indigenous population in Siberia. Historically speakers of a Mongolic language, Buryats live mainly in southeastern Siberia around Lake Baikal. The 2002 all-Russian census, the most recent at the time of my field research, recorded 445,175 Buryats as living in the Russian Federation at that time.[4] Buryat enclaves can also be found in the north of Mongolia and in Inner Mongolia in China. Within the Russian Federation, Buryats constitute the titular nationality of the Republic of Buryatia and, as I began this project, were also designated two smaller national territories: Ust'-Orda Buryat Autonomous Okrug to the west of Baikal and Aga Buryat Autonomous Okrug to the east of the republic. Autonomous okrugs, formerly dotted across Siberia, were small federal territories designated as homelands for indigenous peoples and encapsulated within larger administrative territories. Ust'-Orda Buryat Autonomous Okrug lay within the boundaries of Irkutsk Oblast, while Aga Buryat Autonomous Okrug was situated in Chita Oblast. *Oblast* is often translated as "province," and most are purely administrative territories with no titular nationality. Both Ust'-Orda and Aga Okrugs were merged with their surrounding oblasts in 2008, and the process of unification is detailed here in chapter 5. This book draws primarily on fieldwork undertaken among the population usually referred to as Western Buryats, living both in Ust'-Orda Buryat Autonomous Okrug and parts of Irkutsk Oblast in Cisbaikalia. As the book shows, however, the relationship between Buryat institutions west of Baikal and the history and cultural institutions of the republic have always been important to the way that cultural forms have developed.

Historically, Western Buryats identified with one of several large clan groupings as well as belonging to more localized lineage groups. Affiliation to all of these groups was defined through patrilineal descent. (See chapters 1 and 3.) These affiliations have proved remarkably tenacious despite the complete reorganization of social life under Soviet communism. Consequently, I pay particular attention to kinship as a form of social belonging in this book. Since the late twentieth century, social anthropology has moved away from studying discrete societies, in the way that was once common, and from describing social groups, such as clans and lineages, as concrete and immutable ways of ordering social life. Instead a greater focus has been on networks of relations and the way that personhood is constituted through these relations.[5] This has been evident in recent studies of Inner Asia, and the classic descriptions of kinship institutions have sometimes been critiqued as outdated. (See chapter 3.)[6] Yet in the Western Buryat communities where I worked, belonging to clan groups and the obligations of kinship seemed so central to the discourse of my Buryat interlocutors that these institutions warranted serious consideration. Rather than produce a functionalist account, however, I hope to show the experiences through which these institutions come to be meaningful, the ways that they have changed and been creatively mobilized in different historical contexts, and the way that kinship overlaps, intersects, and contrasts other forms of belonging—such as civic and national belonging—as social actors move between roles and obligations.

BURYAT NATIONAL CULTURE

Misha's distinction between the song and dance found within the walls of Erdem theater and the practices of shamanism exemplified by *tailgan* ceremonies reflects a common differentiation that was institutionalized in Soviet policy. In the early years of Bolshevik rule in Russia, national minorities were mandated to undertake processes of *cultural national construction*. Through the 1920s and 1930s, indigenous intelligentsias led the development of official national cultures that conformed to European formal conventions and enshrined communist ideology within their content. These processes included the codification of written national languages and the creation of new literary and artistic forms, such as a national theater, opera, and dance. All of these forms were developed in state-run ensembles and academies, practiced in theaters and houses of culture (*dom kul'tury*), and systematized by professional artists and scholars who came to be regarded as cultural specialists. As the Soviet leadership's drive against religious practice gathered momentum in the 1920s, the new cultural institutions and professionals provided focus for an officially sanctioned Buryat culture. This culture increasingly excluded content explicitly related to shamanism and Buddhism, the religions hitherto followed by Buryats. In chapter 4 I describe the state institutions of Buryat culture and their role in re-energizing Buryat national consciousness in the late Soviet and post-Soviet eras.

While the delineation between official Buryat culture and wider cultural practice takes a distinctly post-Soviet form in Western Buryat communities, the distinction resonates with long-standing anthropological investigations into definitions of culture and the relationships between public and intimate practices. The distinction parallels the tension between English-language discourse that takes culture as a synonym for the arts and a broader anthropological understanding of culture famously described by Edward Sapir as "any socially inherited element in the life of man."[7] This book refers to *Buryat national culture, institutionalized culture,* or *public culture* as those practices objectified within state ensembles, galleries, museums, films, and publications to draw attention to a definition that is created discursively and institutionally in contemporary Russia. The terms are used here to distinguish these objectified forms *within* the more heterogeneous array of practices that constitute Buryat culture in the wider sense. In differentiating national culture from local ritual practices then, my aim is not to reproduce a restrictive definition of culture but rather to reflect the way that the term is used locally, as outlined in depth in chapter 4. In recent years ritual practices have been brought into the public domain and, increasingly, have been included in a definition of Buryat national culture, a phenomenon documented in chapter 7.

SHAMANISM AMONG WESTERN BURYATS

The ritual practices discussed in this book fall under the broad heading of Buryat shamanism, the dominant form of religious practice among Western Buryats. Shamanism is understood here as a belief in incorporeal spirits and the practices involved in mediating between those spirits and the corporeal world. The term has been critiqued as a cross-cultural category, given the huge range of spirit beliefs, ritual practices, cosmologies, and practitioners considered within the term, a point that has led some anthropologists to write about *shamanisms* in the plural.[8] In comparing local rural practice with the work of large, city-based shamans' associations, it might also be possible to talk of plural Buryat shamanisms. Instead I follow Caroline Humphrey in noting that shamanism in Inner Asia is intrinsically heterodox and "dispersed"—practiced in a variety of contexts by a range of practitioners with no central authority.[9] Historically, studies of shamanism often focused on the person and practices of the specialist shaman.[10] More recently, however, anthropologists have decentered the shaman to take account of everyday ritual practices and relations with spirits as well as the role of alternative ritual practitioners, such as clan elders.[11] This is an approach I follow in documenting analogies between everyday offerings to spirits and collective ritual events in Buryat communities.

Buryat shamanism has many beliefs, practices, and terms in common with those of other peoples across Siberia and Inner Asia. The most significant spirits that reside in the landscape of the Baikal region include ancestral spirits of given clans, deceased shamans, and master spirits of places, such as sacred mountains, hills, rivers, and lakes. Spirits can belong to a particular household or be powerful mythical ancestors of large territorial clans. Nineteenth-century ethnographers described a pantheon of spirits worshipped across the region. This pantheon included ninety-nine *tengeri* spirits (forty-four black *tengeri* of the western sky and fifty-five white *tengeri* of the eastern sky), blacksmith spirits, and mythical ancestors of the largest Buryat clans.[12] In more recent times, I found reverence for this pantheon to be more common within the rituals of professional shamans' associations from the Republic of Buryatia and described in revived shamanism among Buryats in Mongolia than in local ritual practice on the Ust'-Orda steppe, a phenomenon I explore in chapter 7.[13]

Before the Soviet repression of religious practice in the 1930s, professional shamans could be found across the Baikal region. In common with other parts of the Mongol world, specialist shamans were initiated to nine levels of expertise, though clan elders and noninitiated shamans also led rites.[14] The high Stalinism of the 1930s saw the execution or forced recantations of many Buryat shamans and led to a decline in healing rites and séances. Myriad offering rites to spirits in the landscape have proved resilient, however. Most Buryats I know offer a little tea or vodka to the spirits when drinking in return for protection and good fortune. Local people regularly make libations at sacred places on the road when traveling, and heads of households make annual offerings to their ancestors and household spirits on behalf of their families.

Shamanist cosmology and ritual remains an important means of mediating Buryat kinship. As I detail in chapter 3, Western Buryat clan groups regularly make collective offerings to their ancestral spirits in a rite known as the *tailgan*, which has been practiced openly since the collapse of communism. During the rite, sheep, goats, or horses are slaughtered and the meat shared among kin and their protector spirits. I found *tailgan* rites to be ubiquitous in Ust'-Orda okrug in the mid-2000s, when kin relations were vital for economic survival following the collapse of collectivized agriculture.

The fall of Soviet communism and the accompanying religious freedoms have led to shamanist practices reappearing in the public life of the region. Chapter 7 compares the institutionalized shamanism that appeared in the post-Soviet era with local forms of shamanist practice. The chapter examines how the relationship between these forms has developed and how local shamans in Ust'-Orda have responded to the increasing presence of professional shamans in the region.

THEORETICAL CONVERSATIONS AND HISTORICAL CONTEXT

My observations of Buryat cultural practices in this book are, throughout, brought into dialogue with some of the classic theorists of ritual, symbolism, and performance. Those theorists are mostly drawn from the European tradition of social anthropology, which has tended to focus on social institutions and relations as a point of departure. These classic theorists might be seen by some to be part of an outdated functionalist model of anthropology—according to which discrete societies and cultures were seen to have a range of social institutions (legal, economic, religious, etc.) that functioned in equilibrium. The approach is fairly critiqued today as too often depicting an ahistorical notion of traditional societies, often occluding the colonial context in which these societies—and European ethnographers—operated.

A similar observation can be made about many of the Russophone ethnographers (many themselves Buryat) on which this book draws. In a political context that banned religious practice, Soviet ethnographers of Buryat culture almost universally depict a Buryat culture described as belonging to "the late-nineteenth and early-twentieth century." This situated ritual practices in an age before Soviet enlightenment was deemed to have rendered them redundant.

In making a critical application of work from both of these traditions, my aim is to suggest that their insights still have some purchase. However, while I make theoretical use of concepts such as liminality, communion, and communitas, I aim to do so in a historicized way, trying to understand how ritual, dance, kinship, and belonging were experienced in a rapidly changing political context and how cultural forms are reshaped in relation to state institutions and policies in different eras. Bringing these theories into relationship with paradigms for the study of performance provides scope to analyze the way that these forms are framed and new meanings are generated in the contexts of particular enactments.

PERFORMANCES AND RITUALS AS SIGNIFICANT EVENTS

There is a long history of regarding performance and ritual events as comparative phenomena in anthropology. Milton Singer famously invoked the category of *cultural performances* to describe public events that express a shared identity. Singer identified a broad range of practices that foster shared cultural consciousness, including "plays, concerts, and lectures ... prayers, ritual readings and recitations, rites and ceremonies, festivals and all those things we usually classify under religion and ritual rather than with the cultural and artistic."[15] One of the key pioneers of this field, Victor Turner drew on Van Gennep's model of rites of passage to identify both ritual and performance events as *liminal*.[16] Much as neophytes undertaking rites of passage undergo a period of withdrawing from everyday activities and existing between social identities, Turner suggests that during certain events, participants suspend their engagement in day-to-day activities and a liminal context is established from which the social order can be viewed, critiqued, and reaffirmed. During Buryat *tailgan* rites I attended, the hierarchies and social roles that participants adhered to in everyday civic life were suspended such that the ritual space was, in effect, a liminal one. In subsequent chapters I look at the ways that performance events are marked out from everyday practice—by the stylized practices employed by participants and the conventions of staging and public presentation.

Alongside Turner's own writings on ritual and theater, the legacy of his theoretical project can be found in the work of Richard Schechner, who was instrumental in developing the field of performance studies, and the writing of anthropologists such as Don Handelman, who sees in both rituals and theatrical performance "models and mirrors" for the social order.[17] In making Buryat ritual and performing arts the focus of this ethnography, I follow this tradition within anthropology. Here I consider events that seem to be marked out from quotidian life as special moments in which social forms, relationships, and identities are made visible, reaffirmed, or challenged. As I noted above, however, my aim is not to restate the comparability of ritual and performing arts as holding similar social functions in different cultural contexts. Instead, I seek to compare the mobilization of both artistic performances and ritual events in a particular time and place. I explore some similarities in the way that these events effect a sense of belonging to social collectives, but I also suggest some important differences in the ways that kin-based Buryat rituals and the public performances of institutionalized art forms articulate relations to place and space; differentiate or unify skilled specialists, participants, and audiences; and engage public media in broadcasting political messages about Buryat political autonomy.

In order to understand where commonalities of form can be found and how shamanist rites are mobilized as display, I follow more recent work that sees performance and ritual as modes of action found in all kinds of events and practices. Some of these events may be referred to as rituals and some as performances, but they commonly contain elements of each kind of action, often in combination.[18] Discerning performance and ritual—or *performativity* and *ritualization*—in multiple events led to my use of inward-facing and outward-facing forms as a heuristic to compare kin-based and public practices in terms of form and experience rather than simply describing their nominal function.

RITUAL, FORM, AND EXPERIENCE

In anthropological writing, ritual denotes formalized and repeated activities that seem to be demarcated as particularly important or meaningful to social actors. In Western Buryat communities, ritualized practices included the everyday act of dabbing a little tea or vodka on the table for spirits when drinking; formal hospitality practices in which a vodka glass was passed around according to strictly followed rules; and large-scale *tailgan* ceremonies—communion rites at which animals were slaughtered and butchered and meat was shared among kinsmen and their ancestral spirits.

Ritual actions have a predefined form to which actors adhere, even when the original logic or meaning of those acts has been lost or remains obscure. Humphrey and Laidlaw observed that in ritualized action, you "are and are not the author of your acts."[19] This pithy formulation evokes well the combination of an actor's agency in deciding to undertake a ritual act with submission to a form that is predefined. Though the logic of these actions may be obscure and highly variable for actors, it is ultimately the adoption of a "ritual stance" that demarcates the special attention to a formalized act as important.[20] Since ritualization demarcates certain acts as meaningful and important, ritual practices often privilege moments in which social relations and social values are expressed and constituted.

The Buryat practices analyzed here can mostly be understood as ritualized acts of reciprocity and sharing. The invocation of incorporeal spirits in such relations is underpinned by shamanist cosmology, and although the meanings of some individual elements of offering rites remained obscure for participants, this spectrum of Buryat ritual practices were all undertaken with a sense of moral obligation to share and reciprocate. Identifying ritualized acts in everyday life not only helps to explain the tenacity of shamanist beliefs despite decades of persecution but also illuminates an ethos that pervades Western Buryat sensibilities.

Ritual events are commonly rich with symbolism. Insofar as ritual often represents cosmological and social orders, the process of interpreting and explaining symbolic action forms a large part of ritual analysis. Buryat rituals are no exception, and in chapters 2 and 3, I document the ways that social relations of reciprocity and sharing among both corporeal kinsmen and clan spirits are expressed in the formal exchange and consumption of vodka, milk, and meat and the offering of butchered meat to clan spirits via ritual pyres. There are recurring motifs and analogies of form between everyday hospitality practices on the one hand—in which a shared glass is passed in a sunwise direction, the table is a fetishized object, and the hearth a place of offering—and collective rites on the other, which follow the same sunwise pattern of circumambulation, sacralize the table as a place of offering, and are focused on a ritual hearth.

Yet I also wish to account for the intense shared experiences that engender strong feelings of social belonging as powerfully as any symbolic references that those events contain. There is a long-standing, if punctuated, anthropological tradition of analyzing collective events in this way. At the turn of the last century, Emile Durkheim famously described a "collective effervescence" achieved through community activities;[21] in the mid-twentieth century Victor Turner used the term *communitas* to describe the intense feelings of togetherness experienced in ritual;[22] and in the past two decades, kinship studies have recognized that commensality and conviviality are as crucial to cementing kinship and social belonging as the genealogies and metaphors of relatedness that have long dominated the topic.[23]

Among Western Buryats powerful communal experience was evident in the *tailgan* rites I attended among local clans. Clan members worked together at these events to build and stoke fires, butcher animals, and cook the *tailgan* meat. They also drank vodka, caught up with news, cheered on relatives in wrestling competitions, and consumed the *tailgan* meat together in acts of communion.

Moreover, the form of ritual events was crucial to the generation of such experiences. The semicircular lines in which *tailgan* participants faced the offering fire during prayers at ritual events, the collective circumambulation of the pyres as clan members offered vodka and meat to their ancestors, and ritual circle dances—later appropriated as a secular symbol of Buryat identity—both represent collective belonging and provide the means to experience and instill that sense of belonging in participants.

Influential ethnographic studies have sought to demonstrate the ways that spatial forms reflect and model social structures and institutions. This idea of *isomorphism* can be found in Durkheim and Mauss's early-twentieth-century studies of Native American encampments and resurfaces through different tropes in the late twentieth century, including Pierre Bourdieu's research among Kabyle in North Africa and Clifford Geertz's influential ethnography of Balinese performance and ritual forms.[24] The analysis of Buryat practices in this book follows broadly in this line by emphasizing the spatial form of rites and performances as constitutive of different kinds of social belonging. The inward-facing, closed sociality of kinship rituals is evident in the focus on the clan hearth and the circular and semicircular lines that participants make as members of a collective. This contrasts the outward-facing form of official public performances when placed on the stages of civic venues.

FRAMING PERFORMANCE, STAGING RITUAL

Anthropologists and scholars in related disciplines have addressed the subject of performance, performances, and performativity in varied and sometimes contrasting ways, so it is worth giving a brief resume of that work by indicating how I use the associated terminology in this book.

The verb "to perform" was originally used in English to mean enacting, or carrying something out. The term's use in denoting music, dance, and theater as *performing arts* led to the evolution of a second meaning: that of showing or communicating to an audience. Erving Goffman famously used theatrical metaphors of "frontstage" and "backstage" to explore the way that people present a social persona in everyday life.[25] The understanding of performance as display typifies popular use of the term. We often talk of someone conspicuously acting to create an effect as giving a performance. This sense of performance has enjoyed the greatest currency in anthropology, wherein scholars concerned with acts ranging from oral forms of storytelling to shamanistic healing have analyzed these acts as performances in which people consciously present their actions to others to cement social status or inform social relations.[26]

Some confusion is occasionally brought about by the use of "performatives" as professed by linguist J. L. Austin. Austin's performatives denote the social effects of particular speech acts—what the act does—in contrast to the expressive element of an act that Austin denotes the "constative."[27] In this respect Austin holds the performative to the original meaning of performance as achieving or enacting something. Judith Butler's influential writing on "performativity" in relation to gender draws on both Goffman and Austin to show the ways that gender identity is constituted through both display (particularly the presentation of the body) and the enactment of gender roles.[28] From this perspective, performance (or performativity) is both enactment *and* expression, showing *and* doing—whether it takes place in the course of everyday life or in specially bounded contexts.

In this regard, performance can be understood as a quality of action evident in a variety of activities. In this book I use performance to denote the intentional moments of display found in a range of Buryat ritual and artistic activities, as evident in the practices of shamans leading offering rites that cement their social status as in the dances of folk ensemble members expressing their national identity. Combining analysis of ritual and performance allows us to discern when and why ritual acts are mobilized to communicate with an audience—whether those audiences are the spirits to whom shamanist rituals are addressed, a younger generation of Buryats interested to learn of their cultural history, or a wider public in a heated political context.

Gregory Bateson's terminology of *framing* an act for privileged communication offers a helpful starting point for analyzing performance. Framing, in Bateson's coinage, is a metaphor for the way that certain behavioral cues or linguistic descriptors create a "psychological frame" privileging the communicative message of a particular act and indicating the character of that act—as play, ritual, or performance, for example.[29] The terminology of framing was adapted by Goffman to explore a range of different communication practices and by anthropologists such as Webb Keane, whose influential ethnography of Anakalangese communities is notable in documenting how formalized ritual speech frames certain acts as important and authoritative.[30] Goffman built on the metaphor in describing the *theatrical frame*—the spatial conventions of staging that lead an audience and performer to understand that they are engaged in a process of performance.[31] The framing metaphor is therefore particularly helpful in analyzing different instances of performance—whether in everyday interactions or public events.

There were a number of performative framing strategies evident in events that I analyze in this book. For example, there were the bodily and vocal cues that demarcated an act as intentional display and drew the attention of an audience. Gestures and use of the body were often formalized and exaggerated, particularly in the stylized physical actions of theater and dance. Vocal techniques from the declamatory speech used to recite Buryat verse and the singing employed by professional artists similarly delineated performance media from everyday communication. The costumes and props that demarcated performers from spectators provided another means of performative framing, evident in the colorful national dress of Buryat folklore ensembles and the shamans' robes and drums seen at public ceremonies. In his discussion of the theatrical frame, Goffman illustrates the ways that demarcation of space can define and draw attention to performance acts by means of a physical, sometimes literal, frame. The stage raises up the skilled performer as worthy of attention, differentiated from their audience. Public events also undergo a broader process of framing in public discourse and media. Following the traditions of Soviet civic culture, concerts in Cisbaikalia were often preceded by speeches from local dignitaries. When events took place in the public domain, they were advertised in advance and reported in print or broadcast media afterward, framing that often provided a particular narrative about their meaning.

Performances of Buryat national culture in the early twenty-first century usually took place in the proscenium arch auditoria of houses of culture and municipal theaters. The theatrical frame defined those on stage as cultural specialists and objectified specific practices as part of an official Buryat national culture, a symbolic reference point for national and civic belonging. Events were often heralded and discussed in local news media, particularly in the context of the referendum on unifying Ust'-Orda Buryat Autonomous Okrug with Irkutsk Oblast. These framing strategies provided opportunities for public expressions of belonging—both explicit and implicit—but they were also replete with tensions and paradoxes.

In chapter 4 I describe *theatricalized* rituals performed within folklore concerts. These staged reconstructions featured declamatory speech and stylized gesture and contrasted the intimate rituals of kinship that I attended in the countryside, where the emphasis was on participation and communion rather than the skilled displays of specialists. The Buryat circle dance, the *yokhor*, provides a further paradoxical example of a staged form. Formerly a participatory activity danced in the context of clan rituals and weddings, the *yokhor* was adapted as part of Soviet national culture and is now performed mostly by folklore ensembles. Danced by specialists in traditional costume, the *yokhor* forms part of civic events and is framed as a symbol of national belonging when placed on the stages of theaters and concert venues. Yet, as I argue in chapter 6, the intense collective experience of dancing the *yokhor* and its circular sunwise motion give the form continued resonance with Western Buryat ritual. This aesthetic is rooted in the shamanist practice and kinship that Soviet culture sought to replace. The dance takes both an inward- and outward-facing form, allowing for multiple meanings to flow from its experiential power, its contested symbolic structure, and the context of its performance.

In the post-Soviet era, Buryat activists have sought to bring shamanism back into the public sphere and into a definition of Buryat national culture. In doing so, a more institutionalized form of shamanism has developed that often draws on the performative techniques and frames of Buryat national culture. Shamans' associations based in the Republic of Buryatia enact public rites that are highly performative. During these ceremonies attendees are spatially separated from ritual practitioners who engage in stylized gesture and song while wearing colorful costumes, all of which demarcate practitioners as cultural specialists. The outward-facing public nature of these rites resemble closely the performing arts developed during the Soviet era. Indeed these elements of ritual have led to the associations' rites to be dismissed as "theater" by some local shamans in Cisbaikalia, who have critiqued both the authenticity of the practice and the presence of those they regard as outsiders practicing in Western Buryat homelands.

While eschewing the more spectacular and performative elements of institutionalized shamanism, local shamans in Ust'-Orda formed their own organization, known as *Sakhilgaan*. The organization has used print media to advertise and report on their large-scale ceremonies. While the rites retain the inward-facing form and character of local *tailgan* rituals, this public framing gives the ceremonies a place in public discourse and, like the *yokhor*, a Janus-like quality of being similarly inward and outward facing. In this case, the longstanding meanings of the events for participants were augmented by public expressions of religious authority and authenticity.

Framing events in public discourse often provide for contextual meanings to be attached to particular enactments. The fact that individual performances hold *pragmatic* meanings—inferences that relate to their context rather than to symbolic structure of a form—has been a key feature of performative analyses of ritual.[32] Buryat song and dance constitute symbols of national belonging, but in the context of concerts and events convened to support the cause of unifying Ust'-Orda okrug with Irkutsk Oblast, they held additional meanings, as chapters 5 and 6 recount. Preceded by speeches by local dignitaries widely reported in local media, they signaled support for unification by Buryat activists and a promise to respect Buryat culture by the state. Conversely, newspaper articles documenting Sakhilgaan's *tailgan* rites in 2007–8 allowed the organization to develop narratives about their role as local custodians of land as territorial autonomy was eroded. (See chapter 7.) In the final chapter of the book, I document the invocation of indigeneity and conservation discourses alongside the mobilization of shamanist ritual on the sacred hill of Mankhai following damage to the site from illegal quarrying. These metanarratives were crucial in a context where overt political opposition to the state agenda was effectively repressed and issues of land, autonomy, and belonging were played out in the cultural sphere.

BELONGING, TERRITORY, AND PLACE

A further theme that runs throughout this book is the way that ritual and performance mediate belonging to land as well as to different social aggregates. I opt to write more commonly of *belonging* to evoke an affective attachment to people and place than I do of *identity*, which connotes a more consciously deployed differentiation between self and other.

In comparing kinship and national belonging among western Buryats, I found myself returning repeatedly to yet another dichotomy: place and territory. Anthropologists have often explored the relationship between *space* and *place* in the way that social actors perceive and relate to the land. In scientific thought space was once invoked to render the broad environments in which humans live and move as value neutral, measurable, and given meaning only through human perception.[33] Places, on the other hand, came to be understood as meaningful phenomena in human experience, localities inscribed with meaning through human activities and relationships.[34] In this schema, state projects are frequently described as treating land as depersonalized space, apportioning and administering it as territory through technologies of mapping and overlooking the meaningful places that are contained within.

In Western Buryat communities, significant places root a sense of belonging within the Cisbaikal landscape: Each clan has its own sacred hearth, where offerings are made to ancestral spirits that remain there. Further key sites, in particular sacred hills, are the focus of large-scale collective rituals. These sites form part of what I term a *shamanist topography* for Western Buryats, a plurality of ritually constituted places where relations between spirits and corporeal kinsmen are reaffirmed and renewed.[35]

The anchoring of Buryat kinship in ancestral villages has continued long after clan settlements—known as *ulus* communities—were depopulated under collectivized agriculture. As migration from the countryside to the cities of the region accelerated during the late-Soviet and post-Soviet eras, atomized kin groups continued to return to depopulated *ulus* sites to honor ancestral spirits and reconstitute ties of kinship. The obligations of kinship and reciprocity between kin held increased salience after the collapse of collective agriculture—with urban Buryats relying on rural kin for milk and meat in the shortages of the 1990s and increasingly impoverished villagers turning to wealthy relatives for financial support in the 2000s.

If kinship is rooted in place, then national belonging is more commonly equated with territory. Under the Russian federal system, particular territories are assigned to titular nationalities, such as the Buryats. In chapter 4, I recount how an official version of Buryat national culture was developed in the early years of the Soviet Union. Under Soviet nationalities policy national cultures were homogenized and the symbols of national identity distributed across national spaces in the form of performing and material arts, national literatures, and codified languages. To serve this aim, the state had its own topography of houses of culture, theaters, galleries, and libraries. From the stages of civic institutions, the performing arts were projected outward into public space as symbols of Buryat national culture—a culture and space seen as coterminous with designated national territories.

These comparisons and contrasts between place and territory, inward-facing rites and outward-facing public culture crystallized for me over the course of two years of field research. I followed Misha's urging to better understand the summer rituals and went to live in the villages in the north of Ust'-Orda okrug later that spring. From those locations I reversed my previous pattern of short visits to Ust'-Orda from the city as I instead accompanied my Buryat hosts to attend Buryat cultural events in the city with the local folklore ensemble, gaining new insights into civic and national belonging as it was experienced in the countryside. I also met a steady stream of urban Buryats returning to Ekhirit-Bulagat Raion for offering rites and *tailgan* ceremonies.

The 2006 referendum on the dissolution of Ust'-Orda Buryat Autonomous Okrug, recounted in chapter 5, saw relationships between people and land brought sharply into focus. The proposed unification of Irkutsk Oblast and Ust'-Orda okrug represented a significant departure from the equation of nationality with territory established under Soviet federalism. The argument that Buryat national culture would be supported under the paradigm of *National Cultural Autonomy*, a policy that explicitly divorced nationality from territorial sovereignty, led to serious questions about the way that relations to land might be preserved. In this context, the increasing public framing of rituals that inscribed a relationship to the land was striking. The displays of ritual authority made by professional shamans tapped into the performance conventions of outward-facing forms to give Buryat culture a renewed profile in the regions to the west of Baikal. Meanwhile the increasing institutionalization of local shamanist practice gave many rites a Janus-like character, maintaining their status as inward-facing rites of communion while publicly framing activities in print and broadcast media to assert Buryat custodianship of local sacred places.

The changing way that the state recognized Buryat relations to land gave rise to new forms of placemaking. In the final chapter of the book, I document the ways that Buryat appeals to protect the sacred hill of Mankhai combined the assertion of reciprocal relations to ancestral spirits with discourses of indigeneity and the conservation of material heritage. These emerging tropes suggested ways that sacred places and ritual practices might be protected in an era when national territorial autonomy no longer exists to guarantee the cultural practices revived and reinvigorated since the end of the Soviet era.

WESTERN BURYAT EXPERIENCE IN GLOBAL PERSPECTIVE

While the phenomena described in this book take a particular post-Soviet form, they are comparable to the stories of indigenous peoples and territories colonized by European empires across the globe. The pattern of colonization comprising traders (in this case the fur trade) being followed by military power, missionaries, and the church—and ultimately mass settlement of European peoples—is a familiar one to indigenous peoples throughout the Americas, Scandinavia, and Oceania. While Soviet communism sought to reframe the Russian Empire as a union and native peoples as *national minorities*, contemporary historians have increasingly viewed both Russia and the Soviet Union as imperial polities.[36] The post-Soviet era has seen peoples of Siberia increasingly engaging with global discourses of indigeneity and finding common cause with indigenous peoples around the world.[37]

Public performances of Buryat culture, like those of indigenous cultures in many contemporary nation-states, are often loaded with paradoxes and tensions. Reshaping indigenous practices according to the framing conventions of a dominant national majority, or European settler culture, can provide a site of recognition and respect for minority communities. Moreover presentations of "traditional culture" are often a precondition of access to resources and land rights. As such, the emergence of indigeneity as a global concept in the decades after World War II and the Eurocentric regimes of recognition in modern states mean that indigeneity and performance have been intrinsically linked in contexts where these discourses have been invoked. In many instances, indigenous communities are expected to fill a European ideal of tradition and nativeness in their performances. However, these performances may, ironically, lead to accusations of inauthenticity—from both within and outside those communities.

In southeastern Alaska, for example, Kirk Dombrowski recounts that the terms of the Alaska Native Settlement Act require adherence to traditional culture and subsistence to secure access to land and resources and, as such, has seen a proliferation of indigenous dance troupes in the years since the act. However, this has invited critiques of authenticity and created tensions with those native Alaskans who have converted to Christianity.[38] Elizabeth Povinelli's work among indigenous Australian communities shows that in order to be granted resources these communities are ironically expected to meet a standard of traditional culture that colonization and forced relocation have made impossible.[39] In Amazonia adherence to traditional culture and dress can be necessary for securing land title, funding from international development organizations, or attention from global media in highlighting environmental catastrophe, but this may require deployment of body adornment or cultural practices that fit a European / North American stereotype of native culture.[40] In all these cases, the stakes of cultural recognition are extremely high.

The same tensions, paradoxes, and double binds were in evidence during the referendum campaign on the merger of Ust'-Orda Buryat Autonomous Okrug with Irkutsk Oblast in 2006. Performances of Buryat song and dance at specially arranged concerts were seen by some as complicity with the Russian state's agenda to dissolve the okrug, while others saw the opportunity for recognition and the leverage of guarantees for cultural preservation. Public, highly performative shamanist rituals were critiqued by local ritual practitioners as "theater" or "a big show" in a way that questioned their authenticity, while Western Buryats who were intimately involved with civic cultural institutions again saw this public-facing work as vital for public recognition. At this moment, when territorial autonomy was to be replaced with a policy of National Cultural Autonomy, oil pipelines were being proposed in the Ust'-Orda steppe and sacred sites were found to be illegally quarried for stone. In 2006, then, being recognized as custodians of the land was a process with especially high stakes for Western Buryats.

Discussion of indigenous rights and land title are often framed in terms of *sovereignty*, yet in some quarters both indigeneity and sovereignty are terms that are questioned and problematized. Critiques of the former hinge partly on the question of first-ness and who really can claim to be indigenes in contexts where generations of migration and displacement preceded European arrival. The latter is problematic since local notions of belonging might be understood less as sovereignty and more as a reciprocal relationship with the spirits of the landscape. Such a situation was evident in Ust'Orda in 2007, when the protection of the sacred hill of Mankhai hinged less on Buryats claiming to be the "first" peoples to live on the Ust-Orda steppe and more on being able to mediate with the spirits of earlier peoples—spirits who might have been deemed the true sovereigns according to the local shamanist cosmology.

In chapter 8 I describe how discourses of indigeneity and environmental conservation were mobilized by a small group of Western Buryats in the protection of Mankhai. Embracing this discourse not only shows the identification of Western Buryat experience with other indigenous peoples but also the need to find new, globally recognized discourses for expressing the rights and needs of Buryats in a context where the old Soviet tropes of territorial autonomy, or *national self-determination*, no longer held sway.

THE STRUCTURE OF THIS BOOK: A ROADMAP FOR READERS

Chapter 1 outlines the historical and geographical contexts that have shaped Western Buryat experience. From imperial Russian rule to the establishment and later division of the Buryat republic in the Soviet era, the chapter documents the territorial arrangements that saw Ust'-Orda Buryat Autonomous Okrug established in Cisbaikalia. The chapter also introduces Buryat communities in the cities of Irkutsk and Angarsk in the post-Soviet era and the relationship of Western Buryats to the Republic of Buryatia and the city of Ulan-Ude to the east of Baikal. In the final sections of the chapter, I introduce the villages of northern Ekhirit-Bulagat Raion, where I undertook rural field research. I detail the kinship groups to which local Buryats belong and recount the movement from small *ulus* communities to collective farms in the Soviet era, the gradual migration from the villages from the late Soviet period, and the collapse of collectivization in the 1990s.

In chapter 2 everyday Buryat ritual practice is described in the sprinkling of vodka for spirits when drinking, making roadside offerings, and the formalized sharing and exchange of vodka associated with hospitality. This chapter also documents the annual household rites, including offerings to ancestors and the practice of *feeding the mongol*, usually made at family hearths and commonly undertaken in the sites of depopulated *ulus* communities. Ritualized reciprocity is at the heart of many Western Buryat practices—between neighbors in everyday hospitality, families and clans in wedding gift cycles, and people and the spirits of the landscape, who require offerings in exchange for good fortune. Acknowledging critiques of reciprocity as a ubiquitous trope in anthropology, I nonetheless argue that it is a salient concept for describing the organizing principles of Western Buryat sociality and shamanist cosmology.

Chapter 3 recounts experiences of attending *tailgan* offering rites with clan communities during which animals are slaughtered and the meat shared between attendees and spirits through dedicated offering pyres. The ceremonies contain many analogues with ritualized hospitality and are often described in the same terms. My analysis of the rites emphasizes communion over definitions of sacrifice that focus on ritual substitution or abnegation. In describing the experience of attending *tailgan* rites, I also draw on Victor Turner's classic descriptions of *liminality* and *communitas*. The inward-facing spatial form of these ceremonies, at which clan groups line up to face the ritual hearth while making offerings, reflects the bounded nature of Buryat kinship. While classic descriptions of patrilineal kinship have been critiqued by scholars who have emphasized the role of the Russian imperial state in forming *ulus* clan communities, I argue that whatever the historical contexts of their evolution, patriliny remains a core principle of reckoning kinship, while ritual is a key means of constituting kinship. Ritual can also be understood as a form of placemaking in a context where belonging to people and the land are closely linked, even in an era when ancestral homelands are largely depopulated.

In chapter 4, I observe that Russian conceptions of culture often denote arts and literature as distinct from everyday practices and the category of folklore. As such, the construction of a Buryat national culture under Soviet communism saw forms developed according to European conventions and stripped of any religious content. I suggest that the outward-facing nature of these forms contrasts the intimacy of Buryat ritual practice. I also describe the way that Soviet policy linked culture to territory and the development of a state infrastructure. I describe an apparent decline in the institutions of Buryat culture in the decades following the removal of Western Buryat territories from the Buryat republic in the 1930s. However, I also recount the "national cultural renaissance" recalled by Buryats in the late Soviet period through to the 1990s in both the okrug and the cities of Irkutsk Oblast—a time when civic communities were still meaningful in Ust-Orda and before the collapse of collectivized farming.

Chapter 5 details the mobilization of Buryat cultural institutions to support the cause of merging Ust-Orda Buryat Autonomous Okrug with Irkutsk Oblast in the spring of 2006. The campaign gave cultural activists in the cities of the region unprecedented visibility as the government sought to show that support for Buryat culture would continue even after unification of oblast and okrug. The chapter records how the principle of National Cultural Autonomy was invoked to replace territorial autonomy, and the decoupling of culture and infrastructure was evident in the promises made for regional economic development if the territories unified. A shift in influence from Ust'-Orda to Irkutsk occurred at this time in coordinating Buryat cultural activities in the newly unified territory—a move that some in the former okrug resented.

Chapter 6 focuses on a particular genre of performance: the Buryat circle dance known as the *yokhor*. The dance is of particular interest as a ritual form that was adapted for the stage in the Soviet era. I detail multiple interpretations of the semantic content of the dance and speculations as to its origin. I suggest, however, that elements of movement and form that are analogous to shamanist ritual provide critical insights into the dance's power. In this respect, sensibilities forged through habitual and embodied practice inform an aesthetic of belonging, comparable to the *communitas* and shared experience found in offering rites. The framing of the *yokhor* as a national form thus gives it a simultaneously inward- and outward-facing character (described here as Janus-like) with personal meanings experienced by dancers that may run alongside the official narratives used to frame the *yokhor* in the context of the 2006 referendum.

Chapter 7 looks at the increasing ways that Buryat shamanism has drawn on the presentational conventions of official national culture and the rise of shamans' associations—a process described here as *institutionalization*. In Cisbaikalia at the time of my field research, the placemaking practices of local shamanists extended to the demarcation of family and clan hearths with ceremonial tethering posts (*serge*). The chapter looks in depth at ritual practice that made shamanist topography visible in a way that could not have been possible in the Soviet era. The chapter compares the work of local shamanist organization Sakhilgaan and that of Tengeri, an association based in the Republic of Buryatia but increasingly active in Cisbaikalia. I argue that Tengeri's work drew much more on performative framing—a move derided by some as "theater" but promoted by others as a means through which shamanism has gained recognition as a crucial element of Buryat culture. Sakhilgaan drew less on these presentational conventions, instead seeking to assert long-standing relationships of reciprocity with local spirits in the public domain, giving inward-facing forms a Janus-like character as they sought public recognition for local forms of practice.

Chapter 8 recounts an expedition to the sacred hill of Mankhai in Ust'-Orda Buryat Autonomous Okrug after illegal quarrying for stone had damaged famous petroglyphs found there. The chapter chronicles efforts by local shamanists and activists to have the hill designated as a national park, invoking both indigenous culture and heritage conservation as rationales for doing so. I stress that indigeneity in this context is asserted not as absolute first-ness but rather a relationship of custodianship and reciprocity with spirits of the land. This contrasts ways that state policies have conceptualized and used the land over the last century. In a context where territorial autonomy was soon to be dissolved and the material base of the local shamanist topography was under threat, these efforts highlight the tensions between indigenous cosmology and the policy of National Cultural Autonomy, which decouples culture from land.

In the concluding chapter, I draw together the threads and arguments made throughout the book and place Western Buryat experience in the global context of indigenous experience. I recount return trips to Siberia several years after the events described in the main part of the book, noting that trends toward institutionalizing shamanism and deploying tropes of indigeneity to gain recognition for Buryat culture had developed further during the intervening years. I also attempt to place the dissolution of the Buryat okrugs in the historical context of two decades in which Russia has seen greater centralization of power, domination of public discourse by official government messaging, and ultimately, tragic military action beyond the country's borders.

NOTES

1. Goffman, *The Presentation of Self in Everyday Life*; Schechner, *Performance Theory*; Turner, *From Ritual to Theatre*.
2. Smith, "The Nationalities Question in the Post-Soviet States"; Balzer, *The Tenacity of Ethnicity*; Grant, *In the Soviet House of Culture*; King, *Living with Koryak Traditions*.
3. Humphrey, "Janus-Faced Signs."
4. ROSSTAT, *Natsionalnyi Sostav Naseleniia Po Irkutskoi Oblasti, Vkliuchnaia Ust'-Ordynskii Buriatskii Avtonamnyi Okrug.*
5. See, e.g., Empson, *Harnessing Fortune*.
6. Sneath, *The Headless State*.
7. Sapir, *Selected Writings*, 309.
8. Atkinson, "Shamanisms Today."
9. Humphrey and Onon, *Shamans and Elders*.
10. See, e.g., Eliade, *Shamanism*.
11. Humphrey and Onon, *Shamans and Elders*.
12. Khangalov, *Sobranie Sochinenii, Vol. 1*.
13. Buyandelger, *Tragic Spirits*; Quijada, *Buddhists, Shamans, and Soviets*.
14. Mikhailov, *Buriatskii Shamanizm*, 98–102.

15. Singer, *When a Great Tradition Modernizes*, 71.
16. Turner, *The Ritual Process*; Turner, *From Ritual to Theatre*.
17. Turner, "Are There Universals of Performance in Myth, Ritual, and Drama?"; Turner, *From Ritual to Theatre: The Human Seriousness of Play*; Schechner, *Performance Theory*; Schechner, *Between Theater and Anthropology*; Handelman, *Models and Mirrors*.
18. Bauman, *Verbal Art as Performance*; Rostas, "From Ritualization to Performativity."
19. Humphrey and Laidlaw, *The Archetypal Actions of Ritual*, 96.
20. Ibid., 94.
21. Durkheim, *The Elementary Forms of the Religious Life*.
22. Turner, *The Ritual Process*.
23. Carsten, *Cultures of Relatedness*.
24. Durkheim and Mauss, *Primitive Classification*; Bourdieu, *Outline of a Theory of Practice*; Geertz, *Negara*.
25. Goffman, *The Presentation of Self in Everyday Life*.
26. Bauman and Sherzer, *Explorations in the Ethnography of Speaking*; Bauman, *Verbal Art as Performance*; Atkinson, *The Art and Politics of Wana Shamanship*; Schieffelin, "Performance and the Cultural Construction of Reality"; Keane, *Signs of Recognition*.
27. Austin, *How to Do Things with Words*.
28. Butler, "Performative Acts and Gender Constitution."
29. Bateson, "A Theory of Play and Fantasy."
30. Goffman, *Frame Analysis*; Keane, *Signs of Recognition*.
31. Goffman, *Frame Analysis*, 123–55.
32. Tambiah, "A Performative Approach to Ritual."
33. Casey, "How to Get from Space to Place in a Fairly Short Stretch of Time."
34. Ingold, *The Perception of the Environment*, 125.
35. Long, "Shamanist Topography and Administrative Territories in Cisbaikalia."
36. Lieven, *Russia as Empire*; Hirsch, *Empire of Nations*.
37. Anderson, "Nationality and 'Aboriginal Rights' in Post-Soviet Siberia"; Vitebsky, Piers, "The Northern Minorities"; Gray, *The Predicament of Chukotka's Indigenous Movement*.
38. Dombrowski, *Against Culture*.
39. Povinelli, *The Cunning of Recognition*.
40. Jackson, "Culture, Genuine and Spurious"; Conklin, "Body Paint, Feathers, and VCRs."

MANKHAI, OCTOBER 2005

I MADE MY FIRST TRIP to Ust'-Orda settlement in October 2005 to meet Aleksei, a journalist, local historian, and shaman. We had been put in touch by a mutual friend, Nikolai. Who felt that Aleksei would be a good contact for me. Aleksei had recently coordinated a project to map sacred sites in the district. He came from a line of well-known shamans and had, since the death of his father, fulfilled his own shamanic calling.

The day was taken up with a trip to the mountain of Mankhai, a little to the north of the settlement, with two of Aleksei's colleagues. The trip turned out to be my first experience of the offering rites I was to participate in on many occasions over the next few years. After drinking a round of vodka at the base of the mountain—being sure to offer a little to local spirits by sprinkling a few drops on the dashboard of our jeep—we drove steadily to the top. There Aleksei built a fire and cleansed a ritual area by burning scented grass. We each drank a little milk and vodka before pouring some onto the fire as offerings to the master spirit of Mankhai. As we did so, Aleksei addressed the spirit out loud, requesting my protection in the area during my fieldwork. Carrying the vodka with us, we made a walking tour of the mountain. A striking feature of the mountain was the large, circular plateau overlooking the Kuda River, which snaked along at the foot of the slopes. Walking around the plateau, Aleksei showed me ancient petroglyphs carved into flat rock faces of red and gray stone. The pictures, fifteen in all, depicted horses and men brandishing spears. We stopped in several places while Aleksei sprinkled libations of vodka on the rock next to the petroglyphs, both of us drinking a little as we stumbled our way around. As we paused to take in the view of the Kuda River below, stunning even with the steppe an autumnal brown, Aleksei surveyed the scene wistfully and talked emotionally about the importance of this place as his homeland. I did not begin to appreciate the specific resonances of homeland for him, or the rites that we had undertaken, until I became fully engaged in fieldwork the following year.

ONE

WESTERN BURYATS IN CONTEXT

BURYATS AND THEIR NATIONAL HOMELANDS

BURYAT MONGOLS WERE NOMADIC HERDERS living in the steppe areas around Lake Baikal at the time of Russian expansion into Siberia in the seventeenth century. The lands to the west of the lake saw several centuries of migration and population displacement preceding Russian arrival. Tungusic-speaking Evenki are thought to have dwelled in the area in earlier centuries and to have been pushed north by the arrival of Turkic and Mongolic-speakers.[1] The many cultural and religious practices that these groups have in common leave historians disagreeing about whether today's Western Buryats are descended from Mongols who displaced earlier Turkic residents, Turks and Mongols who intermingled, or Turks who adopted the Mongolic language.[2]

The origin of the Buryat ethnonym is also contested by scholars. A version of the term may have originally referred to a smaller grouping than the Buryat people as construed today, with a Russified variant later applied by imperial authorities to a broad population of Mongols who previously had no shared identity. By the turn of the twentieth century, the ethnonym had come to mean any of the Mongolic-speaking people living north of the border between Russia and the Manchu Empire. The vernacular form of the ethnonym is *Buryad*. Buryat dialects are distinct from Khalkha Mongolian, the language of today's independent Mongolia.[3]

Buryats have historically belonged to a number of concentric groupings, usually referred to as clans in English. The equivalent Russian term, *rod*, denotes groups that range from closely related lineages to larger collectives, sometimes described as "tribes" or "clan-confederations" in historical literature.[4] The Bulagat, Ekhirit, Khongodor, and Khori constitute the largest of these groups, each with its own myth of origin. Bulagat is said to have been a son of the deity Bukha Noyon (Lord Bull). Ekhirit is in some myths Bulagat's brother and in others the son of a fish, specifically a striped burbot. The Khori Buryats living to the east of the lake claim descent from a swan maiden from Baikal, while the fourth of the largest clans, the Khongodor, are recorded as drawing on different aspects of these myths at different times.[5] A number of smaller groupings also exist in the region, some of which have their origins among the Khalkha Mongols to the south. Buryats also belong to more localized clans and lineage groups, all of which theoretically trace their genesis to single ancestors. As this book details, group membership is ritually constituted through rites of offering. These rites are usually known as *tailgan* rites in the western Buryat regions and *obo* rites to the east of Baikal.

In 1708, the administrative division of the Baikal region into the Irkutsk Governorate (*Irkutskaia Guberniia*) to the west of Baikal, and the Transbaikal Governorate (*Zabaikalskaia Guberniia*) to the east, exacerbated already existing cultural and religious differences between Eastern and Western Buryats. The western Ekhirit-Bulagat dialect is distinct from the eastern Khori dialect, which later became the official Buryat language of the republic. Western Buryats living on the increasingly crowded Cisbaikal steppe experienced an influx of Slavic settlement and subsequently became more sedentary than their counterparts in Transbaikalia over the course of the nineteenth century.[6] During this time winter settlements increasingly resembled Russian villages with wooden houses and fenced enclosures. While shamanism had previously been the principal faith of the Buryats, in the eighteenth and nineteenth centuries Christianization, and Russophone church schooling, was promoted by authorities in the west, while conversion to Buddhism was widespread in the east.[7] Russian Orthodox education led to greater uptake of the Russian language in Cisbaikalia, and retention of the Buryat language remains greater among Eastern Buryats today than in communities to the west of Baikal. Buddhist missionaries from Mongolia were kept out of the Irkutsk Governorate in the eighteenth century, while several Buddhist monasteries were established in Transbaikalia at that time.[8] The form of Buddhism that developed in the region was, like that in much of Inner Asia, highly syncretized with shamanist beliefs and existed alongside shamanist practices. Later attempts to spread Buddhism west of Baikal met with limited success.[9]

By the early twentieth century, however, a common Buryat identity had been internalized by an emerging intelligentsia that began undertaking political activities under the banner of Buryat nationhood. This intelligentsia founded a Buryat national committee, *Burnatskom*, which became a de facto Buryat government during the civil war that followed the Bolshevik Revolution of 1917. Buryat intellectuals were instrumental in the Soviet project of constructing a coherent Buryat national identity after the establishment of Bolshevik power.[10]

The Buryat-Mongol Autonomous Soviet Socialist Republic (ASSR) was founded in 1923 as a republic within the Russian Soviet Federative Socialist Republic, itself a constituent part of the USSR. As with other national groups in the Soviet Union, the development of a Buryat national culture was promoted in the 1920s under a policy of *korenizatsiia* or "indigenization." The policy encouraged the formation of national identities in the hope that national elites would ally themselves with the Bolshevik cause.[11]

Buryat Mongolian ASSR 1923–1937

The Buryat-Mongol ASSR originally included the steppe lands of Ust'-Orda to the west of Baikal and Aga to the east, but these were removed from the republic in 1937, and each was designated as a "Buryat-Mongol National Okrug." Meanwhile a smaller republic continued to exist, shorn of its eastern and western wings. This exercise reduced Buryats as a proportion of the republic's population, and the new territorial divisions ensured that the Buryat regions were not territorially contiguous. Stalin's fear of pan-Mongolism has often been cited as a cause for the split, and it took place at a time when national minorities were repressed and members of the national intelligentsias were exterminated across the USSR. The new borders left many Buryats outside the newly created okrugs. Ol'khon Raion in Cisbaikalia, an area that includes the sacred Ol'khon Island on Lake Baikal, was simply left as a raion within Irkutsk Oblast. In 1958 the republic and both okrugs had the term *Mongol* removed from their names, and in 1978 Ust'-Orda and Aga were redesignated "autonomous" rather than "national" okrugs, a change made to all of the okrugs in the USSR.[12]

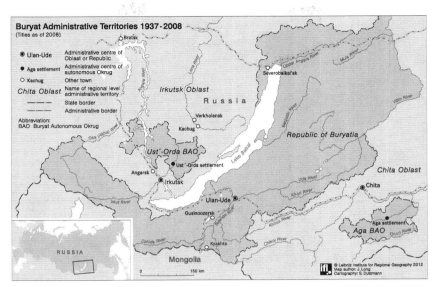

Buryat Administrative Territories 1937–2008

This book focuses on Western Buryat communities living in Cisbaikalia, the geographical area to the west of Baikal. It also takes into account the relationship of Western Buryats to the institutions and culture of the Buryat republic to the east. Cisbaikalia was the site of changing political territories at the time of my field research. In April 2006, a referendum was held in Ust'-Orda Buryat Autonomous Okrug and the surrounding Irkutsk Oblast to decide whether the two political territories should be unified. This followed the broader Russian policy of unifying autonomous okrugs with larger oblasts at the time. The outcome was in favor of unification, and on January 1, 2008, Ust'-Orda Buryat Autonomous Okrug ceased to exist as a politically autonomous region within the Russian Federation (see chapter 5).

CITIES OF THE BAIKAL REGION

The city of Irkutsk is the administrative center of Irkutsk Oblast, a large federal territory. The city is located where the Angara River, flowing out of Baikal, meets the Irkut River, a Russianization of the Buryat name *Erkhüü*. Irkutsk was founded in 1652 as a Cossack base for the collection of *iasak*, the tax in furs levied on the native peoples of Siberia by imperial Russia. The post became fully fortified in 1686 as provision for the garrison stationed there grew. In the early years of Russian presence in the region, resentment at paying *iasak* led Western Buryats to persistently raid and sack Russian forts in Cisbaikalia.[13] This fate was suffered by Irkutsk in 1695–6. As the city grew, it became a major center of regional trade and Russian imperial power. In the administrative reforms of 1736, when Siberia was divided in half, Irkutsk became home to the governor of eastern Siberia. The city became the seat of the second bishopric in Siberia in 1727 and served as a base for Christian proselytizing from that point onward.[14] The towers and domes of orthodox churches, several of them reconsecrated since the fall of Soviet atheism, still peppered a skyline of Soviet apartment blocks and ever-more-elaborate high-rises at the time of my field research. Slavic settlement of Siberia increased in the second half of the nineteenth century, further aided by the coming of the Trans-Siberian Railway at the turn of the century. At this time, Irkutsk experienced massive growth as a point of trade, especially between Russia and China.[15] The acceleration of mineral extraction in the region and rapid industrialization under Soviet communism all added to the city's size and standing. Today Irkutsk also has a large student population with several higher education establishments within the city.

I found that Irkutsk's identity as an essentially Russian city gave rise to a negative reputation among some Buryats, particularly in the Republic of Buryatia. If its long-standing status as a symbol of Russian power informed this reputation, it is likely to have been exacerbated by the fact that Irkutsk, despite its location on land occupied by Buryats prior to Russian conquest, was never part of territories designated as Buryat national homelands by the Soviet system. Many Eastern Buryats who I knew talked very negatively of Irkutsk as a rough or dangerous place and felt it inhospitable compared with Ulan-Ude in the Republic of Buryatia, where Buryat cultural institutions are highly visible. The 2002 census, the most recent at the time of my research, registered only 10,795 Buryats within Irkutsk's population of 593,604, representing 1.8 percent of city dwellers. Slavs (ethnic Russians, Ukrainians, and Belarusians), by comparison, numbered 556, 214 (93.7 percent).[16] The neighboring city of Angarsk did not appear to have the same baggage as Irkutsk in Buryat reckoning, mainly because it is a relatively new city built up in the Soviet era as a center for manufacturing. However, in 2002 only 3,859 Buryats lived there, which was just 1.6 percent of the city's population of 247,118.[17]

Irkutsk was my official base throughout two prolonged stays in the region from August 2005 to October 2006 and from May to October 2007. During this time I was based at Irkutsk State Technical University. In 2005 I took classes to improve my Russian language while undertaking some preliminary visits to Ust'-Orda Buryat Autonomous Okrug to meet local culture workers and attend cultural events. I also began to locate and study Russian-language ethnographies of the Buryats at the library of Irkutsk State University.

Studying in Irkutsk also gave me the opportunity to attend events and activities hosted by the city's Center for Buryat Culture (*Tsentr Buryatskoi Kul'tury*). These included celebrations for *Sagaalgan*, the Mongol New Year, in February 2006, after which I joined a Buryat language course running at the center. The class was mainly attended by young Buryats who wanted to learn the language of their parents and grandparents. As a British student learning Buryat, I was something of a curiosity. Being present at the center twice a week and talking to the teacher and administrators, I gradually got to know the small but energetic group of Buryat cultural activists in Irkutsk and their colleagues in Angarsk, which featured a cultural center and ensemble of its own.

When a large delegation of performers, activists, scholars, and artists from the center attended the all-Buryat *Altargana* festival in the Republic of Buryatia in June 2006, I was honored to travel as a member of the delegation in a specially commandeered railway coach. I later sat in on rehearsals of the center's two song-and-dance ensembles and interviewed performers and the choreographer. I initially had little chance to speak to Andrei, one of the most visible and busy activists, during my time as a student in the Buryat language course, but he became supportive of my research and gave me a lot of precious time when it later turned out that he was from Khuty, the village where I would undertake much of my rural fieldwork. After my attendance at a summer *tailgan* ceremony there and in light of Andrei's warmth toward me after doing so, I began to appreciate the power of Buryat kin networks.

While this book focuses on Buryat communities in Cisbaikalia, any study of Buryat national culture requires an understanding of the relationships of Western Buryat communities to the Republic of Buryatia, the crucible of Buryat national culture. The former fortress and trading town of Verkhneudinsk was nominated capital of the Buryat-Mongol ASSR. The city was renamed with the Buryat name of Ulan-Ude in 1934, reflecting the city's status as the center of Buryat culture.

Western Buryats were instrumental in establishing the Buryat republic, aided by the fact that a greater number were literate in Russian thanks to orthodox church schools in Cisbaikalia. Western Buryats continued to migrate to Ulan-Ude even after the territorial changes that saw them removed from the republic's territory.[18] It is not surprising that the more Buryatized character of Ulan-Ude remains attractive to students and migrants; indigenous culture and political leaders are more visible than in Irkutsk, and many have kin who have already settled there. During my field research, I made a series of trips to Ulan-Ude for interviews and to attend events. I quickly found that the city did indeed have a markedly more Buryat feel than Irkutsk, reflected in both the material culture of the city and the cultural events and institutions found there. While the tower blocks where people live are characteristically Soviet, many are emblazoned with the Mongol eternal knot motif. Around the city are statues of Buryat figures, such as the epic hero Geser Khan and a Buryat girl offering a silk scarf known as a *khadag*, the traditional Mongol greeting. The city's Theatre of Opera and Ballet has a self-consciously Inner Asian architectural style. There is a busy calendar of Buryat cultural events and numerous institutions of Buryat national culture, including a Buryat language theater and the Baikal state song-and-dance ensemble. Several academic institutes and university departments specialize in Buryat and Mongol studies, including the Russian Academy of Science's Institute of Mongolian Studies, Buddhology, and Tibetan Studies and the Eastern Siberian Academy of Culture and the Arts.

UST'-ORDA BURYAT AUTONOMOUS OKRUG

The terrain of the former Ust'-Orda Buryat Autonomous Okrug is principally steppe pastureland. Local Buryats were cattle herders before the arrival of Russian settlers. The chief economic activity, even under Soviet economic development, was cattle farming, with some arable agriculture. The entire population is classed as "rural" for Russian census purposes. Like all the nominally Buryat regions, Slavs actually constitute a majority in the okrug. Of the total population of 135,327 in 2002, 53,649 were Buryats (39.6 percent), while 73,646 were ethnic Russians (54.4 percent).[19] The okrug had six constituent districts or raions—Baiandai, Ekhirit-Bulagat, Bokhan, Osa, Nukutsk, and Alar. My research was undertaken principally within villages in Ekhirit-Bulagat Raion and the okrug's administrative center, Ust'-Orda settlement, which falls within the same raion.

The Buryat communities in Ekhirit-Bulagat Raion are often referred to in historical and ethnographic literature as the *Kuda*

Buryats, after the principal river in the area. The appellation owes much to the imperial system at the turn of the twentieth century, when the Buryat communities around Ust'-Orda settlement made up the Kuda Native Administration, while the Novonikolaevsk area formed the Upper Kuda Native Administration. Buryats in the north of the raion mainly belong to the Ekhirit clan, while the southern part is home to Bulagats and various smaller clans who do not belong to either of these larger groupings.[20]

Ust'-Orda settlement is approximately eighty kilometers north of Irkutsk, a journey I often made either on the daily bus or on one of the many private minibuses (*marshrutki*) that waited around the bus station until they had enough passengers. In 2007 the settlement had a population of just over fourteen thousand and was growing rapidly. More and more homes were being added to the maze of wooden houses and fenced enclosures sprawling out from the center as families moved from deeper in the countryside. Some households still kept cattle, which wandered along the crumbling roads out to pastures beyond.

My initial contact in the okrug was Nikolai, a local activist for the preservation of Buryat culture who had links with international networks of indigenous peoples. Nikolai put me in touch with two colleagues he thought would be able to help me with my research: Aleksei, the local historian and shaman with whom I traveled to Mankhai on my first trip to the okrug, and Misha, the artist with Steppe Melodies who hosted my many visits to the professional song-and-dance ensemble. Nikolai also took me to his home village of Khuty in the okrug to introduce me to his cousin Vitali and other relatives and friends in the area.

THE NOVONIKOLAEVSK RURAL ADMINISTRATION

In 2006 and 2007, I spent several months living in two different villages—Khuty and Novonikolaevsk—in the north of Ekhirit-Bulagat Raion. Both come under the jurisdiction of the

Novonikolaevsk Rural Administration (*sel'skaia adminstratsiia*), formerly the Novonikolaevsk State Farm *(sovkhoz)*.

The area comprises several villages made up primarily of wooden houses with their distinctive Russian-style painted wooden shutters. Households generally have a fenced enclosure that includes yards and stables where inhabitants grow vegetables, keep private cattle, and store hay and firewood for the winter. Though all homes were supplied with electricity, there was no running water and there were no phone lines in the villages at the time of my field research. Homes were heated by brick stoves in the center of the house. Water was collected from a communal well in Novonikolaevsk and the river in Khuty. Cattle were mostly turned out to graze on the steppe around the villages, and the families I knew had allocated land where they could cut hay in the summer.

Until the early twentieth century, households usually herded together in groups referred to as an *ulus*. The term *ulus* is found in Mongolic and Turkic languages and has been applied to many different kinds of social and political categories in Inner Asia. The term also applies to the appanages that Chinggis Khan's thirteenth-century empire were divided into and is used to refer to subterritories of the Oirat-Jungarian polities of the fourteenth to seventeenth centuries.[21] The Khalkha Mongolian term *uls* today refers to the Mongolian state, and in the Sakha Republic of northeastern Siberia, *ulus* has come to refer to district administrations.

In the Buryat context, the term historically referred to a herding collective, specifically the collection of nomadic households that spent their winters together and were, in many cases, groups of kin.[22] The term is also applied to the winter encampments that later became villages—one of many ways that people and place have become elided in Buryat thinking. In the eighteenth and nineteenth centuries, the Buryat *ulus* became a unit of administration and taxation under the imperial Russian government and came to include households that were not necessarily kin.[23]

Ulus communities survived until the early Soviet era, when the first wave of Soviet collectivization saw collective farms (*kolkhozy*) established in the district. Kin-based property ownership was anathema to communist definitions of collectivism, though discussions with Buryat interlocutors seem to suggest that in Cisbaikalia *kolkhozy* were often, in fact, *ulus* communities that were given a new title.

In the 1950s and 1960s, collectivization was reorganized across the USSR. Much larger state farms (*sovkhozy*) were established to incorporate several villages and further collectivize labor. Across the Cisbaikal steppe, wheat and barley agriculture was promoted and meat production was organized on an industrial scale. This period saw small communities across the USSR forcibly relocated to *sovkhoz* centers.[24] The Novonikolaevsk *sovkhoz* was established in 1966 and incorporated the villages of Novonikolaevsk, Khabarovsk, Muromtsovka, Shertoi, and Khuty. At this time local people recalled how several *ulus* communities in the area, including Khertoi, Khara-Nur, and Darbai, were forcibly depopulated, and their residents moved to work in the larger industrial farming units at Muromtsovka and Novonikolaevsk. These larger villages saw Buryats and Slavs increasingly living side by side, working together on the *sovkhoz*. Most of the villages remain home to a mix of nationalities to this day, with cross-cultural friendships and marriages not uncommon.

The relocations were still resented by older Buryats locally, however. I knew several former Khertoi residents who bitterly recalled being forced to move. As I illustrate in the next chapter, *ulus* identities are still important and known locally. Moreover older *ulus* names are still used for local villages that have been renamed. The coming of increasing numbers of Slav settlers to the steppe in the nineteenth century saw some villages established with Russian names, while others were renamed in the Soviet era. Locally, I almost always heard Buryats refer to the village of Khaborovsk by its former *ulus* name, Shikhi. Novonikolaevsk was

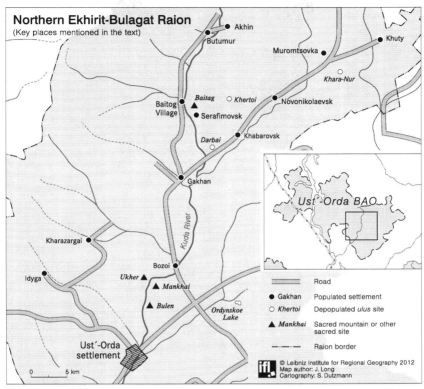

Northern Ekhirit-Bulagat Raion

likewise referred to as Adyk, a Buryat *ulus* that existed close to the current settlement that bears the more Russian name.

At its height the Novonikolaevsk *sovkhoz* was remembered by local inhabitants as having had twelve thousand head of cattle, and I was often told how the institution was known throughout the region as a rich and successful collective that won many awards. In 1996, however, as with the rest of the USSR, the state no longer found itself able to support collective farming, and the workers of the *sovkhoz* were laid off and most of the cattle sold off for slaughter.

Novonikolaevsk was the administrative center of the area with an administrative office (*sel'sovet*), post office, secondary school, and house of culture (*dom kul'tura*) that was home to a small library, a folklore ensemble, and the village's youth club. Built in 1990 to replace an older *klub*, the *dom kul'tura* stands on top of a hill—the one brick building among a mass of wooden houses. At the village sports ground, a sports center stands half-finished after funding for construction ran out with the collapse of the USSR, a "monument to Soviet power" as one friend jokingly described it. There are three shops in Novonikolaevsk and two in Muromtsovka but none in Khuty or Shertoi, each lying ten kilometers from Muromtsovka and twenty kilometers from Novonikolaevsk. Muromtsovka and Khabarovsk still have their own primary schools as does Novonikolaevsk, where there is also a secondary school. Declining numbers, however, led to talk of the two schools merging and ultimately being amalgamated with the schools in Gakhan, some fifteen kilometers to the south.

As I walked around Novonikolaevsk with Nikolai on my first time there, the most striking thing to note was the number of empty houses visible on every street. Every second or third house seemed to be either an empty shell with hollow window frames or neatly boarded up as though waiting for some possible future when it would be required once more. Beside the road were pieces of farm machinery in various states of disrepair, including several old combines. There was no evidence of arable farming on the surrounding steppe at that time. On the hill to the east of the village stood derelict machine sheds, their roofs stripped of corrugated iron, now providing little more than shade for passing cattle. "This was once a very rich *sovkhoz*," lamented Nikolai, almost apologetically, as I gradually took in the view. It was a refrain I was to hear often over the next two years.

The sense of melancholy engendered by that first impression was reinforced by the way I would later find people talking about the declining population and nostalgically remembering the days of the *sovkhoz*. I lost count of the number of conversations that began with, "When it was the *sovkhoz*..." Friends told me of the

Novonikolaevsk, May 2006.

workers' canteen and communal bathhouse that had been in the village. One elderly lady told me of the days when lorries would come from Irkutsk every day and bring fruit and fresh produce.

The local population was rapidly declining and aging as young people who left for higher education had little reason to return after graduation. Most people remaining in the area survived through small-scale animal husbandry, selling meat and milk products at Irkutsk's indoor market. There was also a herd of horses in Novonikolaevsk that was collectively managed, and privately owned individual animals were kept for meat.

Khuty is perhaps the most remote spot in the former *sovkhoz*. Although a herding brigade remained there until the 1980s, many residents of the village—still often referred to as Khuty *ulus*—gradually moved to work in Muromtsovka and Novonikolaevsk. When I resided there in 2006, only four households remained, and the village had a population of twelve. It was hard to imagine that the road leading to a little huddle of wooden houses was once lined with homes and paddocks. I was amazed when I was later shown old photographs that pictured a village shop and even a primary school there.

Having arranged a stay with Vitali, I attempted to make my way to Khuty in early May 2006. After reaching Novonikolaevsk, however, where Nikolai was staying, I had no luck finding anyone to drive me to Khuty because of the evident shortage of petrol. Since the collective farm had collapsed, the nearest petrol station was sixty kilometers away. As an outsider, I did not yet have any local networks to draw on for favors.

My week in limbo in Novonikolaevsk gave me my first insight into some of the dynamics of the area. I stayed with Nikolai at Uncle Igor's place. A kindly older man originally from Khuty himself, Igor had space in his house since his children had all moved away to Irkutsk and Ulan-Ude. After a week of trying, Igor managed to procure enough petrol to put into his large truck to deliver me to Khuty. On the way to Vitali's house, Igor showed me the remains of his former home, a boarded-up house standing in the middle of the steppe. It was one of a few buildings left standing in Khuty, where, unlike Novonikolaevsk, most abandoned houses had been pulled down.

Vitali was a former tractor driver for the *sovkhoz* and the last member of his family remaining in the village. He lived on an invalid's pension after an accident working with agricultural machinery several years ago and kept one milk cow that he calved each year. He made occasional trips to Muromtsovka for provisions, where he caught up with relatives and friends. His four brothers and sisters all had families and moved away. Vitali, a bachelor, had remained in Khuty with his mother, who had died three years prior to my stay. Vitali's nephews often come to stay with him, however, and in the summer while I was there, his younger brother's son, nine-year-old Bora, came to stay with us. Vitali was respected within his family as a keeper of the family hearth, a role I discuss in chapter 2. He is always known as *Diadia Vitia* (Uncle Vitia) among family and neighbors, a name by which I soon came to know him.

Khuty, May 2006.

I enjoyed the peacefulness of Khuty and the relatively slow rhythm of life. In May and June, I helped Vitia to clear out the cow's winter stall and chopped and stacked wood for the next winter. Later in the summer, I assisted with cutting the hay by scythe in Vitia's fenced meadows and gathered mushrooms and berries in the taiga that surrounded the Khuty steppe. While I initially wondered if I would get much of a sense of traditional cultural practices in that isolated spot, these fears were soon assuaged. I was surprised by the frequent appearance of Khuty people on the steppe on weekends in May and June. Most had traveled from Irkutsk, Angarsk, and Ust'-Orda settlement and called on Diadia Vitia to make ritual offerings for them, a process I describe in the next chapter.

My initial stay in Novonikolaevsk had a very fortunate consequence in that it gave Nikolai a chance to introduce me to a local couple, Dmitri and Erzhena. Knowing of my interest in the performing arts, Nikolai thought that I might be able to get to know the local folklore ensemble through them as both were members. Dmitri was a schoolteacher in the village, while Erzhena was employed part time at the *dom kul'tura* to help run the ensemble and lead youth groups learning the Buryat language, song, and dance. An extremely kind and welcoming couple, Erzhena and Dmitri generously invited me to return to Novonikolaevsk to join their clan's offering rites that June.

Dmitri's family originally came from Khertoi, one of the *ulus* communities depopulated in 1966. Khertoi is located about six kilometers west of Novonikolaevsk, and I joined Dmitri on several trips there to undertake offering rites, which I describe in this book. Erzhena had grown up in the Republic of Buryatia but moved to Novonikolaevsk when marrying Dmitri after they met at teacher-training college in Ulan-Ude.

I visited again to join the folklore ensemble when they performed in Irkutsk that summer. Given the difficulty of coming and going from Khuty, I ended up staying with them on these occasions. I also ended up drawing on their hospitality when undertaking the four-hour walk from Khuty in order to catch the early morning minibus to Irkutsk for cultural events. Occasionally I joined Erzhena in getting a lift to the city, where she traveled to sell milk products at the Thursday market. Gradually Erzhena and Dmitri's place became my second home in the countryside. I stayed many times in 2006 and for much of the summers of 2007 and 2008. I attended Dmitri's clan *tailgan* in June 2006, joined delegations to cultural events in Irkutsk and Ust'-Orda that summer, and attempted to make myself useful fetching water from the well and digging potatoes in the autumn. Dmitri and Erzhena have three children, all of whom were students in Irkutsk at the time of my fieldwork and whom I often met up with. During periods when I was based in Irkutsk, I would visit the market on Thursdays, along with Dmitri and Erzhena's children, to get news from the villages or send messages. I rarely left without a bag of potatoes and cartons of milk and sour cream because Erzhena could not bear the thought of me eating supermarket food.

MIGRATION TRENDS IN EKHIRIT-BULAGAT RAION

The effect of forced relocations, the collapse of the *sovkhoz*, and the rapid migration from steppe to city have had a profound effect on rural communities in the Novonikolaevsk area. Table 1 indicates the extent of these changes in six sample communities within the area. The years I have taken examples from are not evenly distributed but were the years that I could find records for in the okrug archives. Until 1966 Novonikolaevsk, Muromtsovka Khuty, and Khara-Nur fell under the jurisdiction of *Burovskii* rural administration, then part of neighboring Baiandai Raion. Khertoi and Khabarovsk were part of the Gakhan administration to the south until 1972. In 1966 the new *sovkhoz* was created. The administrative center appears to have been Muromtsovka until 1973.

The population figures clearly show the relocation of many people in the late 1960s and early 1970s. For example, Khertoi went from having thirteen households in 1968 to being depopulated completely by 1971. There are no records of Khara-Nur after 1965, which seems to indicate an extremely rapid relocation of many people. Looking at the simultaneous large jump in population for Muromtsovka, a village that lies very close to Khara-Nur *ulus*, it seems to me that the Khara-Nur households may have been directly relocated there or that statisticians simply began to count Khara-Nur as part of Muromtsovka at that time. The *ulus* was certainly uninhabited when I attended the initiation of a local shaman there in 2006. Khuty's population began to decline in the 1970s, but a rapid reduction between 1975 and 1986 suggests that this was when the Khuty brigade was disbanded. At this time Diadia Vitia began commuting to Muromtsovka to work as a tractor driver. Increasing populations for the villages of Novonikolaevsk, Muromtsovka, and Khabarovsk in the late 1960s and early 1970s reflect the relocations from *ulus* communities. The populations of these larger villages peaked in the early-to-mid-1970s.

Table 1 Population change in settlements of northern Ekhirit-Bulagat Raion by number of households (HH) and population (Pop.).[1]

	Novonikolaevsk		Muromtsovka		Khabarovsk		Khuty		Khertoi		Khara-Nur	
	HH	Pop.	HH	Pop.	HH	Pop.	HH	Pop.	HH	Pop.	HH	Pop.
1965	101	478	90	406	64	260	37	197	15	60	42	169
1966	101	490	120	531	71	304	32	185	15	48	–	–
1968	133	621	120	554	87	410	28	187	13	53	–	–
1971	172	825	98	143	104	498	24	148	–	–	–	–
1975	176	854	98	395	104	492	27	148	–	–	–	–
1981	177	631	84	261	86	311	16	47	–	–	–	–
1986	173	652	77	260	85	305	7	17	–	–	–	–
1990	204	686	94	258	97	351	5	9	–	–	–	–
1996	197	652	96	258	110	293	3	7	–	–	–	–

1. The following documents from the state archive of Ust'-Orda Buryat Autonomous Okrug (*Gosudasrtvenyi Archiv Ust'-Ordynskogo Buryatskogo Avtonomnogo Okrug*) were used to compile the population statistics in table 1: 1968 R-51-229. *Svidenie o chislennost' naselenii okruga v razreze naselenikh punktov za 1961–1968gg*; 1975 R-51-357 *Svidenost' naselenii okruga v razreze naseleníkh punktov za 1971–1975gg*; R-51-545 *Svidenost' naselenii okruga v razreze naseleníkh punktov 1/1/1981*;1986 R-51-643 *Svidenie o chislennost' naselenii okruga v razreze naseleníkh punktov 1/1/1986*; 1990 R-51-775 *Svidenost' naselenii okruga v razreze naseleníkh punktov 1/1/1990*; 1997 R-51-813 *Svidenie o chislennost' naselenii okruga v razreze naseleníkh punktov 1/1/1997*.

An overall reduction in population across the district began from the late 1970s onward and continued throughout the 1980s. Locally, people speak as though the decline of the rural community began with the collapse of collective agriculture under Yeltsin, but statistics point to a steady rural exodus that actually began much earlier. Caroline Humphrey's analysis of late Soviet-era population dynamics observed that the beginning of large-scale outmigration from rural districts to cities was already observable in the 1960s and 1970s as industrial development progressed, particularly in Ulan-Ude. Migration by Buryats from Irkutsk Oblast and Ust'-Orda Buryat Autonomous Okrug to Ulan-Ude was particularly noticeable during this era. Although the higher birth rate among Buryats compared to ethnic Russians makes the overall impact of this migration hard to quantify, Humphrey has noted that between 1970 and 1979, the Buryat population of Ulan-Ude increased by 56 percent compared with an overall population increase of 18 percent. She suggests that this tendency might be seen as a result of "national consolidation." The Soviet state's creation of a national identity for the diverse groups classified as Buryats was coming to fruition at this time, and an increasing number of Buryats attending higher education institutions preferred to live and study in "their" capital.[25] In chapter 4, I suggest how these processes of migration and national consolidation might have influenced the beginnings of a national cultural revival in Ust'-Orda BAO in the late Soviet period.

BURYAT KINSHIP IN NORTHERN EKHIRIT-BULAGAT RAION

Buryats have an array of terms relating to kin groups of various sizes, and there is a degree of flexibility in their use. The Russian term *rod*, usually translated as *clan*, is applied to everything from carefully delineated patrilineages to herding collectives such as the *ulus* and wider territorial groupings. It is worth examining the different groupings to which the term was historically applied while noting that the slippage between these different terms reflects the malleability of practices that define kinship, as I explore in chapter 3.

The Western Buryat term often used for a closely related lineage is *yahan*, meaning bone, a term historically related to the symbolic notion of patrilineal essence being transmitted as bone, while the female essence is blood. It is usually stated in ethnographic literature, and people often expressed to me, that lineages consist of anyone related within eight generations of a common ancestor and that every man should know their ancestry through the paternal line to eight generations. There is, however, a good deal of slippage between various kinship terms. I have seen *yahan* employed to describe wider kin groupings; Buryat ethnographer Margarita Khandagurova notes use of the term *soloi* to refer to lineages within wider clan groups in the area; and I have also heard lineages described as *ail*, a term that generally refers to a nomadic household or encampment in the wider Mongol world.[26] That these encampments were often made up of close relatives in nomadic contexts perhaps explains the interchangeability of the term with that of a kin group.

I found some genealogies to be broken at less than eight generations. Diadia Vitia only knows his lineage back four generations, for example. His family's earliest known ancestors are two brothers who settled in Khuty at the turn of the twentieth century. Caroline Humphrey's historical analysis of Buryat kinship records that even in the nineteenth century, the most immediate lineage groups in Cisbaikalia only consisted of three to four generations. In that era, Humphrey argues, competition for pasture meant that lineages segmented in order that junior members could make claims on land, denying the authority of lineage seniors over resource distribution.[27]

In northern Ekhirit-Bulagat Raion, I found that the term *rod* most often referred to the Buryat *ulus*, and this seemed to be the collective among whom *tailgan* rites were most frequently held. The Khuty *ulus* still hold *tailgan* rites together—as do the Khertoi. I heard the Khertoi clan referred to as both *ulus* and *ail*. Probing deeper, I found that the clan are all descendants from a single ancestor named Khertoi, who came to the *ulus* site from Akhin, across the hills to the north. The Kharazargai *ulus*, whom I joined for a *tailgan* in 2008, are comprised of three *ail* groups who each slaughter their own ram on the occasion of the *ulus tailgan*. From the place that *tailgan* took place, one clan member could point to each site in the surrounding pastures where the three *ail* groups spent their summers.

Buryats of the Novonikolaevsk area all belong to the wider clan known as the Bura. Descended from a single ancestor of that name, the clan is often Russianized as *Burovskii*. The area is often referred to as "Bury," and as I noted above, prior to the reorganization of collective farming in 1966, the local administration in Muromtsovka was named the *Burovskii sel'sovet*. The Bura are, in turn, part of the wider Ekhirit grouping.

The principle of patriliny defines membership of all of these groups. Where many local people have mixed Slavic and Buryat heritage—and mixed marriages were not uncommon even before the Soviet era—it is through the paternal line that local people would be identified as belonging to a lineage or *ulus* group.

The ubiquity of lineages and clans within Buryat society, and in Inner Asian society in general, was famously described in the work of Lawrence Krader. Drawing on the wealth of Russian ethnography of the nineteenth and twentieth centuries, much of it by Russian-educated Buryat scholars, Krader summarized concentric affiliations to lineage, *ulus*, and broader territorial clans in pre-Soviet Buryat society.[28] Krader is among a number of mid-twentieth-century scholars criticized by contemporary anthropologist David Sneath for perpetuating an idea of kinship society existing as a kind of pre-state social order, independent of state intervention. Sneath argues that genealogical reckoning of kinship was historically for the preserve of the aristocratic strata of Inner Asian society rather than common herders and that the division of a population into clans was essentially a form of statecraft imposed for purposes of taxation and military conscription. Sneath's chief purpose is to critique the analysis of kinship and state activities as discrete phenomena and question evolutionist discourses that use terms such as *tribe* and *clan* to downgrade indigenous forms of aristocratic statecraft as primitive.[29] In considering clan and kin identities in Cisbaikalia, it is therefore important to account for the role of imperial policies in reifying certain kinship categories.

Russian colonial policy certainly institutionalized the *ulus* as a collective identity. In 1822 the Siberian governor Speransky issued statutes for the administration and taxation of native peoples. Under this system each *ulus* formed the basis of a "clan administration" (*rodovaia uprava*). In some cases small herding communities were grouped together to gain the necessary minimum of fifteen households for an *ulus* administration.[30] Yet the Speransky reforms retained existing indigenous social orders and forms of law, and it has been argued that the structure of *ulus* communities was largely left alone. Helen Hundley, for example, has pointed out that the Buryats were the indigenous group that Speransky was best acquainted with when he drew up the code of 1822.[31]

In considering contemporary kinship, I contend that however far back the Buryat *ulus* may date as an institution, or however much colonial administrations may have tinkered with the precise makeup of given *ulus* communities, the *ulus* remains meaningful as a kinship group today, and belonging to *ulus* communities is cemented through the ritual practices described in chapter 3. Moreover, the availability of different possibilities for kinship groupings afford license among Buryats to choose between different definitions of group belonging, particularly where genealogies are broken or unknown. Ultimately state collectives and kinship groups *are* meaningfully differentiated among Buryats of Cisbaikalia today. This testifies to the role that Soviet statecraft had in separating the two social forms, a differentiation that I investigate through the analysis of ritual and performance media in subsequent chapters.

FROM ANXIETY TO INSIGHT

My initially frustrating experience at being unable to procure petrol in Novonikolaevsk was the first of many occasions when I began to wonder if I was ever going to manage to live in the area, let alone be able to gather any kind of useful material. After finally making it to Khuty and spending time with Vitali on his quests for petrol and material help in the villages, I began to appreciate the importance of personal networks for survival in the countryside. The exclusive nature of reciprocal relations seemed, at first, to be coupled with a closed attitude to a curious outsider.

Dmitri and Erzhena's invitation to join their *ulus* offering rite proved to be an important turning point in getting to know many local people. Even once I became a known quantity however, friendliness and hospitality seemed to coexist with reluctance toward explanation of ritual or genealogy. On the occasions when I asked someone for an interview or to sit down with a questionnaire, they usually told me that they had no time, that they didn't know anything that would be useful to me, or that they didn't know any "stories" or "folklore," the traditional interests of the Russian ethnographer.

On some occasions when I asked questions about offering rites or genealogies, I was told, "Oh you need to speak to so-and-so," or, "My mother will tell you about that." In fact, I soon learned that ritual or genealogical knowledge is often kept by a few clan elders and not always known by all, so I think these answers were often genuine, but given a general reluctance to talk to me, I did not normally push for meetings for fear of annoying or alienating people.

A second factor was the dubious reputation enjoyed by some regional ethnographers. In the Russian ethnographic tradition, scholarly expeditions are mounted to collect material in a short space of time. I was told by friends that ethnographers in the past had been given a great deal of folklore material from Novonikolaevsk teachers who had painstakingly recorded and collected it but that it had been published with little credit and certainly no remuneration.

My approach of long-term participant observation was novel, then, and the longer I stayed, learning to cut hay, dig potatoes, and take part in everyday life in the villages, the more acceptance I seemed to gain from locals. Returning in subsequent years seems to have been particularly important in cementing locally the idea that I was serious in learning about the way of life there.

I resigned myself to simply participating in things as much as possible while keeping formal questioning to a minimum. When people were relaxed and happy to discuss things, I did so but did not push them to talk to me. I can identify four particularly key interlocutors in all of my material on rural ritual. Erzhena and Dmitri proved to be very important informants in the villages, explaining rites and events that I had attended and patiently answering questions. Vitia gradually drip fed information about ritual practice to me when he felt that I was ready. On one occasion toward the end of my second summer, he sat down for a long talk with me about his practices. Aleksei, the shaman based in Ust'-Orda settlement with whom I had contact throughout my fieldwork, provided me with very detailed material on his own shamanic practice. I was honored to be invited to Aleksei's *ulus tailgan* in 2008.

When I was invited to attend rituals, I did so. I did not seek to document guarded information, like the words for offering rites or genealogies unless offered them. Establishing just where these private-public boundaries were was revealing in itself. Some knowledge is simply considered private or best left to specialists. On one occasion, Diadia Vitia took me to meet a local shaman in Muromtsovka who wrote down the words that I should use in Buryat to make offering rites, if I wished to, though I was told not to publish them. Diadia Vitia felt anxious about me having them, however, and later asked me to give him the piece of paper. When I attended Aleksei's *ulus tailgan* in 2008, I found him being quizzed by a number of his elderly relatives at one point. They wanted to know how much he had told me about them. "I don't tell him. He simply watches," insisted Aleksei. When I asked Aleksei about this later, he told me of the difficulty he felt in gauging how much to tell me, mindful of a Buryat proverb: "Never teach another's son." The learning of ritual practice, genealogies, and the constitution of kinship are essentially closed, private practices. One of the key points I wish to make in the following chapters is that kin groups are meaningful precisely because they are bounded and thus able to fulfill the demands of reciprocity and mutual support that larger social aggregates, like nationalities or civic communities, after the collapse of the *sovkhoz* no longer can. They necessarily require a definition of insider and outsider.

If I compare my experiences in the countryside with those of interviewing urban cultural practitioners, especially those with a political agenda, the contrast is striking. Ensemble directors, performers, and culture workers, particularly those of the younger generation, were used to discussing cultural practices that were reified in official discourse. I carried out a number of interviews with dancers, performers, choreographers, ensemble directors, and culture workers in Ust'-Orda, Irkutsk, Angarsk, and Ulan-Ude. These interviews brought forth considered and clearly articulated answers about cultural identity, the agendas of cultural organizations, and the forms that they presented. Interviewees were usually happy to put their words on record. This reflects the contrast between local ritual practice and an objectified national culture. The performing arts and folklore are part of that national culture. They were approved and institutionalized by the Soviet and post-Soviet states. Shamanist practice and kin rituals took place largely outside the sphere of official culture and were not subject to the same articulations. The work of urban shamans' associations and the public rituals they conduct (documented in chapter 7) has been largely moved into the public domain, however. Representatives of these associations were, like most culture workers, only too keen to be interviewed and place on record their outlooks and agendas.

The contrast, then, between the closed, private, and inward-facing world of kin-based ritual practice and the outward-facing performance of national identity and belonging was evident not only in the cultural forms that I analyze here but also in the research methods needed to understand each one. The former required time, talking to people steadily, digging potatoes, mucking out stables, and most importantly, eating and offering together. The latter engaged people through conducting interviews, following broadcasts, and reading print media. These differences illuminate local understandings of what constitutes "culture," which practices are public and which are closed, bounded, and intimate.

NOTES

1. Forsyth, *A History of the Peoples of Siberia: Russia's North Asian Colony.*
2. Nanzatov, *Ėtnogenez Zapadnykh Buriat: VI–XIX Vv.*
3. Nanzatov, "K Voprosy o Rannei Etnicheskoi Istorii Bargu-Buriatskoi Obshnosti"; Bolkhosoev, "K Voprosy ob Obshikh Istokakh Proiskhozhdeniia Etnonimov 'Buriat,' i 'Bulagat.'"
4. Krader, "Buryat Religion and Society"; Krader, "Principles and Structures in the Organization of the Asiatic Steppe-Pastoralists."

5. Baldaev, *Rodoslovnye Predaniia i Legendy Buriat*, 1:11–12; Mikhailov, *Buriatskii Shamanizm: Istoriia, Struktura i Sotsial'nye Funktsii*, 28–32; Humphrey, "Some Ritual Techniques in the Bull-Cult of the Buriat-Mongols," 17.

6. Humphrey, "The Uses of Genealogy: A Historical Study of the Nomadic and Sedentarised Buryat."

7. Hundley, *Speransky and the Buryats: Administrative Reform in Nineteenth Century Russia*.

8. Atwood, *Encyclopedia of Mongolia and the Mongol Empire*, 61–62.

9. Humphrey, "The Uses of Genealogy: A Historical Study of the Nomadic and Sedentarised Buryat."

10. Rupen, "The Buriat Intelligentsia"; Rupen, "Cyben Zamcaranovic Zamcarano (1880–1940)"; Montgomery, *Buriat Language Policy, 19th c.–1928: A Case Study in Tsarist and Soviet Nationality Practices*.

11. Smith, "The Nationalities Question in the Post-Soviet States"; Smith, *The Bolsheviks and the National Question, 1917–23*; Martin, *The Affirmative Action Empire: Nations and Nationalism in the Soviet Union, 1923–1939*; Hirsch, *Empire of Nations: Ethnographic Knowledge and the Making of the Soviet Union*.

12. Tarmakhanov, Dameshek, and Sanzhieva, *Istoria Ust'-Ordynskogo Buriatskogo Avtonomogo Okruga: Uchebnoe Pocobie Dlia Obshscheobrazovatelʹnykh Uchebnykh Zavedenii*; Humphrey, "Buryatiya and the Buryats"; Chakars, *The Socialist Way of Life in Siberia*, 77; Balzer, "Dilemmas of Federalism in Siberia."

13. Collins, "Subjugation and Settlement in Seventeenth and Eighteenth Century Siberia," 39; Forsyth, *A History of the Peoples of Siberia: Russia's North Asian Colony*, 89.

14. Forsyth, *A History of the Peoples of Siberia*.

15. Ibid., 190–91.

16. ROSSTAT, *Natsionalʹnyi Sostav Naseleniia Po Irkutskoi Oblasti Vkliuchaiia Ust'-Ordynskii Buriatskii Avtonomnyi Okrug*.

17. Ibid.

18. Humphrey, "Population Trends, Ethnicity and Religion among the Buryats"; Chakars, *The Socialist Way of Life in Siberia: Transformation in Buryatia*, 91–95.

19. GOSKOMSTAT, *Ust'-Ordynskii Buriatskii Avtonomnyi Okrug v Sifrakh i Faktakh (1990–2002)*.

20. Baldaev, *Rodoslovnye Predaniia i Legendy Buriat*, 1:368–69.

21. Riazanovskii, *Customary Law of the Nomadic Tribes of Siberia*.

22. Krader, "Principles and Structures in the Organization of the Asiatic Steppe-Pastoralists."

23. Raeff, *Siberia and the Reforms of 1822*.

24. Grant, *In the Soviet House of Culture*, 120–43.

25. Humphrey, "Population Trends, Ethnicity and Religion among the Buryats," 152–57.

26. Khandagurova, *Obriadnost' Kudinskikh i Verkholenskikh Buriat vo 2 Polovine XX Veka (Basseinov Verkhnego i Srednego tTcheniiarek : Kuda, Murino i Kamenka)*.

27. Humphrey, "The Uses of Genealogy: A Historical Study of the Nomadic and Sedentarised Buryat."

28. Krader, "Principles and Structures in the Organization of the Asiatic Steppe-Pastoralists"; Krader, "Buryat Religion and Society."

29. Sneath, *The Headless State : Aristocratic Orders, Kinship Society, & Misrepresentations of Nomadic Inner Asia*.

30. Raeff, *Siberia and the Reforms of 1822*, 117–19.

31. Hundley, *Speransky and the Buryats: Administrative Reform in Nineteenth Century Russia*.

TWO

HOSPITALITY, RECIPROCITY, AND EVERYDAY RITUAL

IN THE VILLAGES OF EKHIRIT-BULAGAT Raion, I found everyday life to be suffused with ritualized activity. Drinking tea with breakfast or vodka when visiting others always entailed offering a little for local spirits. Formalized hospitality involved a complex set of rules for sharing vodka—rules I learned in the time-honored ethnographic tradition of getting it wrong a lot and being chided and corrected until I got it right. As I traveled the area with my hosts and friends, frequent stops for offerings at the roadside emphasized Western Buryats' obligations to the spirits in the landscape. Obligations of reciprocity—between people, and between people and spirits—pervaded local sociality.

In the introduction to this book, I defined ritual not as a type of event but as mode of practice—in everyday life and on special occasions—in which people act according to predefined and repeating forms. This formalization marks out ritual practices as significant. Acts of reciprocity, hospitality, and commensality were ritualized in this way by my interlocutors, underscoring the mutual obligations that they implied as ethical imperatives in Western Buryat sociality. The recognition of incorporeal spirits in these acts manifested shamanist cosmology in everyday practice and sacralized those obligations.

SPRINKLING FOR THE SPIRITS

The most common ritual acts that I came across were the offerings to spirits referred to as *sprinkling*. The verb "to sprinkle"—*bryzgat'* in Russian or *turiakha* in the Ekhirit-Bulagat dialect of Buryat—denotes a wide variety of practices. In everyday life the verb describes offerings made whenever someone sits down to drink. Whether entertaining guests with vodka or simply drinking tea at breakfast time, my Buryat interlocutors poured a little on the table "for the spirits." Sprinkling also referred to roadside offerings when traveling and the ritual offerings Western Buryats are expected to make every year at their family's ancestral homeland. Furthermore, sprinkling occurred within larger-scale clan and lineage rituals, such as the *tailgan* ceremonies I describe in chapter 3, where vodka and milk products were offered to clans' ancestral spirits by pouring libations onto ritual fires. The Western Buryat term for a spirit is *burkhan*, in common with Turkic and Tungusic-speaking peoples in Siberia. The word is used across the wider Mongolian region for both Buddhist and shamanist deities.[1]

Sprinkling vodka, milk, or tea for the spirits is a common activity across Siberia and Inner Asia, and it is possible to observe many regional variations in practice. In Mongolia, for example, I have seen vodka flicked in the air with the ring finger of the right hand before drinking. As a guest of Khori Buryats, I witnessed the senior male present take the first glass of vodka from a bottle to a window, cover his head, and cast offerings to the sky. Among Western Buryats, however, drinks taken in the household were always poured onto the stove or directly onto the table. This reflected the focus on the table and the hearth in Western Buryat hospitality, a focus that was replicated at different scales of ritual practice.

RITUALIZED HOSPITALITY

My time living with Diadia Vitia in the isolated location of Khuty was punctuated by forays into the neighboring villages of

Muromtsovka and Novonikolaevskto get provisions from the local shops, make ritual offerings on behalf of fellow Khuty people who had moved to the bigger villages, or make social visits to relatives and friends. We usually made our way there on Vitia's *motorola*, a three-wheeled motorcycle with a trailer fitting on the back, where I bumped around as Diadia Vitia navigated the unmade roads.

Whenever we called in on people, no matter what time of day or however informally, tea was usually poured immediately and some food laid out on the table. The table is an important focal point of the household in the Cisbaikal villages where I lived. The Buryat children who I knew were chided if they did not sit properly or behave well at the table. Hospitality and the sharing of food and drink between neighbors, kin, or friends is valued in Buryat communities and incorporeal spirits are included in these practices.

A whole genre of table songs in Western Buryat communities reflects this emphasis on the table as center of the household—a place for the family to gather, a place where a healthy herd yields meat, and a place where the good fortune of having guests (and by implication good relations with others) is fulfilled. The following example, collected by Buryat ethnographer M. D. Urmaeva in Ekhirit-Bulagat Raion gives a good illustration of this:[2]

Dürben khültei ostooldo	At the table with its four legs
Düüreed huukhan haikhyema	Gathering to sit down is lovely
Dürben Teeshee uraguudaaraa	With relatives on four sides
Zygaalaad huukhan haikhyema	Conversing and sitting is lovely
Aduun sookhi moridtnai	Your horses are in the herd
Ar'bantai dalantai yabag le	Let them have fat lining their abdomen and withers![3]
Aiagtaikhan beyetnai	Have a cheerful nature!
Ashatai gyshatai üteleg le	With grandchildren and great grandchildren you live to old age.

Nuurai tanai dulaanda	[If] your lake is warm
Nygahan shubuun er'esetei	Then ducks fly in
Nugain tanai haikhanda	[If] your meadow is beautiful
Ailshad tandaa er'yesetei	Then guests will come to your household

Commensality—the act of eating and drinking together—is a salient feature of Western Buryat sociality. My friends in Cisbaikal villages followed a strict procedure for the ritual sharing of vodka, an important medium of cementing and symbolically expressing good relations between kinsmen, neighbors, and friends.

When visiting someone, or when entertaining visitors, a bottle of vodka was almost always given as a gift to the master of the house, usually referred to by the Russian term *khoziain*. The ritual precedence of the *khoziain* was evident throughout such occasions. The bottle would be presented with the right hand and often with a glass that would be used for sharing. The *khoziain* would then take charge of pouring and passing the glass around.

The first glass was always sprinkled at the hearth for the spirits of the household. This usually meant pouring a few drops onto the brick stove, even if it was not lit. In apartments without stoves, I saw vodka poured on electric cookers and even on radiators in offices or workplaces.

The single glass was then refilled and passed to each person at the table in turn by the *khoziain*. The sequence always ran clockwise, the direction the sun is said to travel (*Rus. po-solntsu*). Each person's glass was known as their *khubi* (Buryat for *share* or *portion*) and as each person received their *khubi*, they were expected to sprinkle a little vodka on the table for the spirits. The glass was always passed with the right hand, usually supported by the left held under the right elbow.

As the glass was passed around the table, people present undertook symmetrical exchanges with their *khubi*. While the glass was someone's *khubi*, they could show respect to another person present by offering them their glass after first putting it to their own lips. The *khoziain* would usually take precedence, or else a senior clan member or honored guest if present. The recipient was then expected to drink to the bottom of the glass in order to show respect to the person who passed it, or at the very least put the glass to their lips. If the glass was finished, it was to be returned to the pourer, who would refill it and pass it straight back to the person who had just drunk, who would again place it to their lips before returning it to the person who offered them their *khubi*. The giver was also expected to drink to the bottom, ensuring a symmetrical relationship of reciprocity and respect.

When the last glass was poured, it was proclaimed *khabain* and passed sunwise (clockwise) around the table with each person taking a small sip. At this point everyone present in the house was expected to be at the table. Even those not drinking were obliged to put the glass to their lips, and children are also called to the table to dab their ring finger in the glass and place it on their foreheads. If the bottle was gifted to the *khoziain*, this last glass was passed first, along with the empty bottle, to the person who brought the bottle so that the cycle began and ended with that person.

The sequence often proved baffling as glasses were passed backward and forward. Buryats from other regions commented on their own confusion at times. I finally felt that I had "got it" on an occasion when distant relatives visited Khuty from Chita Oblast and Diadia Vitia took pride in instructing me to guide his visitors through the drinking process.

When guests come from far afield, or friends marked special occasions, the register of hospitality practices was elevated by formal gift giving. The traditional Mongol practice of welcoming guests with the presentation of a silk scarf (*khadag*) had its analogue in Cisbaikalia of giving shirts to honored male guests and shawls to honored female guests. When these items were given, guests were dressed in their new clothes by their hosts (over what they were wearing) and given their own bottle of vodka to share.

On special occasions—such as birthdays, anniversaries, or graduations—the families with whom I lived slaughtered a sheep. At these celebrations special guests, senior members of the clan, or important figures in civic communities were honored by being served with the *toolei*—the sheep's head. These honored guests were expected to cut a piece of meat for the spirits and place it on the fire or stove. On such occasions the *khoziain* usually stood to address the honored guest, expressed the auspicious nature of the occasion, and emphasized the strength of the relationship between guest and host.

Seniority and precedence depended on the character of the event. When I brought a bottle of vodka to a gathering after a Khertoi *ulus* ritual, I was instructed to present the bottle to Ivan Petrovich, the senior male present within the hierarchy of the clan. When I joined a number of local cultural activists after the village *Sur-kharban* (Buryat traditional sports competition), the chief administrator of the Novonikolaevsk rural administration was presented with the first bottle of vodka. Following this, vodka was presented to two retired teachers who were respected within the community and founded the local folklore ensemble. In civic contexts such as this, practices were adapted to reflect seniority and respect in public life.

The code of conduct surrounding Buryat hospitality exemplifies the role of ritual in day-to-day life: the symmetrical exchanges, the special direction for passing the glass, and the use of the right hand supported by the left all formalized these practices and demarcated them as significant. Hospitality was an important means of ensuring good social relations, and reciprocity was vital to everyday life in the countryside, where help was often required from neighbors and kin. Neighbors were often called on for help with management of the domestic herd or homestead and quick favors, such as lifting heavy things, pushing a car out of the mud, or borrowing tools. Neighbors in both Khuty and Novonikolaevsk were occasionally asked to herd cattle home in the evenings when people were away, help with milking, or assist in finding lost animals. Ritualized hospitality underscored the moral obligations of reciprocity.

In everyday ritual practice, sprinkling acknowledged the presence of spirits and included them in relations of reciprocity. Spirits were an omnipresent force, able to effect changes in the fortunes of all present and likely to inflict misfortune if not properly acknowledged. Strictly ordered hospitality practices not only reinforced the principle of reciprocity in relations between neighbors and kinsmen but, in including spirits, sacralized them.

Duties of reciprocity and the obligation to participate in hospitality rituals were often manipulated when favors needed to be pulled. When traveling to Novonikolaevsk or Muromtsovka from Khuty to buy supplies or visit the *sel'sovet*, Diadia Vitia always carried a small vodka glass with him. He often purchased a bottle of vodka on arrival and would share it with friends and acquaintances if he met them on the street or called on them. This was a good way of renewing friendships, after which he could more comfortably ask people if he could buy petrol from them. With petrol being in very short supply in the district, Vitia often relied on getting it in order to make it back to Khuty and always had a length of hose ready to siphon off a couple of liters if the opportunity arose. Vitia thus relied on the social ties consolidated through hospitality customs in order to maintain his mobility.

Theorists of hospitality have long noted some of the tensions inherent in such practices. Julian Pitt Rivers famously recorded the tensions surrounding a moral obligation to receive guests with no expectation of return in Mediterranean contexts.[4] This tension has been observed in the wider Mongolian context by Humphrey, who describes the heavy obligation of providing hospitality to strangers who may also not ultimately reciprocate.[5] During my fieldwork I occasionally heard complaints about those who took advantage of hospitality but did not return it. In one extreme case, I saw a man known locally as an alcoholic chased out from a household where he had turned up when he saw other guests arriving. The hosts told me that he just looked for opportunities to drink but never brought a bottle himself or hosted other people. Also underpinning tensions in Buryat communities are the ongoing expectations of reciprocity and the fear that relations may be asymmetrical. That same tension underpinned the often-voiced fear that powerful spirits may be vengeful or invoke bad fortune if they are forgotten or offended by local Buryats who do not show the requisite recognition through sprinkling and making offerings in return for their protection.

OFFERINGS AT THE ROADSIDE

Traveling with Buryat friends, I soon came to know dedicated sites along the road, where we were expected to make offerings for spirits. Each site, known as a *bar'sa* (fully *barisa* or, informally, *bar'sazhka*) was recognized as a place to sprinkle in return for safe passage. In everyday travel between villages, *bar'sa* sites were usually acknowledged by casting a little tobacco out of vehicle windows, sounding the horn, or simply raising a hand in acknowledgment. For more significant journeys—such as traveling to clan rituals, weddings, and civic events such as folklore festivals or sports competitions—my Buryat hosts usually stopped to offer vodka or tobacco and drink and smoke themselves. On my first trip into the area with Aleksei, I produced a bottle of vodka to share with my hosts, only to find a horrified reception: Aleksei explained to me that we should not have passed sacred sites while carrying vodka without stopping to share some with the spirits, who would be offended that we had not done so. Offerings were quickly made, and we made a point of stopping at every *bar'sa* on the return journey.

Most *bar'sa* sites in the area were not marked by tethering posts, cairns, or ribbons tied to the trees as they are in other parts of Inner Asia; they were simply known by local people. At the border of the okrug on the road from Irkutsk to Baikal, a decorated ceremonial tethering post and shelter had been erected for tourists to make offerings on the way to Baikal. Most Buryats I knew did not stop there, however, but at the "real" *bar'sa*, unmarked, a few hundred meters along the road. Some people I asked explained roadside offerings as being for any spirits that may be encountered along the road. I found most *bar'sa* sites were, however, explicitly dedicated to the master spirits of sacred places near to the road or to the spirits of deceased shamans whose funeral sites were close by.

The sharing of tobacco or drink in return for safe travel echoes the obligations of reciprocity constituted through ritual hospitality and reminds travelers of the presence of spirits in the landscape, protecting local people and determining their fortunes. These relationships are made more explicit still in the annual ritual cycle undertaken by the Buryats among whom I lived.

HOUSEHOLD SPRINKLING RITES

Over the summer months I spent in Khuty, work or daily activities were halted on several occasions by the arrival of kin and former villagers returning to the *ulus* from their homes in the city or neighboring settlements. Vitia's relatives appeared, household by household, to sprinkle in the places where their parents' or grandparents' homes used to stand.

Local Buryats referred to their ancestral villages—mostly former *ulus* sites—by a variety of terms. In everyday Russian, my interlocutors talked of their *malaia rodina* (little homeland). In Buryat the term *toonto nyutag* was occasionally used, a term historically used to define the place where someone's afterbirth was buried. In more general terms, people referred simply to their *nyutag* (homeland) and sometimes to their clan or family *hearth* (Rus. *ochag*).

Most Buryat heads of household I knew undertook offering rituals every year on behalf of their families. The sprinkling was sometimes led by the head of household himself, alternatively a senior relative or clan shaman was asked to officiate. Most who sprinkled in Khuty asked Vitia to conduct the offerings, and I was able to observe and take part on a number of occasions. I was also able to join Dmitry in making offerings at his home *ulus* of Khertoi, now completely depopulated. The rites were usually referred to simply as sprinkling, but Dmitri also referred to his annual offering rite in Buryat as *gaza dosoo hukha*, meaning "to sit outside and inside." The term perhaps refers to the historical practice of offering both at the household hearth and the summer pastures. Most coming to offer in Khuty offered at the site of their former family homes. Those still living in their home villages, or who had relatives who did, sprinkled at the household's stove as their family hearth. All of Vitia's brothers made their offerings in his kitchen, for example.

The basic form of the rites was very similar on the occasions I observed them. Once the site of a former household was established, ritual participants usually began by gathering three stones and placing them in a triangle before constructing and lighting a ritual fire between the stones. When Diadia Vitia carried our offering rites within his own house, he lit a small fire on top of the stove. Participants then burned scented grasses (usually a grass known in Russian as *bogorodskaia trava* and in Buryat as *hükhrehen'*). Anyone present cleansed themselves in the fragrant smoke before beginning offerings. Men did this by waving each foot in sunwise (*po-solntsu*) circles over the fire, women by smoking their hands in the same sunwise circles. Burning scented grass was also used to cleanse the area where offering rites took place—either by waving it around the room where sprinkling was taking place or circling the designated ritual area outside three times. Householders also cleansed any milk products or vodka to be sprinkled in the smoke of the ritual fire, again by moving it in sunwise circles.

Offerings consisted of a clear spirit—either vodka or *tarisun*, a drink distilled from milk that was a Buryat staple before the availability of mass-produced vodka. Milk and a milk product such as *salamat* (a cream prepared with oil) were also offered. The senior male presiding over the rite—the shaman, elder, or head of household—poured each product in turn into a glass or wooden bowl before addressing requests to ancestral spirits to look after the family for the coming year, naming each member in turn. After each of these prayers, the officiant poured some of the product on the fire before drinking a little himself. He then filled the glass or bowl for each person present, who was also expected to pour a little on the fire and drink. During prayers, those present would show their concurrence with the requests uttered by raising their right hand, half cupped, usually in front of their chests.

After the sprinkling had finished, everybody present shared any remaining food and vodka. Buryat friends explained to me on several occasions that vodka left over from sprinkling rites should be finished as soon as possible after the rite. Often neighbors or friends were invited to help finish the vodka, and on several occasions, I visited neighbors with Vitia or Dmitri and Erzhena to partake in this activity. As with any invitation, it would have been seen as unusual and problematic if such a request to help finish the vodka were refused.

Household practices also include an annual ceremony known as *feeding the mongol*, which follows much the same pattern but is addressed exclusively to the family's *mongol-burkhan*. At the turn of the twentieth century, the ethnographers Petri and Zhamsarano recorded that *mongol-burkhan* was understood as the spirit of those who lived on the land before the Buryats came.[6] Today the *mongol* is generally explained as the spirit of the household, including the family herd. Most of my interlocutors explained the rite as being made in order that nothing bad happens to the household. In principle the *mongol* is the spirit of the current household, but many people also carry out the rite at their

Feeding the *mongol* with vodka and *salamat* at a former *ulus* site, Ekhirit-Bulagat Raion, June 2007.

ancestral homeland.[7] Some people I knew carried out this rite as their main annual offering, while others observed both feeding the *mongol* and offerings to their ancestors in separate rites.

Dmitri, whom I accompanied to feed the *mongol* in June 2007, sprinkled in four places: at the site of his former family home in Khertoi; at the Khertoi summer pastures; at a *bar'sa* site approaching Khertoi; and in the yard in Novonikolaevsk. On the occasion that I accompanied Dmitri, he invited along his older brother, Sasha, and Vanya, a Khertoi kinsman who owned a car and was able to drive us to Khertoi. As well as helping to consume the vodka, Sasha and Vanya were able to add their prayers to Dmitri's and ensure that everything was done correctly. Erzhena emphasized to me that Dmitri and his brothers were particularly meticulous about sprinkling correctly as, on the death of Dmitri's father a few years ago, it had been revealed that he had not sprinkled in all of the required places in Khertoi.

Dmitri's offerings consisted of three liters of vodka as well as milk and *salamat*. After sprinkling at the *bar'sa* on the road to Khertoi from Novonikolaevsk and then at one of the springs that rise in Khertoi, the first task was to find the site of the former family home. This was located by looking at patterns of nettle growth and pacing out the distance from the nearest track. Offerings at this site were made in three places in the shape of a triangle. At each site three stones were placed in a triangle, a fire was lit, scented grass added, and offerings of vodka, milk, and *salamat* made. After each address, Dmitri poured milk, *salamat*, and vodka on each of the stones and then on the fire while naming each family member in turn. The process was then repeated at the summer pastures and finally in the yard of their current home. Erzhena stressed to me that all these offerings had to be made in the course of one day, before sunset.

On that occasion Dmitri and his companions explained to me some of the rules regarding sprinkling rites: Once every five years, Khertoi families feed the *mongol* with a ram. If a live ram is not available, meat may be offered but must include offerings from each part of the body. Once a son is married and heads his own household, he is no longer named in offerings but must make his own. According to the principle of patriliny, once a woman is married, she becomes a member not only of her husband's household but of his clan as well. Consequently, a married woman is no longer named in prayers at her homeland but at that of her husband's. A woman will usually return to make offerings at her own homeland once every five years after marriage, however.

Sprinkling rites conforming to the patterns described above are observed at other times of year. On *Mikola*, formerly an orthodox Christian festival for St. Nicholas on the 23rd of May, it is common to sprinkle for the growth of the grass into hay as the steppe finally emerges from the thaw of spring. People also offer libations tied to particular personal events. Aside from assisting with annual sprinkling rites, Vitia was called on by neighbors to sprinkle on the birthdays of children away studying in Ulan-Ude and for the success of a relative enrolling in university. I also knew Khertoi friends to make offerings for success in exams or before making long journeys. When in Khuty I looked at the calendar one day and remarked that it was my sister's birthday, Diadia Vitia insisted that we sprinkle for her.

Over the course of several rites and discussions, I was told of a number of prohibitions and rules that govern all sprinkling rites: Bottles in which vodka is carried should be plain with a straight neck. The label around the neck must be cut off. Men should wear belts and women, if present, should cover their heads and wear skirts. Rites must not be carried out if a member of the household is menstruating, as the house is then considered unclean and offerings will not be heard by the spirits. On days when offerings are made, visiting other households is avoided in case those houses are unclean and participants become polluted. It is to be ensured that visitors to the household before the rite are also "clean." When purchasing vodka it is checked that the shop is clean. Rites cannot be carried out in a year when a family member has died until after *Pokhrov*, another formerly orthodox festival on October 14, as members of the household are also seen as being unclean. This reflects a wider year-long taboo on death that prevents clans in which a death has taken place from attending *tailgan* rites, making offerings, marrying, or building. *Pokhrov* is considered the beginning and end of the shamanist ritual calendar, and household rites may be made at any time after this date. January is seen as a month when no offerings should be made, and local shamans told me they were able to rest. In practice most offerings are made in the summer.

It is often noted by ethnographers that while ritual acts can be identified by submission to a designated form of action, the reason why that action takes that form is often obscure to participants.[8] I found this to be true of many elements of local ritual practice in Cisbaikalia. Few people could tell me exactly why there had to be three stones around a ritual fire, why a bottle had to be a certain shape, or why three liters were necessary, just that this was the way it must be done. Moreover, the offering practices varied considerably. As Diadia Vitia explained, exasperated, when I tried to pin down some exact rules: "Everyone does it differently. Some people sprinkle at the summer pastures; some don't. Some people feed the *mongoi*; others don't. I am nearly fifty, and I don't know exactly how it should be done!" However obscure the origin of some actions, the necessity of these practices was clear to almost everybody I asked: offering at a hearth, on the road, or at the table constitutes a duty to recognize spirits in return for protection and good fortune.

WEDDINGS AND GIFTS

Just as formal reciprocity governs relations between neighbors and households, it can also mediate relations between clans through the exchange of wedding gifts. Caroline Humphrey's Soviet-era ethnography of Buryat collective farms notes the tenacity of cycles of reciprocity between families and kin groups in Buryat weddings.[9] In two weddings I attended in Ekhirit-Bulagat Raion, practices of reciprocity and ritualized hospitality remained central to proceedings.

When Erzhena and Dmitri celebrated the wedding of their son, Vadim, in 2011, Dmitri's Khertoi kinsmen assembled a week early to slaughter sheep for the feast. The butchery was accompanied by Dmitri continually sprinkling and exchanging glasses of vodka with those who had come to help. The bride and groom's families took it in turns to host wedding celebrations. The night before the feast hosted by the groom's family, I assisted with unpacking and preparing around two hundred shirts and scarves for guests who were all personally presented and dressed with these over the course of the feast. All reciprocated with gifts of money for the young couple. Following the wedding, Dmitri's kin hosted the bride's family at their homes as celebrations continued over two days. The most honored guests at the wedding were the family of the bride. At both the weddings I attended locally, the bride and groom took a relatively passive role in proceedings—receiving gifts and drinking with guests. The key symbolism of obligations between families was carried out by clan elders: Dmitri's oldest brother, the senior member of his family, accompanied Vadim as a guest of the bride's family before bringing her to the civil ceremony and celebrations. At another wedding I attended in Ust'-Orda, clan elders enacted exchanges of belts and tobacco to symbolize the relationship between the bride's natal clan and her new relatives. In this regard, wedding ceremonies both marked the formal transition of a bride from her natal to marital clan and cemented relations of reciprocity between clans and neighbors.

During the course of Vadim's wedding feast, different local families made speeches announcing their gifts to the couple—usually considerable sums of money. One of the wedding party recorded all the gifts given before the guests in question came forward to the top table to share in a round of vodka drinking with the married couple. Erzhena explained to me that the combined gifts of money provided young couples with the means to set up a home. She stressed the importance of recording the gifts since the families of the married couple would be expected to gift at least as much back when members of the guest's family married. "You see," she exclaimed, "Buryats are always in debt!"

RECIPROCITY AND OBLIGATION

The concept of reciprocity has been a dominant trope in anthropology for over a century. Since Marcel Mauss's landmark *Essay on the Gift*, ethnographers have observed multifarious ways that social relations are built through reciprocal obligations. Marshall Sahlins famously created a typology of reciprocity that included both direct reciprocal exchange and a more "generalised reciprocity," which evokes ongoing mutual obligation.[10]

In recent times the ubiquity of reciprocity has been critiqued from a number of perspectives. Some scholars have stressed that the principle of sharing is often overlooked where food, particularly the spoils of hunting, is given out with any social obligation or expectation of return. Others have critiqued the projection of Western notions of transactional exchange or debt onto contexts where material transfers are not perceived in those ways.[11] Nonetheless, I found the notions of exchange, return, and mutual obligation traditionally associated with reciprocity to be pervasive in Western Buryat practice. The direct and symmetrical exchanges of vodka and gifts are particularly formalized in ritual practice, but they underlie a broader ethos of the generalized reciprocity described by Sahlins in eliciting favors or material support in everyday life.

In a similarly critical vein, theorists have sought to distinguish between *hospitality*, which is used to mediate relations with strangers, and *hosting* others who may be known or tied into ongoing relations of reciprocity.[12] Particularly striking in the Western Buryat context is that while the register of these practices may change—at times involving the giving of gifts or a particularly elaborate spread—the underlying form remains the same, whether reconstituting ongoing relationships with kin and neighbors or invoking the possibility of new relationships or future return from strangers and new acquaintances.

These social obligations are emphasized through the ritualization of everyday hospitality and consumption. This formalized practice draws attention to acts of reciprocity as crucial to Buryat social life. The recognition and inclusion of the incorporeal spirits that dwell in the Cisbaikal landscape sacralizes these principles. As the next chapter shows, this ritual form and its underlying ethos were writ large in the collective rites I attended in the summer months. The notion of reciprocity and mutual support not only underpins relations between individuals, spirits, households, and clans but is a crucial obligation *within* kin groups.

NOTES

1. Laufer, "Burkhan."
2. Urmaeva, "Zastolnye Pesni Ekhirit-Bulagatskikh Buriat."
3. Horse meat, especially the fat, is a valued dish among Western Buryats. Horses and children have often been explained to me as signs of wealth in Buryat culture.
4. Pitt-Rivers, "The Law of Hospitality."
5. Humphrey, "Hospitality and Tone."
6. Cited in Khandagurova, *Obriadnost' Kudinskikh i Verkholenskikh Buriat vo 2 Polovine XX Veka*, 33.
7. Khangalov, *Sobranie Sochinenii, Vol. 1*, 478; Mikhailov, *Buriatskii Shamanizm: Istoriia, Struktura i Sotsialnye Funktsii*, 282; Shaglanova, "Kul't 'Mongol-Burkhanov' v Sovremennom Predstavlenii Buriat-Ekhiritov"; Khandagurova, *Obriadnost Kudinskikh i Verkholenskikh Buriat*.
8. This phenomenon is well-documented in Humphrey and Laidlaw, *The Archetypal Actions of Ritual*.
9. Humphrey, *Marx Went Away—But Karl Stayed Behind*.
10. Mauss, *The Gift*; Sahlins, *Stone Age Economics*; Gregory, *Gifts and Commodities*; Strathern, *The Gender of the Gift*.
11. Widlok, "Sharing"; Weiner, *Inalienable Possessions: The Paradox of Keeping—While Giving*; Sneath, "Transacting and Enacting"; Graeber, *Debt: The First 5000 Years*.
12. Chau, "Hosting as a Cultural Form."

THREE

KINSHIP, RITUAL, AND BELONGING IN WESTERN BURYAT COMMUNITIES

WALKING THROUGH THE VILLAGE OF Novonikolaevsk one afternoon, I met an older man passing the other way. We exchanged a polite greeting before he stopped, looked at me quizzically, and asked, "*Ty chei*?" The question was not "who are you?" but "*whose* are you?" I explained that I was a student from the UK, an ethnographer, and told him that I was living at Zhambalov's in Khuty. It was only the last piece of information that really seemed to be of interest to him, however. "Ah, I know Alexander Zhambalov," the old man said, nodding (in fact referring to Diadia Vitia's late father). His curiosity sated by having placed me in the local scheme of things, the man moved on.

In a study of belonging in Evenki and Dolgan communities of Siberia, David Anderson evokes the "subtle mix of possessive attributes which signal the relationship between a person and other people or a person and the land."[1] Such a formulation could well describe kinship and belonging in Western Buryat communities. Unlike the nomadic communities described by Anderson, many Buryats no longer have a day-to-day relationship with their ancestral homelands but constitute their relationship with people and place through ritual practice.

Relatedness to others in the villages of Cisbaikalia was often expressed in idioms of possession, such as that used by the older man. The question *ty chei?* is typically asked of children and young people. The prefix *nash* (our) is widely used in Russian to differentiate one's own from outsiders. Within families, first names are often prefixed with a possessive pronoun, such as *our* Sasha or *our* Vania. I often heard these phrases used to denote affinity to Buryat clan groups with the possessive pronoun qualified by someone's *ulus* identity. Vania from Khuty was thus *nash Khutskii Vania* in Russian or *manai Khutin Vania* in Buryat. The possessive pronoun is situational, however, and might be employed to express mutual belonging to any number of social groups. These prefixes may denote kin or clan affiliations; at sports or folklore competitions, they may be extended to members of one's village or district team to reflect attachment to civic communities; or they may be used to differentiate Buryats or fellow Russian citizens from foreigners.

It soon became clear to me that placing someone according to *whose* they were implied a host of expectations related to that social positioning. Belonging to a Buryat clan comes with obligations of reciprocity to the ancestral spirits that provide protection and between kin, among whom mutual support is necessary. These relations are sacralized through shamanist ritual practices that emphasize mutuality and reciprocity, namely the *tailgan* ceremonies that take place periodically. While kinship is reckoned through patrilineal descent, it is practically constituted through ritual commensality and exchange. These ritual forms are socially exclusive. They define who is *ours* and who is not, and they inform social obligations within bounded groups. Furthermore, *tailgan* rites embed kinship in ancestral homelands and maintain relations with the spirits that remain there, constituting a distinctively Buryat sense of belonging to people and place.

TAILGAN CEREMONIES

Tailgan rituals have been well-documented in Russian and Western studies of Buryat shamanism. These rites involve the offering of sheep, goats, and occasionally horses to local spirits in return for the protection and well-being of clan members.[2] *Tailgan* rites may take place for a closely related lineage, an *ulus*, or larger clan groupings. The larger rites are termed *ekhe tailgan*, Buryat for *big* or *great tailgan*. Most *tailgan* rites I witnessed or heard about occurred at a dedicated place on the *ulus* site, but big *tailgan* ceremonies were held on common ritual sites, such as the sacred hills of Kapsal, Mankhai, and Baitag along the Kuda River valley.

All sacred sites had their own master spirits named foremost in offerings. In common with other Mongolic peoples, Buryats refer to these spirits as *ezhen*. Western Buryats also use the Russian term *khoziain* to describe these master spirits, a word used to denote both a head of household and a host. Sometimes master spirits are clan ancestors, sometimes individuals associated with that place in local myths. In many instances the identities of spirit and place become merged such that both are revered when named in offering rites, and both are evoked by the toponyms. My friend Nikolai argued that when his kinsmen offered at Khuty, they were recognizing both spirit and place as a kind of unity. Similarly, Khertoi was the founder of an *ulus*, but the name now references the *ulus* site—in particular its spring—as well as the ancestor and clan.

Offerings are also made to a number of other spirits associated with particular places. When offering at Khertoi, Dmitri recounted that prayers are made to former shamans of the clan, including one significant "grandmother." He explained that when Ekhirit clans of the upper Kuda valley go to make offerings on the sacred hill of Baitag, prayers were dedicated to the ancestor of the

Bura clan—himself named Bura—and his eight sons, the *Buriin naiman* (*Bur.* the Bura eight) from whom several local *ulus* clans are said to be descended. When I asked Aleksei, the shaman from Ust'-Orda settlement, to whom his prayers for the Kharazargai clan were dedicated, he spoke of the spirit master of Mankhai and also notable ancestors of his own clan: "We pray for the prosperity of our native land.... We make requests to our own ancestors that all our prayers are taken to higher spirits. They should pass on these pleas like a relay. And we name our ancestors: seven initiated shamans and five grandmothers—shamanesses."

The grandmother spirits mentioned by both Dmitri and Aleksei are a common phenomenon locally. Most *ulus* clans have their own *toodei* (grandmother) named during *tailgan* rites and sometimes designated an offering site of their own. *Toodei* spirits are either powerful female shamans or women who have borne many children and have been important matriarchs within a clan.

Offering rites are thus dedicated to a variety of spirits of place, shamans, and ancestors. As I will argue below of kinship and relatedness more broadly, the crucial relationship between clans and spirits is one of recognition and reciprocity enacted through offering and feeding.

I have attended three lineage and *ulus tailgan* ceremonies in the Kuda valley—as a guest of Khuty, Khertoi, and Kharazargai friends. I have also participated in six *big tailgan* ceremonies across the Baikal region, some of which are documented in chapter 7. All the local rites I participated in followed a similar form. Below I illustrate this form through description of an *ulus tailgan* I attended in 2006. First it is worth noting how ritual authority is manifested in such events.

LOCAL SHAMANS AND *HOLDERS OF THE CUP*

At *tailgan* ceremonies in Cisbaikalia, participants usually referred to the senior clan member leading the prayers as their shaman.

Yet while these elders clearly garnered a great deal of respect and reverence, they were not the flamboyant figures that are often associated with shamanism.

The popular image of the Siberian shaman is one of a robed figure, masked by a veil, calling up spirits with a drum, and adorned with accoutrements, such as a mirror hanging around their neck. Historically shamans of this kind were common to every Buryat community. Initiated through nine degrees of expertise, professional male shamans (*böö*) and female shamans (*idygan*) led offering rites, undertook rituals to counter illness and misfortune, and used trance techniques and drumming to summon and converse with spirits.[3] Like all forms of ritual and religion in the Soviet Union, shamanism was effectively repressed under Stalin, and professional shamans were forced to recant their practice, imprisoned, or even executed.

In the villages of Ekhirit-Bulagat Raion, there were a number of local figures who were called on to lead household sprinkling rites or *tailgan* ceremonies for their clans and who were recognized as religious authorities. These figures were all male and usually referred to as *shaman* in Russian, or as *böö* or *tagsha buryashad* in Buryat. The latter term literally means "the holder of the cup," in reference to the act of sprinkling offerings. Ritual leaders did not wear costumes, use drums, or enter trances. Formal processes of initiation were not common in Cisbaikalia at the time of my field research. Instead, local communities and clans recognized those best qualified to lead ritual practice through their shamanic lineages, seniority within clans, and ritual knowledge.

Narratives of shamanic authority in the post-Soviet era often focus on the issue of who could, or should, have taken up a shamanic initiation but for the Soviet disruption of professional lineages. Buryat shamans have historically been identified by strong *utkha*—a shamanic essence indicated by a history of initiated shamans in the family. This remains an important factor in the recognition of local shamans today. Aleksei was able to trace the path of his *utkha* back through the last initiated shamans in his family, executed in the 1930s, to the past shamans of his clan, who he named in offering rites. Knowledge of the correct rites is particularly important after the repression of religion in the Soviet era left shamanic knowledge somewhat fragmented. While *utkha* legitimated Aleksei's status, he emphasized to me that the *utkha* had come to him because he had a knowledge of Buryat language, ritual practices, and his clan's history. This knowledge was not shared by his older cousins, to whom he felt the *utkha* should rightfully have passed. Narratives of shamanic calling frequently include reference to periods of illness or misfortune once recognized as *shaman sickness*—a sign that the spirits might be punishing a neglected call to duty.

Ritual specialists of this kind have been described across the Buryat and wider Mongol world in the post-Soviet era and recognized as important carriers of knowledge in a world where professional, initiated shamans have disappeared from view.[4] Yet there has always been a role for local practitioners, even before the fragmentation of knowledge and disruption of practice effected by Soviet communism. Humphrey and Onon have described ritual *elders* in Daur Mongol communities, and Buryat ethnographers have also documented the role of noninitiated shamans in pre-Soviet times.[5]

A number of such local shamans lived in the Novonikolaevsk area. At rites I attended with Khertoi friends, participants referred to the oldest man present called on to make the ritual prayers as their shaman. Vitia in Khuty was occasionally referred to as a shaman by other people, though never by himself, and was often asked to lead offering rites by other Khuty families. When I asked Vitia what qualified someone to sprinkle, he told me that any head of household could. Vitia is actually the second eldest brother in his family, but as he remains at the family home and keeps the hearth, it is to him that his younger brothers and cousins turn to lead sprinkling rites for them. As well as his knowledge of the rites, I gained the impression that Vitia was often asked because of his sincerity. After telling me that any *khoziain* could sprinkle, he added, "Anyone can say the words, but it is necessary to believe."

A *TAILGAN* ON BAITAG

In June 2006, Dmitri's clan—the Khertoi *ulus*—organized a *tailgan* to be held on the sacred hill of Baitag. The mountain lies a few kilometers from the *ulus* site and is revered as a sacred place by local Ekhirit clans. All the Khertoi people living locally went to make offerings at the *ulus* site together the preceding week and were joined by relatives from farther afield for the *tailgan*. This earlier sprinkling ceremony was organized and led by Ivan Petrovich, a man of around sixty who lived in Novonikolaevsk. Ivan, I later learned, is the oldest male in a family descended from the oldest son of Khertoi and thus the senior member of the clan.

At the preceding event, Ivan organized donations for the purchase of an animal for slaughter. As he did so, he drew up a list of those who had contributed and were thus entitled to receive a share of the meat, even if they were unable to attend the rite in person. Ivan seemed a little uncertain about having me present and kept his distance throughout. I was generally made welcome by other clan seniors, however, several of whom introduced themselves with the word *diadia* (uncle). The word is often used as a term of both affection and respect in Russia, and here again a Russian idiom is employed in the context of Buryat kinship: within a clan, older men are all referred to as *diadia*.

The *tailgan* was attended by men only. On the morning of the ceremony, all the local Khertoi men gathered in Novonikolaevsk at Ivan's home. Ivan consented to my attendance on condition that I did not photograph or film the rite. His younger brother directed much of the rite on Baitag, telling kinsmen where to stand, overseeing the slaughter and butchery, and instructing younger relatives to chop wood or tend the fires. On this occasion the oldest man present, an octogenarian still living locally, was designated as shaman to lead the offerings. The Khertoi kinsmen left in a convoy of cars and vans with a tractor and trailer carrying firewood, cauldrons, and the animal for slaughter. In this case a ram was to be offered for the clan.

On the way to Baitag from Novonikolaevsk, the entire party stopped at the summer pastures above Khertoi to sprinkle libations. Here the entourage was met by relatives coming from Irkutsk, Angarsk, and Ulan-Ude. One participant had come all the way from Yakutsk in northeastern Siberia to attend the rite. Participants lit a fire, and everybody smoked their feet before the officiating shaman made prayers to the spirit master of Khertoi and the shamans and ancestors of the *ulus* while sprinkling *tarisun* on the fire. All present stood around in a semicircle facing Khertoi with their right hands raised, half cupped, as the prayers were made. A glass was then passed around the entire company, refilled for each person, and all present sprinkled a little on the fire and drank. The process was repeated at the foot of Baitag before ascending the hill. On the way to the top, a birch branch was selected and cut down to be planted in the ground during the rite.

The beginning section of all the large-scale rituals I saw involved a great deal of work. A fire was lit to burn throughout the rite, and the birch branch was planted in the ground with a ribbon tied around it in front of the place where the ram was due to be killed. Birch branches like this, known as a *türge*, were present in every ceremony I attended. Wood was cut and cauldrons were set up to cook the *tailgan* meat.

At the top of Baitag is a large, flat cairn. This was referred to by Dmitri as an *obo*—the name for the circular stone cairns that mark offering places across Inner Asia. Many local people also refer to the Baitag cairn as a stone *sheree*, the Buryat word for both a table and an altar, relating to its role in the ceremony.[6]

KINSHIP, RITUAL, AND BELONGING

Members of a Buryat clan line up to make offerings at their ancestral hearth. Ekhirit-Bulagat Raion, June 2006.

After cleansing our feet in smoke once more, everybody reassembled in a semicircle around the ritual fire and *türge*, facing the cairn with their milk, vodka, and *salamat*. As prayers were made to the spirits, each head of household drank a little of their vodka, named each member of their family, and then cast the rest into the air in the direction of the *obo*, each time drawing the spirits' attention to the offering by calling out, "*Soog!*" After this part of the rite, all the participants processed sunwise (*po-solntsu*) around the ritual fire and then sunwise around the cairn, pouring vodka on both as they went.

Following the initial prayers, the ram was brought in front of the birch, where the officiating elder fed it with a little milk and then poured some along its head and back. The beast was then killed in the traditional way: the Buryat practice, in common with other parts of the Mongolian region, is to lay the animal on its back, cut an in incision in the chest, and pinch the aorta, causing a quick death. Meanwhile the milk from the bucket that had been used to pour on the animal's back was then brought along the line of men, and a little was dabbed on the front of each man's coat. Keeping the dead animal in the same position, the fleeces were cut away and the animals gradually stripped of meat. The intestines were taken away, cleaned out, and then filled with blood to make sausage. All the meat was placed in large cauldrons at the ritual site and cooked straight away.

In the meantime, a rectangular offering pyre was constructed on top of the cairn. These pyres are also referred to as *sheree*, as the place where the meat for the spirits is offered. While the butchery took place, people sat around, chatted, and caught up with each other's news. One of the senior members of the clan brought around vodka for those who were cutting wood or cooking the meat. Each sprinkled a little on the carcass of the ram before drinking. As participants took turns working, relationships of seniority within the clan were noticeable. Older members directed the work and younger members always did as they were told with deference. The hierarchy was entirely based on genealogical and age seniority, roles in civic life were irrelevant. While Dmitri might be addressed respectfully with his patronymic, Dmitri Viktorovich, by Khertoi children at school, he will be known as Diadia Dima during offering rites. Another Khertoi friend, Sasha, whom I knew as senior administrator at the village *sel'sovet* and a respected figure locally, blended quietly into working with his kinsmen, directed by clan elders. As a liminal space in which civic roles and relationships were suspended, the *tailgan* created a context for alternative clan hierarchies to be enacted.

After this period of work and socializing, a portion of each part of the animal was placed in the middle on the pyre, while the rest of the meat was laid out on a plastic sheet and divided carefully into even piles for each household present. Some was also

Clan members sprinkle offerings while circumambulating the fire. Ekhirit-Bulagat Raion, June 2006.

set aside for me and two guests (Buryats from other clans). Each portion of meat was referred to as a *khubi*. One of the senior clan members read out the names of those who had donated money. Each came and collected their meat and bagged it up.

The men present then reassembled in a semicircle facing the pyre with the bags of meat open. The pyre was set alight as the officiating elder made further requests for the spirits to accept the meat. After the elder's last prayer, the company all followed him in turning sunwise on the spot with their arms raised and calling out, *"A-khurai! A-khurai!"* This gesture is usually described as summoning the spirits or asking for their blessings. The birch *türge* was then placed on the fire. Participants again circled the cairn followed by the ritual fire, placing a little of each of their household's *khubi* in the fire. Finally all present were asked to add three stones to the cairn. The company then retreated to a place a little farther back on the mountain. Leftover *tarisun* was passed around while a series of wrestling matches was organized. The atmosphere became more playful as participants lightheartedly goaded each other on and mocked the losers.

After leaving Baitag, the convoy returned to the summer pastures above Khertoi, where a fire was lit and the men again stood in a semicircle with their bags of meat open in front of them. Here the oldest man made final prayers to the master spirits of Khertoi to bless the meat. A last glass of *tarisun* was passed around the entire company before everybody dispersed in various directions. That evening in Novonikolaevsk, Erzhena cooked the meat Dmitri and I had brought home, and we ate it. Erzhena pointed out that the *tailgan* meat should not be shared outside the household and that any leftovers had to be incinerated, not thrown out or given to the dog.

SACRIFICE AND COMMUNION

The *tailgan* has often been described as a *sacrifice* in ethnographic literature.[7] Yet the term has connotations in English that warrant questioning in relation to *tailgan* ceremonies. In some cultural contexts, sacrifice has been analyzed as an act of supplication or substitution—a soul sent to placate spirits, sometimes in place of human life.[8] Often the moment of slaughter is described as crucial, as a violent act denoting the power of the spirit recipient or as a symbolic reference to other significant deaths in local mythology.[9] The common usage of sacrifice implies abnegation—giving something up that is important or valuable to the donor.[10] None of these descriptions of sacrifice quite describe the *tailgan*, however.

The notion that the soul of an animal is a substitute for the soul of a human rests on an attribution of personhood to animals often found in hunting societies.[11] This sense of animal as a person is less discernible in the pastoral milieu of the Inner Asian steppe, however. In the rites I attended, animals were treated as property and primarily a source of meat. Anthropologist Roberte

Hamayon has noted the contrast between Siberian hunting rituals, where spirits of the forest are compensated for meat taken, and pastoral rituals, where the importance of offering meat to ancestors and emphasizing lineage reflects the institution of herds as heritable property.[12]

Since *tailgan* meat is both gifted to the spirits and shared among ritual participants, it is questionable whether abnegation is a relevant principle to apply. In *tailgan* rites the slaughtered animal's value lies in its status as a collectively owned and shared commodity rather than as something rare or special that is given up. Historically, clans are likely to have slaughtered their own sheep as an act of offering. In a milieu where many had left the countryside and kin groups were atomized, the animal for slaughter was collectively purchased. Indeed Dmitri emphasized to me that a sheep should be bought from outside of the clan, but if it does comes from a clan member, it must be purchased from him by collective funds, not donated as the gift of an individual. While a sheep may not be reared within the clan, it becomes associated with clan members by ritual mechanisms: the pouring of milk along its back and the dabbing of that same milk on the clan members' coats, the sprinkling of vodka on the carcass, and the sharing of meat between clan members and ancestors all serve to create association between the clan and the animal for slaughter. Its value, then, does not lie in giving up something precious but in its character as a collectively purchased and consumed item.

One of the earliest writers on this theme, the nineteenth-century Scottish scholar William Robertson Smith, characterized Semitic sacrifices as communion meals, focusing on the collective consumption of meat as the most important aspect of these rites.[13] Smith's notion that in a communion rite a group is consuming their god is less pertinent, but in the Buryat *tailgan*, the communion meal is shared with ancestral spirits and the meat is sacralized through blessing and prayers. The centrality that Smith places on communion as a source of *social fellowship*

A *sheree* (offering pyre) with meat portions reserved for the spirits awaits incineration. Ekhirit-Bulagat Raion July 2006.

seems entirely appropriate, then. The emphasis on consumption is indicative of the value of commensality in Buryat sociality. In the *tailgan*, as in sprinkling rites or ritualized drinking, meat and vodka are not only offered but must be consumed. In the same way that one shows respect by drinking another person's *khubi* in hospitality practice, vodka sprinkled must also be drunk and some of the meat shared with one another.

Where some theorists emphasize the moment of death as a critical focal point of sacrifice, this moment bears less significance for the *tailgan*. While the act of slaughter is carried out in a prescribed way, it is not always the center of attention when it happens. By the time the beasts were laid on their backs and slaughtered at the Khertoi *tailgan*, for example, most people were already busying themselves with fires and cauldrons, pooling the leftover vodka, or even catching up and chatting with each

KINSHIP, RITUAL, AND BELONGING

Portions (*khubi*) of *tailgan* meat are divided up for distribution by household. Ekhirit-Bulagat Raion, June 2008.

other. The moment of death was not accompanied by prayers or any ritualized solemnity; it simply began a workmanlike process of butchering the meat. Greater intensity of focus was evident at the moment, once the meat had been equally divided and taken, when clan members once again fell in line to see the pyre containing meat for the ancestors set alight, thus giving the meat to the spirits for consumption. The *tailgan* meat, like vodka libations made at the roadside or bottles drunk with friends, is consumed *with* ancestral spirits at the hearth of the clan.[14]

In her analysis of Buryat sociality, Caroline Humphrey has suggested that in symbolic terms the idea of dividing the meat of an animal into *khubi* emphasizes the fact that portions, like people, are parts of a whole.[15] In the case of the *tailgan*, that whole is the institution of the clan. That a *khubi* is then drawn into ritualized exchange emphasizes the moral obligations of reciprocity—whether it is a glass at the table being passed back and forth (described in chapter 2) or in the exchanges of meat once it has been divided at the *tailgan*.

GENDER AND DISTRIBUTED COMMUNION

Buryat shamanist practice reflects long-standing cosmological beliefs relating to gender. *Tailgan* rites were, for the most part, male-only occasions. At some large ritual events I attended, women occupied a separate space away from the ritual site, where they prepared food to accompany the *tailgan* meat at a feast at the end of the day. The women's space was a place of female sociality to catch up with news and look after children away from the slaughter and prayers. On occasions when women attended rituals or were present at household offering rites, they were required to wear skirts (sometimes worn over their jeans) and headscarves, while men wore belts and hats, the latter of which were taken off for key prayers. So while I characterize the *tailgan* as a communion, it is important to qualify that this is a distributed communion where male members of a clan represent their households and usually take the meat back to their family homes for sharing or else share it with women of the clan who had joined in the conviviality of the occasion after the main ceremony.

Women are not permitted to enter sacred sites during rituals or climb sacred hills. During *tailgan* rites menstruation carried the same taboos described in chapter 2: Men who had menstruating women in their households were not considered clean or allowed to attend ritual events.

There is a tension, then, between women as outsiders coming into a clan and as potential polluters of ritual spaces on the one hand and their role as crucial progenitors and contributors to clan life on the other. This tension runs throughout Buryat cosmology and ritual practice.[16] Despite these ritual proscriptions, the anticipated resolution to this tension is expressed through reverence for those women who become clan matriarchs and nurture the continuation of a lineage. Where patriliny is symbolized by the idea of bone, women joining a clan are said to contribute blood to their progenies and, ultimately, to their marital clans. Perhaps this reverence for maternal figures within the clan is most evident in the phenomenon of *toodei* spirits, described above. As I recount in the concluding chapter, *toodei* spirits have taken on a particular significance in contemporary Cisbaikalia.

RECIPROCITY AND SHARING

Sharing and exchange feature in Buryat ritual practice at both household and clan levels, and there are formal analogies between the everyday hospitality I described in chapter 2 and the *tailgan* rites that I attended. The sunwise direction of passing the glass, turning to call the spirits, and circumambulating fires and cairns is a recurring motif. The centrality of the fire or hearth as the place of offering is another. The term for a share of meat or drink as *khubi* is also analogous. The relationship to household hospitality is made explicit in idioms used to describe the rites. One Khuty friend explained sprinkling rites as *hosting* the ancestors, even as *laying a table* for them. Reference to the offering pyre and the stone cairn on Baitag as a *sheree* underlines the analogy. There seems to be a paradox in describing the rites as hosting spirits but designating many of the master spirits of place with the Russian term *khoziain*, a term that refers to a head of household and also a host. It seems to me that the blurring of who is host and who is guest serves to emphasize the relationship between incorporeal spirits and corporeal kinsmen as one of reciprocity and interdependence.

Formalized ritual practice draws attention to analogous acts of sharing, exchange, and commensality as significant. Such practices both reflect and constitute mutual obligations between the corporeal humans and incorporeal spirits present. These obligations exist within kin groups, as emphasized in exclusive *tailgan* rites, and between kin groups, as demonstrated in the reciprocal hospitality and wedding gifts described in chapter 2.

I think it is possible to determine two different dynamics at work in the ritual practices I witnessed: First the sharing and division of material goods, such as meat and vodka, constituted a relationship of mutual investment—friendship or neighborliness in instances of hospitality or, in the case of *tailgan* rites, mutual belonging to a single clan. Second, the symmetrical exchange of vodka glasses in hospitality or meat portions at the *tailgan* emphasized obligations of reciprocity in the more traditionally understood sense—an expectation of support between individuals within a clan, households within a community, or between clans brought into relations through marriage.

Despite the critiques of reciprocity as a ubiquitous concept, outlined in the previous chapter, reciprocity remains a salient way of describing social obligation in Buryat practice: The pouring of vodka or division of meat in Buryat ritual practices clearly carry with them expectations and obligations of return. At an individual level, the exchange of vodka glasses in household hospitality and the immediate production of a second bottle from host to guest was described by my friend Nikolai as ensuring there is no debt. At the same time, the reciprocal exchange of wedding gifts described by Erzhena in the previous chapter carried explicit obligations of monetary exchange over protracted periods of time.

EXPERIENCING BELONGING

By emphasizing the communion aspect of the *tailgan*, I wish to place as much stress on the collective experience of the event as on the symbolism of dividing and exchanging meat. In the ceremonies I attended, the time and energy given over to butchery of the animal, stoking fires, and wrestling, all added to a sense of shared endeavor and an experience of togetherness and mutual belonging.

These moments of intense, shared experience have been described in a variety of ways in classic anthropological literature: from Robertson Smith's "social fellowship" in communion to Durkheim's "collective effervescence" and Victor Turner's famous description of *communitas* in ritual events.[17] Turner described *communitas* as a "modality of social relationship," a kind of unmediated "comradeship" that could be brought about in those liminal contexts—such as ritual events—during which everyday activities and social orders are suspended.[18]

Turner's notions of *communitas* and liminality resonate strongly with my experiences of Buryat ritual. While *tailgan* rites include symbolic references to togetherness and reciprocity, it is also important to note the powerful sense of common purpose and enjoyment evident at these events. This was engendered through the dynamics of formalized elements of the rites: joint attention to prayers, the spatial arrangement of bodies in a semicircle, raising of hands together as prayers and offerings were made, and circumambulation of the fire. However this feeling of togetherness was also tangible in less formalized elements of the occasion such as the joint work of stoking fires and butchering and cooking meat. There was a convivial atmosphere as kinsmen caught up with each other's news, taking time out to drink and eat together. The organization of wrestling competitions while the meat cooked also added a ludic quality as kinsmen cheered on competitors, relatives taunted one another, and all matches ended in an embrace and a shared glass of vodka.

The *communitas* I experienced in *tailgan* rites was not an unmediated or egalitarian phenomenon in the way that Turner characterized it. Buryat kin groups have their own hierarchies: elders directed the action, often giving younger members orders or instructing them on how to butcher or prepare the meat. But the sense of mutual engagement in all the events I attended was palpable, and these clan hierarchies represented a departure from the status of individuals in civic life. In traveling to a sacred place, smoking their feet before beginning the rite, and partaking in formal ritualized action, *tailgan* rites were demarcated as liminal events, marked out from everyday life and privileged as significant undertakings.

KINSHIP IN PRACTICE

Tailgan rites both symbolized and constituted the obligations of mutual aid and reciprocity expected within kin groups. They were, in Don Handelman's terms, both a *model* and a *mirror* for social relations.[19] These obligations have been important in the past and remained so at the time of my research. In a pastoral nomadic milieu, it is easy to imagine how important mutual aid was for the collective management of herds. In the Soviet period, Humphrey's fieldwork carried out on two collective farms revealed that kin networks remained important to fulfilling roles such as childcare and partaking in the cycles of reciprocity surrounding weddings. In revisiting these farms in the 1990s, Humphrey recorded the way that rural Buryats helped to alleviate food shortages in the immediate post-Soviet years.[20]

In the more recent context of the former Novonikolaevsk *sovkhoz*, it was possible to see how important kin groups became once again for the rural economy. The collapse of state-supported collective farming led to large-scale migration from the villages and left families distributed over a wider geographical area and villages depopulated. Buryats who remained in the villages relied on each other's help for small-scale farming activities. Families I knew relied on kin from the cities to return in the summer to help cut and stack hay and prepare firewood for winter. I saw firsthand how Khertoi kin supported each other in pooling the use of the few remaining working tractors in the village, obtaining petrol, and helping to transport hay home. Dmitri shared a tractor with his two brothers, who still lived in the village, and resources were pooled when his son and nephews came home from university to help cut the hay in Khertoi and bring it back to Novonikolaevsk. Three of Vitali's nephews were sent to help him cut the hay in July. Where everyday reciprocity was visible between neighbors, kin were called on for these large-scale tasks relating to the annual farming cycle.

Where the state once organized the slaughter, transport, and distribution of meat produced by the *sovkhoz*, personal kin networks seem to be crucial to the distribution of produce from small-scale farming in the post-Soviet period. On one occasion I returned from Khuty to Irkutsk with meat for the market. The older brother of Vitia's neighbor had come by car to help slaughter a heifer and take the meat back with him to Ust-Orda settlement. The next day another Khuty relative drove the meat into Irkutsk's Novolenina market for sale. When I accompanied Erzhena on her Friday trips to market in the city, Dmitri's relatives often turned up to collect milk, sour cream, and curds, much of it for poorer elderly relatives.

Kin involvement remained evident in wedding cycles. As I recounted in the previous chapter, Khertoi kins were instrumental in preparing meat for the wedding of Dmitri and Erzhena's son in 2011 as well as hosting guests and holding feasts over several days.

Relationships with kin from the city were also drawn on for financial help. When the daughter of Khertoi friends received the opportunity to attend a university course in the United States, various members of the Khertoi clan, including professionals from the city, contributed money so that she could go. Following this a Khertoi university lecturer from Ulan-Ude decided to found a homeland association (Rus. *zemliachestvo*) for Khertoi Buryats with a fund for the purposes of supporting younger members of the clan. Another clan member described the student as "our first swallow," explaining that "after that we realized that in the future such help may be necessary again." A Khertoi surgeon whom I knew in Irkutsk stressed that he preferred to give money to clan funds rather than to Buryat cultural associations because he knew where the money was going.

DEFINING AND CONSTITUTING KINSHIP

In my discussions with Western Buryats, patriliny remained the stated principle for membership of kinship groups—whether that was in reference to a lineage, *ulus*, or larger clan grouping. Buryats have long-established genealogical metaphors. As I have noted, patrilineal substance is described as bone (*yahan*), the same term that is applied to lineage groups, and genealogies are remembered by counting off patrilineal ancestors through eight generations, from the finger tips through the joints of the finger, wrist, elbow and shoulder to the neck. The naming of common ancestors in offering rites makes this principle explicit.

Descriptions of kinship systems based on genealogical descent have been heavily criticized in recent decades. Africanist models of segmentary lineage systems, such as that based on Evans-Pritchard's study of the Nuer, have been critiqued for not always following reality and overlooking bilateral alliances.[21] Moreover, Sneath argues that an overemphasis on lineage groups as an organizing principle of society in Inner Asian ethnography has come about from the importation of Africanist models to the field.[22] For this reason it is worth considering patriliny as an ideal way of *defining* Buryat kinship and ritual as a way of *constituting* kinship.

The Buryat ideal of naming one's paternal line through eight generations was not always met in reality. Several people I knew were able to name their paternal lines through eight generations, counting them off in the traditional way. Others, however, would refer me to someone else when I asked. "You need to speak to my mother about that," one Khertoi friend told me as he struggled to remember the details. Indeed, women marrying into kin groups often became keepers of genealogical knowledge. In the

Khertoi *ulus*, Ivan Petrovich was considered a knowledgeable elder who knew the correct ancestors to honor in prayers. In some instances, genealogies are broken or lost, as in the case of Vitia's family in Khuty.

Humphrey observed bilateral kinship relations in Buryat collective farms of the 1960s, contrasting the dominant discourse of patriliny with "practical kinship" among affines, often maintained by women and providing links across clans.[23] The same was observable in Cisbaikalia in the early 2000s. Erzhena, for example, called on two of her sister's sons from Ulan-Ude to come and help with cutting hay in Novonikolaevsk in 2007 and often sent food to relatives there. In the autumn of 2007, I was in Novonikolaevsk to help Dmitri and Erzhena with the potato harvest and several sacks were sent to Erzhena's relatives in Ulan-Ude as a bad harvest in Buryatia had pushed up prices that year. When Erzhena and Dmitri's eldest daughter was young, she was sent to Ulan-Ude for two years to live with Erzhena's sister while Erzhena was working full-time. Later, Erzhena's nephew was sent to Novonikolaevsk for a period when, as a teenager in the city, he had got into trouble and started playing truant.

At both the Khertoi *tailgan* and the Khuty *tailgan* described in chapter 7, I found that a number of relatives were present whose mothers came from the clan in question and were thus classified as *zee*, a Buryat term for affines. One friend, the husband of a woman born into the Khertoi clan, always attended offering rites with his in-laws. This seemed to reflect the fact he had moved from his home village of Akhin (a few miles to the north) to work in the Novonikolaevsk *sovkhoz* and engaged in closer ties of reciprocity with his wife's family than with his own.

Historical analysis shows that this flexibility has long been practiced by Western Buryats. Humphrey's survey of Buryat kinship in the eighteenth and nineteenth century illustrates that Western Buryats regularly found common ancestors of different genealogical distance in order to organize and attend *tailgan* rituals. This manipulation of genealogy and ritual allowed herders to draw on the obligations of reciprocity from different relatives and secure rights to new pastureland.[24]

In looking beyond genealogical descent as the sole means of defining kinship, anthropologists at the turn of this century sought to identify diverse ways that different communities identify relatedness. In so doing, they have emphasized, for example, the importance of commensality and shared hearths, ongoing relationships with given land and places, and narratives and stories.[25] In the Buryat context, it is possible to see that while patriliny remains the ideal through which kinship is reckoned, ritualized commensality, communion, and *communitas* are essential for understanding the ways that kinship is constituted and practiced.

In his analysis of ethnographic literature on Inner Asia, Sneath expresses concern that clan and kin groups are often contrasted with state institutions as a hangover from a past juridical-political order. In Sneath's view, this overlooks the role of state taxation regimes in concretizing forms like the *ulus* in the nineteenth century.[26] Rather than gloss over that history, I wish to illustrate that the principle of patrilineal descent is adapted in such ways that state-influenced forms, like the *ulus*, have become meaningful as kin groups, in part through ritual practice. While *ulus* communities were crystallized by Russian imperial policy, the collective offering to spirits of place has provided a tenacious focal point for those communities beyond both the imperial regime and later resettlement. Where genealogies are broken, as with Diadia Vitia's family in Khuty, long-term reciprocal relations with local spirits underpin group membership and belonging to place. Whatever the question over a group's origin, membership is continued through patrilineal descent. Where the Buryat terms *ulus* or *ail* might historically have referred to pastoral herding units or collectives for taxation rather than denoting biological kinship, I found group members to regard one another as relatives (Rus. *rodstvenniki*) whatever the clarity of their origin.

While the ritual constitution of kinship allows for a certain amount of flexibility, both genealogical knowledge and ritual practice remain ways of bounding kin groups and differentiating *ours* from others. Ritual forms exclude people as effectively as they include them. The symbolism of commensality and the experience of communion both play a part. As described above, *tailgan* meat must not be shared outside the household. Humphrey records the symbolic smashing of a communal cooking pot as a way that clan segmentation was historically carried out.[27] In 2008 I attended a big *tailgan* led by Ekhirit and Bulagat shamans and my friend Aleksei was keen to accompany me. As Aleksei belongs to the Ashabagat clan, a group that were originally part of the Bulagat clan but dissociated themselves after internecine conflict, his clan elders allowed him to attend only on the condition that he ate none of the *tailgan* meat.[28]

EMPLACED KINSHIP

The ritual practice described in this chapter not only cements ties of kinship between people but also creates a deep connection with place, rooting kinship in the ancestral homeland. In an era of rapid urbanization and the atomization of kin groups, communion with ancestral spirits requires a return to the landscapes where those spirits remain.

Anthropologists have often explored indigenous peoples' relationships to landscape, constituted in a range of dwelling activities and movements across the land.[29] For most Buryats in twenty-first century Siberia, ancestral landscapes are no longer experienced in day-to-day activities or pastoral practices. However, rituals such as feeding the *mongol* or *tailgan* ceremonies offer connectedness with those landscapes through the intensive experiences they create.

The ways that places are made meaningful have been a subject of broad anthropological attention in recent decades.[30] Places, according to Tim Ingold, are "nodes in the endless comings and goings of people, each characterized by its particular assemblage of relations."[31] In Cisbaikalia, shamanist rites represent a particular kind of placemaking, defining ritual sites as the hearth of a clan, a place where kinship and belonging is experienced.

Western Buryats often talked of their *malaia rodina* with the same kind of emotion and in the same kinds of idioms that they describe their own relatives. Friends talked of *nash Khertoi*, for example, and one younger member of the Khertoi *ulus* told me of how her father had "always taught [her] to love our Khertoi." It helped my relationships with Khuty Buryats I met in the city to know that I had not only lived with other clan members but had spent time living in their home village. It was clearly important for Vitia's brothers that their sons spent time in their *malaia rodina* each summer. I printed many photos for Dmitri and Erzhena in my time in the region, but the most treasured, and most warmly and emotionally received, was a picture of the spring at Khertoi that I had framed for them.

Clan hearths, along with sacred hills and *bar'sa* sites along the road, could be thought of as forming a shamanist topography within the Cisbaikal landscape. This constellation of sacred places was inscribed through ritual practice and provided a material base for relations with the spirits that dwelt there. As my Buryat interlocutors moved around the Cisbaikal steppe, that shamanist topography served as a reminder of the presence of spirits and the obligations to them among the infrastructure and institutions of more recent milieux.

RITUAL FORM AND SOCIAL FORM

The French sociologist Pierre Bourdieu is notable for his insight that symbolic actions, crucial to reproducing the social order, are often habituated into daily embodied practice and inform cultural sensibilities in this way.[32] This was certainly true of the

Western Buryat communities in which I lived, where the everyday practices of drinking, traveling, and hospitality described in chapter 2 took ritualized forms. In the everyday acts of dabbing tea and vodka on the table, raising a hand while passing sacred places, and in regular acts of hospitality, a Western Buryat ethos of reciprocity and sharing was embodied and habitual. Particularly striking in the Western Buryat context is the way that these everyday practices find their formal analogue in larger-scale events that are imbued with the same ethos.

Rituals at every scale had analogous focal points. Prayers always directed to the place where the ancestors were offered food or drink—the household hearth, the ritual fire, or the *sheree* at *tailgan* ceremonies. The analogy between the household table and the *sheree* for hosting the spirits has been documented above and the sunwise motion of passing drinks at the table, circumambulating the ritual hearth, and summoning the spirits adds a further embodied motif that is replicated at different scales.

While there is a continuity between ritualization in everyday life and larger-scale events, there is also a formal demarcation from quotidian matters in *tailgan* ceremonies. The rituals are carefully prepared for: collections for donations are made, a date is set, ritual roles are assigned, and relatives travel to attend. As noted above, the enactment of rites at specially demarcated places, the smoking of feet, and the spatial organization of the event, all created a liminal context in which everyday hierarchies and social orders were suspended. The shared experience of participating constitutes the collective sense of belonging that Buryats feel toward their kin and clan groups.

Ethnographic studies have long documented the ways that spatial forms reflect and model social structures and institutions. In the early twentieth century, Durkheim and Mauss argued that the layout of Native American encampments reflected cosmological orders.[33] This theme of *isomorphism* between cultural forms, cosmologies, and social orders has resurfaced in the work of influential anthropologists ever since—from Bourdieu's analysis of the way that household space mirrored gender relations in Kabyle culture to Clifford Geertz's analysis of Balinese performance and ritual as isomorphic with the social order.[34] Analyzed in this way, the form of the *tailgan* could be said to reflect the social form that it constitutes—the Buryat clan. The way kinsmen lined up in a semicircle to make their prayers and offerings gave the rites what I term their inward-facing form: kin groups are bounded, exclusive, and, like the portions of shared meat, participants can be understood as parts of a whole, instituted through this coming together in one place.

This form featured no spectacular displays of shamanic practice. Rather, ritual leaders designated as shamans took their places at one end of the line of ritual participants. There was little that was declamatory or performative about their prayers and offerings. Indeed, much of what was said was inaudible to other participants. The authority of ritual practitioners came from their knowledge, lineage, and position within the clan rather than the manner of their performance. The intended audience for the shamans' words was the spirits to whom offerings were made.

The focus of attention on the ritual hearth, where the spirits receive their offerings, reflects both the emplaced nature of Buryat kinship and its rootedness in relations with ancestors. Sacred places and the events that constitute them are the center of a centripetal motion as kinsmen return from far and wide to engage in communion, cementing their relations with one another and with their place of origin.

The *tailgan* is not just a symbolic representation of relations as they should be in quotidian life—formalized versions of day-to-day reciprocity—it is also a real-time enactment of those relations. Rituals can be understood as models or mirrors of the social order, but they are, as Handelman has also pointed out, an activity in their own right, worthy of attention in and of themselves.[35] In the coming together of relatives to undertake the act of offering to spirits, *tailgan* rites are kinship in practice.

Clan rites are carefully manipulated to define who can be classed as *ours* and who cannot, who shares meat, and who is obliged to provide support in times of need. Yet, as described in chapters 2 and 3, analogous processes of ritualized hospitality can also be deployed to build mutual relations with neighbors and alliances with other clans. Most important, however, are relations with the spirits of the Cisbaikal landscape that are constituted through the ritual sharing of vodka and meat. These long-standing relations of reciprocity predated and outlasted Soviet communism. In the next chapter, I explore the social institutions and new forms of belonging that emerged in the Soviet era.

NOTES

1. Anderson, *Identity and Ecology in Arctic Siberia: The Number One Reindeer Brigade*, 208.
2. Khangalov, *Sobranie Sochinenii, Vol. 1*; Mikhailov, *Buriatskii Shamanizm*; Tugutov, "The Tailagan as the Principal Shamanistic Ritual of the Buriats"; Humphrey, "The Uses of Genealogy: A Historical Study of the Nomadic and Sedentarised Buryat."
3. Mikhailov, *Buriatskii Shamanizm*, 99–101.
4. Buyandelgeriyn, "Who 'Makes' the Shaman?: The Politics of Shamanic Practices among the Buriats in Mongolia"; Pedersen, *Not Quite Shamans*.
5. Humphrey and Onon, *Shamans and Elders*; Mikhailov, *Buriatskii Shamanizm*, 100–101.
6. Khangalov, *Sobranie Sochinenii, Vol.1*, 478; Mikhailov, *Buriatskii Shamanizm*, 282.
7. Tugutov, "The Tailagan as the Principal Shamanistic Ritual of the Buriats"; Humphrey, "Some Ritual Techniques in the Bull-Cult of the Buriat-Mongols."
8. Hubert and Mauss, *Sacrifice*; Evans-Pritchard, "The Meaning of Sacrifice among the Nuer"; Leach, *Culture & Communication*.
9. Hubert and Mauss, *Sacrifice*; Bloch, *Prey into Hunter*; Lambek, "Sacrifice and the Problem of Beginning."

10. Firth, "Offering and Sacrifice: Problems of Organization."

11. For example, Ingold, *The Appropriation of Nature*; Viveiros de Castro, "Cosmological Deixis and Amerindian Perspectivism"; Willerslev, *Soul Hunters*.

12. Hamayon, "Shamanism in Siberia: From Partnership in Supernature to Counter-Power in Society."

13. Smith, *Lectures on the Religion of the Semites*.

14. Similar observations have been made of *ovoo* rituals in the wider Mongolian region. Humphrey and Onon emphasize the significance of offering (propitiation) among Daur Mongols in *Shamans and Elders*, while Empson notes the importance of consumption among Buryats in Mongolia in *Harnessing Fortune*.

15. Humphrey, "The Domestic Mode of Production in Post-Soviet Siberia?"

16. See Empson, *Harnessing Fortune* for an in-depth exploration of these tensions.

17. Smith, *Lectures on the Religion of the Semites*; Durkheim, *The Elementary Forms of the Religious Life*; Turner, *The Ritual Process*.

18. Turner, *The Ritual Process*, 96–97.

19. Handelman, *Models and Mirrors*.

20. Humphrey, *Marx Went Away—But Karl Stayed Behind*.

21. Evans-Pritchard, *The Nuer*; Holy, *Segmentary Lineage Systems Reconsidered*.

22. Sneath, *The Headless State*.

23. Humphrey, *Marx Went Away—But Karl Stayed Behind*, 289–99.

24. Humphrey, "The Uses of Genealogy: A Historical Study of the Nomadic and Sedentarised Buryat."

25. Carsten, "Introduction," *Cultures of Relatedness*; Bamford and Leach, *Kinship and Beyond*; Bamford, "'Family Trees' among the Kamea of Papua New Guinea"; Ingold, "Stories against Classification: Transport, Wayfaring and the Integration of Knowledge."

26. Sneath, *The Headless State*.

27. Humphrey, *Marx Went Away—But Karl Stayed Behind*, 52.

28. Compare Empson's descriptions of acts of "containment" and "separation" among Buryats in Mongolia in *Harnessing Fortune*.

29. Ingold, "Ancestry, Generation, Substance, Memory, Land"; Anderson, *Identity and Ecology in Arctic Siberia*.

30. Feld and Basso, *Senses of Place*; Hirsch and O'Hanlon, *The Anthropology of Landscape*.

31. Ingold, *The Perception of the Environment*, 145.
32. Bourdieu, *Outline of a Theory of Practice*.
33. Durkheim and Mauss, *Primitive Classification*, 23–59.
34. Bourdieu, *Outline of a Theory of Practice*; Geertz, *Negara*; Handelman, *Models and Mirrors*.
35. Handelman, *Ritual in Its Own Right*, "Why Ritual in Its Own Right? How So?"

FOUR

CONSTRUCTING CULTURE, FRAMING PERFORMANCE

THEATRICAL METAPHORS ARE OFTEN EMPLOYED to invoke a distinction between public display and more intimate and hidden aspects of social life. The sociologist Erving Goffman famously wrote of "frontstage" and "backstage" activities and interactions.[1] Similar analogies have been used by contemporary anthropologists in exploring the differences between the publicly promoted cultures of communities and those practices that are kept out of view.[2] In the Buryat context, to talk of cultural practices that are *on stage* or *off stage* might serve not just as a metaphor but a literal description of the relationship between public performing arts and kinship rituals.

Large-scale collective ceremonies that once formed part of the Buryat ritual calendar were effectively repressed under Soviet communism, when religious ritual was removed from public view. As this chapter and chapter 6 show, however, elements of shamanist culture were developed into art forms for public display and institutionalized as a Buryat national culture under Soviet rule. New performing arts contained aspects of ceremonial practice but were cleansed of any religious content and were reconfigured for the stage as national dance and drama.

The intimate, inward-facing rituals that constitute Buryat kinship and the public presentation of national forms evince social belonging in fundamentally different ways and at different scales. The institutionalization of certain cultural activities through state organs, such as theaters, academies, and houses of culture in the Soviet era, reified this contrast. Consequently, a specific definition of Buryat culture evolved that did not always include day-to-day custom or ritual practice. This chapter traces the process of cultural institutionalization, its legacy in the early twenty-first century, and the ways Buryat culture was framed in the public domain in the mid-2000s.

KUL'TURA, BYT, AND FOL'KLOR

When I was introduced to a cousin of Diadia Vitia's in the spring of 2006, I explained that I was living in Khuty because I was an ethnographer interested in learning more about Buryat culture. "*Khuty?*" She laughed. "What kind of culture do you think you will see there?" Explaining my research to people in Siberia was often quite difficult given that culture and ethnography have particular resonances in Russian.

Kul'tura, I soon realized, had connotations that did not ordinarily include ritual practice, herding, or hunting. The Soviet project of cultural construction identified *kul'tura* with forms such as literature, fine art, dance, theater, and opera.[3] The term does not generally evoke the broader understanding of culture used by English-speaking anthropologists, a category that includes everyday customs and practices typified by Sapir's characterization as "any socially inherited element in the life of man."[4]

From the Europhile reign of Peter the Great onward, imperial Russia's ruling elite sought to patronize the arts according to European models, often in privately owned theaters and galleries. In the nineteenth century, artists and writers began to turn their attention to uniquely Russian themes and to use their native language to a greater degree, a move accelerated by anti-French sentiment after the Napoleonic wars.[5] This Slavophile movement began to adopt the German term *kultur* to describe their activities as the word described a connection between artistic activities and what proponents described as their "national spirit."[6] It is worth noting, however, that although the content of the emerging *kul'tura* was avowedly Slavic, the forms that developed retained presentational conventions that owed as much to Western European sensibilities as the Germanic term used to describe them. Creative efforts were still presented in theaters, galleries, and literary journals. Both the term *kul'tura* and those European formal conventions were later exported to peoples across the Soviet Union to develop multiple national cultures in the 1920s.

Since *kul'tura* in Russian often connotes the arts, there is little wonder Diadia Vitia's cousin was incredulous that I would find any such thing in a village with no state cultural institutions, no schools, and a population of twelve. People I met in the villages of Cisbaikalia were somewhat puzzled why, as an ethnographer, I would wish to spend time living there, cutting hay or chopping wood. Buryats are more used to the idea of Russian academic expeditions, where teams of ethnographers appear and interview as many people as possible in a short space of time rather than someone committing to long periods in the countryside. While trying to explain to some visitors to Khuty one day why I might be gathering berries or mushrooms there instead of ploughing through the archives of an Ulan-Ude library, Vitia filled the pause in my explanation with the assertion that what I was interested in was *byt*. If a broad anthropological definition of culture did not have common currency in Russian, then *byt*, often translated as "way of life" or "everyday life," resonated better. The everyday drinking and hospitality that I describe in this book might fall into this category or might be glossed in Russian as custom (*obichai*). Either way these practices were not generally thought of as *kul'tura*.

When I introduced myself as an ethnographer, Buryat interlocutors often assumed that I must be interested in *fol'klor*: the songs, stories, and sayings that are the focus of much Russian-language ethnography. Talk of *fol'klor* usually elicited an assertion that much had been forgotten, or I would be referred to a grandmother or grandfather who might know a few stories.[7] Folklore in post-Soviet Siberia usually denotes the vernacular songs, stories, and oral epics found in ethnographic texts and preserved in the repertoires of folk ensembles. This category also came to the region via European Russia. The study and collection of folklore evolved with the Romantic-era interest of central European nationalist movements in vernacular forms. Russian intellectuals seeking a distinctly Slavic identity for nineteenth-century Russia followed their lead.[8] In the late czarist era, a Russian-educated Buryat intelligentsia emerged that was highly invested in the study of ethnography. These scholars combined an academic interest in Buryat *byt* and *fol'klor* with the active development of new cultural forms.[9]

ETHNOGRAPHY, NATIONALITY, AND CULTURE

Buryat scholars began recording local traditions and collecting folklore in the late nineteenth and early twentieth centuries. In Cisbaikalia, teachers Ia. A. and N. C. Boldonov, an uncle and nephew, collected material in the lower Nukutsk district. Matvei Khangalov, a graduate of the Irkutsk teacher's seminary, famously described rituals and traditional practices of the Buryats of the Kuda Valley, and V. A. Mikhailov, a St. Petersburg–educated Western Buryat, collected ethnographic material between 1903 and 1918.[10] Zhamsarano, an Aga Buryat scholar, later known as a prime mover in the Buryat national movement, also collected material among Western Buryats.[11] All of this work was undertaken according to a model of ethnography and folkloristics that had been learned from scholars and institutions in European Russia: Mikhailov was encouraged in his work by the well-known scholars Radlov and Shternberg; Khangalov was a member of the Russian Geographical Society and published much of his work in the society's journals; Zhamsarano was decorated by the same society.[12]

This nascent Buryat intelligentsia anticipated Soviet attempts at promoting literacy in their native language by translating famous Russian and European literature into the Buryat language. Three further graduates of the Irkutsk teachers' seminary, D. A. Abasheev, I. G. Saltikov, and I. V. Barlukova, wrote some of the first plays in the Buryat language between 1908 and 1911. These moral tales depicted the need for social order and family values and warned against the dangers of alcoholism.[13] The work began the practice of using the Buryat language within European theatrical forms.

Although Buryats had never been a politically unified population, the educated intelligentsia clearly began to conceive of themselves as having a shared nationality. This sense of national identity was intensified with the coming of the Bolshevik Revolution. Following the February revolution of 1917, a gathering of Buryat intellectuals in Chita in April of that year spawned the Buryat National Committee, known by its abbreviated name of *Burnatskom*. While Moscow's revolutionaries were coming to terms with governing a former empire and fighting the First World War, the committee became a de facto Buryat government. *Burnatskom* oversaw local-level administration of health, education, and public services. Some of the earliest actions and resolutions of the committee concerned the setting up of native-language programs in schools, the training of Buryat-language teachers, and funding the publication of texts in Buryat.[14] Scant resources and a lack of time to properly train teachers in the classical Mongolian script hindered these early attempts at spreading literacy. The intervention of the civil war further limited possibilities.[15] With the foundation of the Soviet Union in 1923, however, the process of *cultural-national construction (kul'turno-natsional'noe stroitel'stvo)* was taken into the remit of the state.[16] This process crystallized an official version of Buryat national culture that was to outlast the Soviet polity.

CONSTRUCTING NATIONAL CULTURE

After the revolution of October 1917, the Bolsheviks inherited an empire of diverse nationalities. Maintaining Russia's territorial integrity therefore required winning over national elites to the communist cause. This meant convincing non-Russian intelligentsias that Bolshevik rule would provide some degree of national autonomy through the Marxist-Leninist doctrine of *national self-determination*.[17]

The ways that the aspirations of national groups could be accommodated within a communist state was debated among revolutionaries long before the Bolsheviks took power. One model open to the revolutionary government was that of extraterritorial *National Cultural Autonomy* advanced by Marxists Bauer and Renner as a model for Austria-Hungary. Renner's 1899 essay, *State and Nation*, proposed economic, legal, and defense policy as the jurisdiction of the federal state, while nations within the state would have control of their own cultural and educational affairs.[18] The National Cultural Autonomy model was favored for Russia by the Jewish Bund prior to the revolution and later by *Muskom*, the committee representing Muslims in the early Bolshevik governments.[19] Stalin's 1913 essay, *Marxism and the National Question*, the blueprint for Soviet nationality policy, explicitly rejected the National Cultural Autonomy approach, however. Stalin's treatise asserted that national identity is necessarily tied to a designated homeland, where nationalities exercise territorial autonomy.[20] This vision informed the territorial structure of the USSR. Under the new federal system, territories of varying degrees of autonomy were demarcated for titular nationalities. Renner's principle of extraterritorial National Cultural Autonomy was largely forgotten in Russia until its resurrection in the post-Soviet era.

After the foundation of the USSR in 1923, the nationality policies initiated by the Soviet government were characterized as *korenizatsiia*, often translated as "nativization" or "indigenization." Stalin famously stated in a 1925 speech, and reiterated often, that national cultures should be "national in form, socialist in content."[21] This involved using local languages, literature, and performing arts to promulgate socialist ideology. Though self-determination was the nominal principle, the development of national institutions proceeded uniformly across the USSR according to formulae dictated by Moscow. The Bolshevik identification of nationalities with designated homelands meant that federal territories were envisaged as cultural spaces. Officially sanctioned national cultures were to be cultivated and, to some extent, homogenized across those territories—culture and territory were implicitly identified as coterminus.

In 1923, the Buryat-Mongol Autonomous Soviet Socialist Republic (sometimes abbreviated as the BMASSR) was established in the Baikal region. M. N. Erbanov, first secretary of the republic's general committee of the communist party, issued his agenda for nation-building in his 1926 speech "Cultural-National Construction of the BMASSR." In the speech he outlined an agenda to publish the literature of Marxism-Leninism in Buryat-Mongolian; to collect, study, and publish folk epics; and to collect, systematize, and publish dramas to be performed in "culture circles." Erbanov further stressed the need to "morally and materially" encourage talented writers in their native language; collect folk songs and motifs and write them down; and find musicians, artists, and singers and educate them so that they could make trips to educational establishments across the region.[22]

STAGING BURYAT PERFORMING ARTS

While language development took priority in the early years of *korenizatsiia*, embryonic versions of new performing arts also began to take shape. The creation of Buryat national dance began in the 1920s, when Gombo Tsydynzhapov first set elements of traditional dance to orchestral backing. Tsydynzhapov also choreographed scenes from Buryat life, such as yurt-building and hunting.[23] Meanwhile, the genre of plays that emerged at the turn of the century to raise issues such as the morality of bride-price was developed to promote a broader turn to socialist modernity.[24] A 1935 report on cultural construction records that in 1929 a theater studio was set up in Verkhneudinsk at the newly founded House of Folk Arts. In 1932 a number of peripatetic theater brigades made their first appearances in the republic.[25]

The new performing arts were created for the stage, following the formal conventions of what performance theorist Erving Goffman termed the *theatrical frame*. Goffman identified the theatrical frame as the spatial differentiation of performers and spectators and the modification of action and movement on the stage so that it is oriented toward the frame and clear to the audience.[26] This form of framing continues to shape Buryat performing arts to this day.

The rituals that I characterize as inward-facing forms engender *communitas* through mutual participation. The spatial arrangements involve participants as a single collective. The outward-facing orientation of performing arts, on the other hand, frames the symbols of nationality for a public audience that is divided from the specialist performers on stage. The proscenium-arch stages that can be found everywhere in Siberia, from large urban theaters to rural houses of culture, allow for the dissemination and replication of these symbolic forms in a public sphere that has a wide territorial reach.

The scale of a nation as a social form means that national belonging relies on mass mediation and replication of symbols in this way. The symbols and narratives that members of a national group are expected to coalesce around are disseminated through education, print and broadcast media, performances, and public events. As well as communicating their meanings to a live audience, performance events are advertised in advance, recorded, and reported in print and broadcast media. As I argued in the introduction, this process can also be thought of as a form of public framing—designating performance events as newsworthy and significant and providing commentary about their meaning. This public framing became a crucial way of imbuing performance events with political significance during my field research, as I will explore in subsequent chapters.

CULTURE, INFRASTRUCTURE, AND TERRITORY

In early Soviet policy, the process of cultural development became tied to the wider civilizing mission of the Bolshevik leadership and the development of a state infrastructure.[27] The construction of national cultural institutions in the Buryat capital was accompanied by the propagation of official culture across the republic. This culture needed a home at a local and a national level, so cultural development entailed the building of schools, libraries, readers' cottages, and houses of culture. The 1931 report *On the Economic and Cultural Position of the Buryat Mongol ASSR from 1928–1930* made a point of listing institutional buildings in the republic as a means of quantifying cultural development.[28]

Vital to this process was the institution of the house of culture (*dom kul'tura*), found in settlements of every size and usually known in small villages simply as a club (*klub*). As collectivization intensified in the early 1930s, the clubs became the social hubs for collective farm communities and bases for literacy circles, libraries, sports teams, artistic ensembles, and local branches of communist youth groups, such as the pioneers and the *Komsomol* (the communist youth league). Clubs also hosted touring ensembles and brigades that came to perform the socialist versions of national culture developed within the institutions of the Buryat capital.[29]

Infrastructural and cultural development proceeded together because both were seen as a precondition for socialist modernity. Erbanov's agenda for cultural and national construction made explicit this link, listing "the backward Buryat-Mongol economy" of cattle pastoralism; the isolation of different regions from each other; over-Russification of some regions; and "the colossal cultural backwardness of the working masses of Buryat-Mongols" as the four key challenges to building socialist modernity in the Buryat-Mongol ASSR.[30] For Buryats, literacy, education, and a national culture became synonymous with the coming of roads, public transport, civic buildings, and the mechanization of agriculture. Because the Moscow government needed national elites to take charge of Soviet modernization, national territorial autonomy was seen as crucial for the fulfillment of this aim. Erbanov's 1926 speech made the link explicit: "It is a fact that Buryatia only really formed as a unit at the time the Autonomous Republic was founded. Only at the moment of creating a single administrative and economic leadership and a single cultural center can we talk about the work of extensive cultural and national construction in Buryatia. Only the sovietization of Buryatia and the foundation of administrative-territorial autonomy allow the possibility for Buryat-Mongols to fully address the development of national culture and uniting it with proletarian culture."[31]

Institutionalized culture, state infrastructure, and territorial autonomy had therefore long been related concepts in the local imagination by the early 2000s.

PURGES, ATHEISM, AND THE DIVISION OF BURYAT HOMELANDS

In the 1930s, the Soviet policies of *korenizatsiia* began to be qualified by a concern that "bourgeois nationalism" may be developing among national minorities. It was made clear by Stalin's government that nationalism would now be regarded as an evil equivalent to the "Great Russian chauvinism," against which policies of *korenizatsiia* had been aimed. The central government of the USSR began to see national elites across the union as a potential threat to Soviet authority. Consequently many thousands of members of national intelligentsias and local party officials across the Soviet Union were arrested and exiled or executed in the Stalinist terror of 1937.[32]

In the Buryat-Mongol ASSR, the twin charges of bourgeois nationalism and pan-Mongolism were the stated rationale for arresting members of the Buryat intelligentsia. The latter charge was particularly ironic given that many educated Buryats had been Moscow's agents in exporting communist ideology to the Mongolian People's Republic.[33] The Stalinist terror saw the execution of Erbanov, who had done so much to define the character of the new Soviet Buryat national culture, and the folklorist and education activist Zhamsarano, who had been instrumental in bringing communism to Mongolia.[34]

This period was also characterized by a sustained assault on religious activity by the Soviet authorities. In 1926, a resolution of the first cultural-national conference of the Buryat-Mongol ASSR identified that "Lamaism and Shamanism are without doubt, factors which retard cultural-national development." A year later, an antireligious commission was formed.[35] In the late 1930s, after a decade of such propaganda, Stalin's purges saw shamans and Buddhist lamas rounded up and forced to recant, sent to labor camps, or even executed.

From the outset, then, the institutionalized Buryat national culture that developed under communism excluded any element of religious practice. Among the new state cultural institutions set up at this time was the Anti-Religious Museum of Ulan-Ude in April 1937. Prior to the revolution, Buddhist temples had been crucibles of literacy. Shamans and lamas were moral authorities in their communities and, as leaders of ritual practice, constituted what might be regarded as *cultural specialists*. The purges of 1937 ensured that the intelligentsia working for state cultural institutions became the only recognized cultural specialists in the Buryat-Mongol ASSR and state institutions the loci of cultural development.

The repression of national elites and religious specialists in the late 1930s was accompanied by territorial changes that sought to curtail any separatist aspirations among national minorities. It is likely that Stalin's fear of pan-Mongolism was the rationale for dividing the Buryat-Mongol ASSR into three separate territories in 1937. This action prevented Buryats from forming a critical mass in any single territory. The territorial division in Cisbaikalia also meant that the newly formed Ust'-Orda Buryat-Mongol National Okrug was no longer contiguous with the Buryat republic. Ol'khon District on the western shore of Baikal, until that point part of the ASSR, was left outside of the official Buryat territories, ensuring that Buryats remained a minority in the newly formed okrug.[36]

CONTINUED *KORENIZATSIIA* AND THE DEVELOPMENT OF NEW FORMS

Although the great terror marked a retreat from unqualified national construction, it did not represent a full departure from the principle of *korenizatsiia*. The process continued in the late 1930s, though it was not trumpeted in the way that it had been in the 1920s.[37]

The new Buryat performing arts flourished toward the end of the 1930s and into the 1940s. The Baikal ensemble of Buryat song and dance was founded in 1937, gaining its official status as a state ensemble in 1942. In 1939 the Music and Drama Theater of Buryatia was made an official state theater, staging programs of Buryat-language theater, dance, and opera. In 1940 a festival of Buryat arts was held in Moscow and opened with the company's performance of the first Buryat opera, *Enkhe-Bulat Bator*.[38]

In the same period, certain forms were designated as traditional *fol'klor* and became enshrined in institutions of culture. In 1936 the Buryat republic's Centre for Folk Arts opened, and after a decree signed by Stalin himself, 1942 was proclaimed the six-hundredth anniversary of the Buryat epic poem *Geser Khan*. The decree included the dictum that the poem was to be published in Buryat and Russian. The same year saw the foundation of an orchestra of Buryat folk instruments.[39] Forms that were preserved in Soviet institutions included the *yokhor*, the traditional circle dance; the *magtaal*, a praise song; and the *uliger*, a Buryat oral epic recited by specialist bards. Despite their museum-piece appearance, these forms were not left unchanged. Religious content was carefully removed and praise for Lenin, the *Komsomol*, and the USSR was incorporated.[40] Versions of the Buryat *uliger* were even written in which Lenin undertakes the archetypal heroic journey before doing battle with "the monster of capitalist oppression."[41] While these adaptations were made to literature and the performing arts, the traditional Mongol sports competitions of horse racing, archery, and wrestling, once part of large ritual gatherings, were adapted into civic sports competitions known by the Buryat term *Sur-kharban*—a Western Buryat term for archery, which came to refer to the games as a whole.[42]

Alongside this carefully curated version of Buryat national culture, the Soviet state developed a union-wide ceremonial calendar and its own topography of significant places nested within the functional infrastructure of the state: these included war memorials; monuments to Soviet leaders and heroes, such as Lenin and Gagarin; civic squares; and theaters and houses of culture, which were home to broader Soviet cultural events as well as Buryat national forms. The naming of roads and buildings after communist figures, historical events, and principles infused public space with Soviet symbolism. Key places were inscribed with meaning through a ritual cycle that commemorated moments in communist history: May Day was marked out as the festival of international workers, and November 9 was the date of the October Revolution. After the end of World War II, Victory Day (on May 9), with its famous military parades, became a focal point.[43]

Buryat national culture crystallized, then, at exactly the same time that the first generation of Soviet Buryat intellectuals, shamans, and Buddhist lamas were being purged. As religious practices were repressed, Buryat literature and high arts were propagated with renewed vigor alongside broader Soviet archetypes. Yet at the same moment the new Buryat forms flourished, Cisbaikalia was territorially and institutionally separated from the artistic and intellectual life of Ulan-Ude and the Buryat republic. Ust'-Orda Buryat-Mongol National Okrug did not enjoy the same institutional support for Buryat national culture until the last decades of the Soviet era, when links with the Buryat capital were renewed.

THE DECLINE AND RENAISSANCE OF BURYAT NATIONAL CULTURE IN CISBAIKALIA

The separation of Ust'-Orda okrug from the Buryat republic in 1937 led to a decline in Buryat cultural institutions in the territory. Later Buryat historians lamented the diminution of native language schools and the poor preservation of traditional culture after the split from Buryatia.[44] An okrug theater set up in 1940 was founded mainly to promote Soviet patriotism during the

Second World War and had fallen into decline by the later Soviet period.[45] According to older Buryats from the region, dancing the *yokhor* and singing traditional songs went on at an unofficial level. This occurred mostly when friends gathered in the clubs for official holidays or at weddings and birthdays. But there were no ensembles and no folklorists preserving and recording traditional material.

By the time of my field research in Ust'-Orda okrug in the mid-2000s, however, institutions of Buryat culture had a considerable public presence. The culture workers who I interviewed talked of a Buryat *national cultural renaissance* (*natsional'noe kul'turnye vozrozhdenie*) in the 1980s and 1990s that led to the reestablishment of Buryat cultural institutions in the okrug. The last years of the USSR and the immediate post-Soviet era are often characterized as a time of revived national consciousness among the nationalities of the former Soviet Union. Local intelligentsias drove cultural revival agendas across the Russian Federation, a phenomenon clearly evident in the Buryat territories. Events and movements in the Republic of Buryatia had important repercussions west of Baikal.

In the late 1980s, members of the Buryat intelligentsia began to take advantage of the new spirit of openness (*glasnost'*) in the USSR to question the degree of autonomy held by the Buryat Republic. During this period key figures within the Buryat intelligentsia began to articulate a nationalist political agenda and call for a revival of distinct Buryat cultural activities and practices. In 1989 *The National Question in Buryatia*, published by a group of Ulan-Ude academics, set the tone for discussions over Buryat national autonomy and cultural revival. The book proposed that Buryatia be raised to the status of a union republic within the USSR—the highest level of autonomy, held by states such as Ukraine, Belarus, and Kazakhstan. It also pushed for the guaranteed sovereignty of Buryat regions, the recognition of Buryat as an equal language of the state, the creation of a center of Buryat culture, and a commission to consider the question of reunifying the Buryat territories.[46]

The collapse of the USSR in 1991 made the demand for union-republic status redundant, but a nationalist political agenda gained momentum briefly in the early 1990s through the activities of two political parties: the Buryat-Mongolian People's Party (*Buryat-Mongol'skaia Narodnaia Partiia—BMNP*) and the Movement for National Unity, known as *Negedel*.[47] Many of these parties' aspirations were voiced at the first All-Buryat Congress for the Consolidation and Spiritual Renaissance of the Nation in February 1991.[48] As the title suggests, delegates from the Aga and Ust'-Orda Buryat Autonomous Okrugs were in attendance. The congress explicitly attempted a pan-Buryat agenda for national cultural renaissance and gave birth to the All-Buryat Association for the Development of Culture, usually known by the acronym VARK (*Vseburiatskaia Assosiatsiia Razvitiia Kul'tury*), still active in the mid-2000s.

Buryat academic Vladimir Khamutaev, a prominent voice in the movement, recounted that the organizers of the congress, drawn from the communist party and republic government, originally tried to restrict the agenda to questions of cultural revival. Ultimately, however, organizers gave way to pressure from delegates to discuss the 1937 territorial reforms and questions of reunifying the Buryat territories. In the meantime, VARK was founded as a way of undertaking mutual projects between the three regions and was supported by state funding. Khamutaev has, however, questioned this move as a ploy to undermine the more ardently nationalist political parties and concentrate on cultural matters.[49]

Negedel and the BMNP remained wedded to more political demands, however. In November 1992, the parties convened an all-Buryat *khural*, a Mongol term used to describe the gatherings of the ancient Mongol aristocratic leaders and the title of the contemporary Mongolian parliament. The 1992 *khural* reiterated the demands for a return to the pre-1937 borders of the Buryat republic, asserted the need to rehabilite the reputations of Buryats who had suffered the brunt of Stalinist purges in the 1930s, and demanded that the republic and its people reinstate their identity as *Buryat-Mongol*.[50] In June 1993 a proclamation entitled *On the Rehabilitation of the People of Buryatia* was issued by the republic's government, criticizing as "unconstitutional" the territorial changes of 1937, which had taken place without consultation of the people. The document stopped short of demanding a return to the pre-1937 borders, a move that politicians in the okrugs did not support at the time, possibly fearing a loss of their own autonomy to Ulan-Ude.[51]

Elena Stroganova's comprehensive analysis of these events considers as a single phenomenon what she terms the *Buryat national-cultural revival project*. Stroganova summarizes the key features of the "official" project as follows:

- The declaration of sovereignty by the Buryat Autonomous Republic in January 1992 and its renaming as the Republic of Buryatia.
- The adoption of official symbols and an anthem by the republic.
- The creation of a people's *khural* and the office of president.
- The declaration rehabilitating the Buryat people and declaring illegal the territorial changes of 1937.
- The birth of a nationalist movement in the shape of the political parties *Negedel* and the BMNP.
- The first all-Buryat congress and the birth of VARK.
- The adoption of *Sagaalgan* (Mongol New Year) and the *Surkharban* (festival of traditional sports) as official holidays.
- The series of jubilees and events in the 1990s, which included the 250th anniversary of Buddhism in Russia (1991), the 70th anniversary of the republic (1993), and the 1000th Anniversary of the *Geser* epic (1995).[52]

In what she refers to as the "unofficial" aspects of national cultural revival, Stroganova documents the way that an archaic character was often attributed to Buryat forms by the scholars and artists involved in their revival. She pays particular attention to the 250th anniversary of Buddhism in Russia and the celebrations surrounding the anniversary of the *Geser* heroic epic in 1995, which VARK played a key role in organizing. In documenting the erection of a series of ceremonial tethering posts and the consecration of an offering place to Geser, Stroganova illuminates the increasing role of shamanist associations and religious movements in creating markers of national identity, a phenomenon I will go on to explore in chapter 7.[53]

In Ust'-Orda okrug, debates over national revival seem to have been less heated than in Buryatia. Discussions about cultural renaissance were initiated by committees of the communist party in a series of meetings to discuss the decline of Buryat national culture in the territory.[54] In the 1990s, initiatives aimed at reviving Buryat national culture in the okrug were supported by the administration. The local intelligentsias in both okrugs were less keen to push for territorial reintegration with Buryatia than activists in the republic itself, however, particularly after 1993.[55] The new Russian constitution of that year gave autonomous okrugs equal status with all other subject territories of the Russian Federation, control over their own budgets, and their own representatives in the federal parliament (*duma*). Reintegration with Buryatia would have left okrug leaders with less autonomy and ended representation at federal level at that point. Khamutaev later recounted that amid economic hardship in the early 1990s, Ust'-Orda Buryats were more concerned with producing food and surviving than with questions of national autonomy.[56] The demographic and institutional landscape of Ust'-Orda should also be taken into account when comparing local cultural revival with that of the republic. With its higher education and cultural institutions, the Buryat capital was home to a sizeable and vocal intelligentsia compared with the largely rural okrug. Furthermore, Buryats constituted a smaller proportion of Ust'-Orda okrug's population, which may also explain the less politicized nature of the national cultural renaissance there.

Though territorial reintegration with the Buryat republic might not have been on the local agenda in Ust-Orda, ties with the republic through cultural events and pan-Buryat organizations were certainly evident. From the late Soviet period onward, my interlocutors recounted how homeland associations (*Rus. zemliachestva*) sprang up in Ulan-Ude through which links were forged between Western Buryats who had settled in Ulan-Ude and their communities of origin. At the time of my field research, each raion of the okrug has its own *zemliachestvo* in Ulan-Ude. The organizations held celebrations for important public holidays, honored notable figures from the raion, and often raised money for schools or charitable projects there. After its formation VARK formed a council of these homeland associations and aimed to consolidate their work.[57] VARK also sponsored cultural and sporting events, conferences, exhibitions, and festivals in Ust'-Orda throughout the 1990s.

Homeland associations, and later VARK, formalized links between the cultural life of Ust'-Orda okrug and the Buryat republic. Yet the roots of cultural revival and the use of models drawn from Buryatia appear to date further back than the *perestroika* era. Interviews that I undertook with cultural activists suggested the stirrings of a revival in the 1970s. In chapter 1 I noted the increased migration from Cisbaikalia to Ulan-Ude from the 1960s onward. It seems likely, therefore, that the growing contact between Ust'-Orda and Ulan-Ude, the continuing center of official Buryat culture, sowed the seeds of cultural revival in the okrug.

In 1970, the folklore ensemble *Magtaal* was formed in Ulan-Ude with a repertoire of exclusively Western Buryat songs, stories, and dances. The ensemble director was Alla Baldaeva, a Western Buryat whom I interviewed in Ulan-Ude. Baldaeva recounted traveling around Cisbaikalia collecting material for *Magtaal*, which later became a state folklore ensemble. In 1976 a group of enthusiasts in Ust'-Orda followed suit and decided to set up a local ensemble for the performance of traditional Buryat song and dance. They received support from the okrug administration in doing so. Professional artists came from Ulan-Ude to advise the group on creating a repertoire. The ensemble, Stepnye Napevy, became an important focus for the Buryat identity of Ust'-Orda okrug. In the 1980s the ensemble, at that time an amateur group, toured various parts of the USSR and Europe.[58] In the 1980s folklore ensembles sprang up in different settlements of the okrug. The ensemble in Novonikolaevsk, for example, was founded in 1982 by two local schoolteachers who collected material from older people in the village and created a repertoire for the group. In the early 1980s, the Eastern Siberian State Academy of Culture in Ulan-Ude founded a course in Buryat national arts. A generation of enthusiastic young Buryats from Ust'-Orda went to undergo training there. Several prominent culture workers in Ust'-Orda whomI interviewed in the 2000s, including Misha, whose words I recounted in the introduction, came from that first generation of graduates.

If the foundations were laid earlier, the zenith of the cultural revival was contemporaneous with that of the Buryat Republic. In conversation after conversation I had with local culture workers, the 1990s were recalled as something of a golden age for Buryat national culture in Ust'-Orda okrug. In 1990 the okrug's soviet decreed that the its main library should be granted national library status and establish a collection of literature on regional studies. In 1992 Stepnye Napevy became a professional ensemble, employing artists from across the Baikal region, most of whom were graduates of the Academy of Culture in Ulan-Ude. A new branch of the Irkutsk Oblast's Centre for the Preservation of Heritage, founded in 1994, worked to map sacred places and archaeological sites of interest.[59] In 1995 the local museum in Ust'-Orda became the Ust'-Orda Buryat Autonomous Okrug State National Museum with a greater emphasis on local customs and ecological issues. In 1996 a center for folk arts was founded that specialized in traditional decorative arts. One of the center's first tasks was the erection of the decorative wooden tethering posts (*serge*) at the border to the okrug, echoing their use as a national symbol in the Buryat republic. The performing arts also continued to blossom. From a total of twenty-four folklore collectives in the okrug in 1991, there were 127 reported in 2002.[60]

When discussing the influence of the Buryat republic on Buryat cultural activities west of Baikal, most local activists preferred to stress the uniqueness of Western Buryat practices. I suspect that this was resistance to the critical discourses that I often heard in Ulan-Ude—that "Irkutsk Buryats" had "lost their culture"— often by citing the lower level of language preservation in Ust'-Orda okrug. It is striking, however, that the initial stirrings of revival came at a time when migration to the republic from the okrug and Western Buryat attendance at higher education institutions in Ulan-Ude were both increasing, as noted in chapter 1. The influence of pan-Buryat organizations in recent decades is also clear. Since 1996 the festival of *Sagaalgan* (the lunar New Year) has been marked with concerts and events in the okrug. The celebration of the holiday in Cisbaikalia is a mark of Buryat national identity rather than the revival of any local celebration. The festival is part of the Buddhist calendar and has long been marked by Eastern Buryats but was rarely celebrated by the predominantly shamanist Western Buryats prior to the post-Soviet era. Few people whom I knew in the okrug marked *Sagaalgan* in their own homes, and several older people in the villages of Cisbaikalia recalled to me its first appearance in the area during the 1990s.

The same decade is reported as an era when a greater interest in pan-Mongol identities and ties were evident in Buryatia as the border with Mongolia became more open. Among Western Buryats with whom I interacted in the mid-2000s, a sense of belonging to the wider Mongol world was something I observed chiefly as a rhetorical assertion. I was told on numerous occasions, usually on first meeting people as a foreigner, that Buryats are "descendants of Chinggis Khan" or new acquaintances invoked their Mongol identity as a way of explaining their ritual or wider cultural practices in differentiation from ethnic Russians.

In Ust-Orda and Irkutsk, I saw few examples of explicit pan-Mongol ties. This is perhaps unsurprising given the distance of Cisbaikalia from the Mongolian border and the fact Western Buryats, unlike the Khori of Buryatia and Aga, do not have a large population of their own clan members, who migrated in the early twentieth century, living just across the border. The exception was my friend Nikolai, who often traveled often between Ust-Orda, Buryatia, and Ulanbaatar, energetically looking to build cultural exchange activities—though these projects were usually constrained by a lack of resources, which may also be the reason for a wider lack of engagement in pan-Mongol cultural activities. Although there was a sizeable population of Mongolian students in Irkutsk, some of whom I got to know, there was little cross-pollination between the events held by that group and Buryat cultural events in the city. Stronger engagement by Western Buryats was visible in pan-Buryat cultural activities, namely participation in the biennial *Altargana* festival, which brought together Siberian Buryats with communities that had migrated after the Russian revolution to present-day Mongolia and China. There was also funding for such activities through the efforts of VARK.

BURYAT NATIONAL CULTURE IN UST'-ORDA BURYAT AUTONOMOUS OKRUG

On a crisp morning in February 2006, I made my way to the house of culture in Ust'-Orda settlement to watch a competition of folklore ensembles from across the okrug. The event was held in celebration of *Sagaalgan*. Audience members sat huddled in

Sagaalgan folklore competition in the house of culture. Ust'-Orda settlement, February 2006.

their overcoats in the rather drafty auditorium as each ensemble took their turn filling an allotted fifteen-minute slot on the stage. Children and adults performed traditional songs and enacted customs. All ensembles danced the Buryat circle dance, the *yokhor*. Performers wore colorful costumes embroidered with decorative patterns, many wearing versions of the traditional Buryat coat, the *degel*. Several female performers wore headdresses with decorated plaits attached, replicating the appearance of Buryat women in pre-Soviet times.

Performances such as these take place on *Sagaalgan*, at the summer *Sur-kharban* competitions of traditional Buryat sports and on federal public holidays, such as May 9, when communities across Russia celebrate victory in the Second World War. On these occasions ensembles represented their local municipal administrations.

In Novonikolaevsk the house of culture, usually referred to simply as the *klub*, was the hub of community activities. The *klub*, built in 1990 to replace an older wooden building, contained a library, an auditorium, and several offices. It was manned by five part-time culture workers (Rus. *kul'turniki*): the highly energetic director, his deputy, the director of the Buryat folklore ensemble, and two further colleagues, one of whom was Erzhena. The ensemble was known as *Bayan Tala*, Buryat for "the rich steppe." In the same municipal administration, a satellite ensemble known as *Dangina*, the Buryat word for beauty, operated in Khabarovsk. Erzhena ran a youth group for children to learn the Buryat language and songs and dances to perform with the ensemble. Most of the adult performers with Bayan Tala were culture workers, teachers at the village school, or retired. Staff at the club also organized the village *Sur-kharban* held each summer, recruited the sports teams, and rallied ensemble members to represent Novonikolaevsk at the raion *Sur-kharban* folklore competition.

The culture workers in Novonikolaevsk were employed—and cultural activities funded—by the department of culture for Ekhirit-Bulagat Raion. Erzhena and her colleagues were answerable to the raion director of culture based at the large house of culture in Ust'-Orda settlement. In that institution, six culture workers ran youth ensembles performing modern dance, drama, and Russian folk dance along with Buryat performing arts. A well-known adult folklore ensemble *Khudain Gol* (Buryat for "the Kuda River") was also based at the Ust'-Orda house of culture. Often culture workers from the villages were called on by the raion administration to perform with Khudain Gol and represent the raion at public events. Okrug-level events and institutions were overseen and funded by the Ust'-Orda okrug Committee for Culture. These included the okrug regional museum, the okrug library, the Centre for Folk Arts, and the Stepnye Napevy professional ensemble.

BURYAT NATIONAL CULTURE IN THE CITIES OF CISBAIKALIA

The cities of Irkutsk and Angarsk have always been outside Buryat national territory, and neither city had any official organs of Buryat national culture during the Soviet period. In previous chapters, I noted the tendency of Western Buryats to migrate to Ulan-Ude rather than Irkutsk in the Soviet era and that Irkutsk is often regarded with disdain by Ulan-Ude Buryats. The increasing Buryat population in Irkutsk and Angarsk in the late-Soviet era, however, meant that the national cultural renaissance of the *perestroika* era became a catalyst for the initiation of Buryat cultural activities. In 1990, Buryat culture centers were founded in both cities.

By the time I arrived in Irkutsk to begin my research, the city's Center for Buryat Culture ran a busy program of events. In spring 2006 I joined a weekly Buryat language class there. The center had its own youth ensemble, *Ulaalzai*, and an adult folklore ensemble named *Ayanga*. The center published an occasional newspaper, *Üür* (dawn). It hosted its own *Sur-kharban* at the city's horse-racing ground each summer and put on an annual *Sagaalgan* concert. Ulaalzai was mainly made up of university students, several from the Buryat republic. The group performed a mixture of Buryat pop music and national dance. Ayanga was formed mainly by retirement-age adults in 2003 and performed folklore material.

The center's small offices in the middle of Irkutsk were a hive of activity every weekend. While my Buryat language class met in the center's main office, people would queue in the corridor outside to see a Buddhist practitioner of Tibetan medicine and Ulaalzai rehearsed their dance routines to a stereo next door. The activists who formed the center's committee came from all over the Baikal region, including the Buryat republic and Aga Buryat Autonomous Okrug. These activists included academics, professionals, and businesspeople.

In Angarsk the Buryat cultural center was something of a cottage industry based at *Tuya*, a canteen serving *buuzy*—traditional meat dumplings. The proprietor funded many of the center's activities and several of the center's activists worked there. The Angarsk center also ran language classes for local Buryat youth, two young-people's ensembles, and concerts in the city. In 2006, the Center published a Buryat language primer.

Though these institutions for Buryat culture were relatively young at the time, they enjoyed a good deal of visibility in public life, asserting a growing Buryat presence and confidence in these historically Russian cities. This visibility was substantially increased during the referendum campaign on the unification of Irkutsk Oblast and Ust'-Orda Buryat Autonomous Okrug described in the next chapter.

RITUAL AND THEATRICAL STAGING OF BURYAT CUSTOMS

While this book makes a broad distinction between the ritual mediation of kinship clan identities on the one hand and the official culture of national belonging on the other, I hope to suggest ways that these phenomena have come to inform one another. This chapter focuses on the mediation of national belonging through state institutions, but it is clear in discussions with Buryat friends that the elements of shamanist ritual that continued under the radar in Soviet times and the visible revival of collective rites also inform a sense of Buryat identity and national belonging.

David Anderson's ethnography of Siberian Evenkis and Marjorie Balzer's study of Khanty people in north west Siberia both see the building blocks of national or ethnic identity in everyday ritual practices.[61] In Balzer's view, the tenacity of indigenous identities can, in part, be explained by the household rituals and shamanist practices maintained out of public view during the period of Soviet communism. It is clear that alongside civic celebrations of culture, the everyday ritual practice and collective ceremonies described in chapters 2 and 3 also provided a sense of Buryat identity and a point of social differentiation from others. It is therefore quite noteworthy that since the 1990s aspects of that everyday practice have increasingly been represented in official culture.

Folklore competitions often specify that presentations include a dramatization, in Russian parlance a *theatricalization* (*teatralizatsiia*), of Buryat customs. I saw many such theatrical stagings over the course of my field research. In 2006, for example, I attended the folklore competition "One Day in Buryatia" at the all-Buryat *Altargana* festival in Ulan-Ude. There I watched the Ayanga and Ulaalzai ensembles from Irkutsk present a theatrical staging of traditional prewedding exchanges of hospitality. Conducted entirely in Buryat, with performers costumed in the traditional Buryat *degel*, the piece was set against the backdrop of a semicircular trellis to evoke the environment of a traditional yurt. The presentation depicted a Buryat bride and groom's families agreeing to the terms of a marriage and featured two ensemble members acting as stereotypical Buryat mothers, exaggeratedly singing the praises of their offspring. The piece also dramatized the exchange of vodka and tobacco between lineage seniors, offerings to spirits at the hearth, and agreements on a date and place for the wedding. The company performed the required circle dance—the *yokhor*—to conclude the piece.

Nastia, one of the culture workers at the house of culture in Ust'-Orda settlement, graduated from the Ulan-Ude academy of culture with a specialization in directing theater performance. She regularly created scenarios for local ensembles. In a joint interview with me, Nastia and her colleagues emphasized the pedagogical value of presenting historical Buryat traditions to a younger generation. Ethnographic texts often provided source material for these dramatizations. Where early Soviet presentations invariably depicted shamans as evil, exploiting their clients for their own gain, today shamanist rites are depicted more positively.[62]

At the Ust'-Orda okrug *Sur-kharban* in 2007, I joined Erzhena's family and a sizeable crowd in gathering around the steps of the okrug administration, where an open-air stage had been created. Here ensembles representing the okrug's six raions each presented theatricalized pieces. Erzhena joined Ekhirit-Bulagat Raion's *Khudian Gol* ensemble in presenting a depiction of a shamanist ritual. The folkloristic sources for the presentation were made clear: before the performance began, the ensemble director announced where, when, and by whom the songs included were collected. The piece was a highly stylized representation of a sprinkling rite. Members of the ensemble slowly circled a mock fire, mimed cleansing themselves with smoke and making offerings, and moved to the front of the stage to recite loud prayers to the spirits. The ensemble then acted out the dedication of a ritual tethering post (*Bur. serge*). The post was placed on the stage by the men before four women came solemnly to the front, holding up silk scarves that were each tied to the post. The actions were narrated in Buryat by two members of the company, each with a microphone. One performer played a shaman. In full costume, including helmet and veil, they danced around the fire and *serge*, banging their drum to a frenetic climax when the costumed figure of a fire spirit eventually emerged. Dressed in a bright robe, the spirit conferred his blessings on the participants before retreating. The presentation again concluded with a rendition of the *yokhor*.

Staged dramatizations of Buryat custom are configured entirely for the theatrical frame as described by Goffman. In his formulation Goffman describes several practices that distinguish dramatic action from the "real life" model. Goffman observes, for example, that "spatial boundaries of the stage sharply and arbitrarily cut off the depicted world from what lies beyond the stage line." He notes the spatial conventions of "opening up rooms," much like the cutaway depiction of a yurt interior, where "participants do not face each other directly... but stand at an open angle to the front" and "one person at a time tends to be given the focus

Theatrical staging of an offering rite. Ust'-Orda settlement, June 2007.

of the stage, front and center."[63] These spatial conventions were all evident in the folklore performance that I witnessed. Action was configured to face outward, the scarves tied to the *serge* were first presented to the audience, and the commentator addressed his narrative to the gathered crowd. These framing conventions constitute, very literally, an outward-facing form. Staged performances used spatial conventions quite distinct from the ritual forms depicted, which face inward toward the fire, hearth, or offering place.

The dramatic action was highly performative in that it was clearly demarcated for purposes of display. Gestures were slow, measured, and larger than life; oratory comprised loud declamations in Buryat. Despite depicting ritual action, the performance was not, in itself, a ritual act. The conscious intent of the performers was one of presenting a theatricalization. It had no ritual purpose. There were no spirits present, only a theatrical representation of one. In subsequent chapters, however, I explore the way that theatrical framing has influenced some public shamanist rituals in Cisbaikalia and how the notion of theatricalization was used to question their authenticity.

CIVIC BELONGING IN RURAL CISBAIKALIA

The development and revival of national culture within the Buryat territories was achieved through local institutions—namely the houses of culture staffed by *kul'turniki* like Erzhena. Yet these institutions are not just repositories of broader Soviet or national culture; they are important focal points for local civic communities. In Novonikolaevsk the team of part-time *kul'turniki* organized local events, such as the village *Sur-kharban*, concerts, and celebrations of public holidays. In the summer the *klub* was opened as a place for young people and students returning to the village to socialize in the evening.

Just as Western Buryats might be said to belong to concentric kin communities, the same is true of civic belonging. Sporting events, such as the summer *Sur-kharban*, were held at local, raion, and okrug levels. When sporting teams or cultural delegations represented these nested communities, I often heard the same idioms of possession—describing a team or ensemble as *nash*—situationally applied to village, raion, and okrug teams.

While there is a qualitative difference between national belonging—expressed in mass-mediated forms that replicate across scale—and kinship—rooted in the immediacy of shared experience and communion—local civic belonging falls somewhere between these categorizations. The sense of community brought through local schools, shared space, friendships, and affinities, all infused events and occasions in the villages of Cisbaikalia. In the Novonikolaevsk area, this appears to have been particularly true of the *sovkhoz*, where local people did not just share a territory but were employed and worked toward the same collective endeavor. Though Humphrey's Soviet-era ethnography suggests that collectivization never obviated the need for kin networks, a sense of belonging to the *sovkhoz* was constituted through collective engagement with the world.[64] In this context civic belonging was celebrated in public events for what appears to have been a particularly meaningful community, and one where Buryats and Slavs lived and worked together. Certainly the *sovkhoz* was spoken of nostalgically after the collapse of collectivized farming had taken a toll on the life of the village.

By that time a civic sense of belonging was less evident. In 2006 the Novonikolaevsk *Sur-kharban* was a small affair. Only two horse races took place, and those present lamented the low turnout compared to the events of yesteryear. As Vitia's neighbor in Khuty expressed, "No one here has any petrol! Who is going to go to the *Sur-kharban*?" In 2007, in the face of dwindling funding from the raion administration and low attendance, the three rural administrations of Novonikolaevsk, Gakhan, and Baitog combined to host a single event in Gakhan.

During my time in the villages, I only saw the full Bayan Tala ensemble perform on one occasion: when I accompanied the Novonikolaevsk delegation to the Irkutsk city *Sur-kharban* in 2006 after funding had been made available by the Irkutsk Centre for Buryat Culture. On that occasion eleven adults turned out—four of them *kul'turniki*, four teachers, and three retired teachers, including the ensemble's founders. Bayan Tala did not attend the raion *Sur-kharban* in Ust'-Orda that summer, complaining that not enough funding had been made available by the raion administration. The following year Erzhena lamented that the adult ensemble had not managed to turn out at all. Ensemble members complained that they were too busy to rehearse or perform. When Erzhena showed me a photograph of the ensemble in the 1990s, I was quite surprised to see how many people had formerly been members. Many of the performers were familiar faces from the village but were no longer involved. The heyday of

Buryat cultural renaissance of the 1990s certainly seemed to be over in northern Ekhirit-Bulagat raion.

If in the mid-2000s the ensemble had trouble putting together a performance, it might be because, following the collapse of the *sovkhoz* and rapid migration from the villages, they no longer represented such a meaningful collective. This was true not just at a symbolic level but also at a practical one: ensemble members claimed they were now too busy to participate because they were tending their own private herds. When the *sovkhoz* provided material and financial income, members had time to rehearse and perform. The decline of civic events in the countryside contrasts the thriving institution of the clan *tailgan*. In *tailgan* rites, long-standing relationships of community and reciprocity were constituted, providing economic support that the state and the *sovkhoz* no longer could.

BURYAT NATIONAL CULTURE IN A CHANGING WORLD

The nation-building policies of the early Soviet period and the national-cultural revival of the late- and post-Soviet eras saw institutionalized Buryat national culture grow and develop. The performing arts that took shape under this banner continued to serve as symbolic reference points for Buryat national identity in the mid-2000s.

The way that national and civic belonging was mediated by performing arts proved markedly different from the way kinship and local senses of belonging were constituted. While local ritual forms effect a sense of belonging to bounded groups through communion and collective activity, the performance events that mediated national and civic belonging were physically framed in a way that differentiated skilled performers from spectators. In these forms, the symbols of national belonging were projected outward from the stage in performance venues across the space identified as Buryat national territory. The institutions where such performances took place—the schools, theaters, and houses of culture—formed part of a wider state infrastructure that intricately connected economic and cultural development in the early Soviet period.

While such performances might have been less meaningful to civic communities that had seen better days by the mid-2000s, the situation in the villages of Cisbaikalia provided a marked difference to increasingly active amateur ensembles and cultural activists of Irkutsk city. Those institutions gained their moment in the spotlight in early 2006, as the next chapter shows. Moreover, as subsequent chapters illustrate, rather than being an alternative to displaying Buryat national belonging in the public sphere, local ritual practice proved to be an important medium for doing just that.

NOTES

1. Goffman, *The Presentation of Self in Everyday Life*.
2. Shryock, *Off Stage / on Display: Intimacy and Ethnography in the Age of Public Culture*.
3. Donahoe and Habeck, *Reconstructing the House of Culture*, x–xi, 1–5.
4. See, e.g., Sapir, *Selected Writings*, 309.
5. Figes, *Natasha's Dance*.
6. Kelly et al., "Introduction: Why Cultural Studies?"
7. Grant, *In the Soviet House of Culture* and King, *Living with Koryak Traditions* recount similar experiences.
8. Cocchiara, *History of Folklore in Europe*.
9. Rupen, "The Buriat Intelligentsia."
10. Khangalov, *Sobranie Sochinenii, Vol. 1*; Tarmakhanov, Dameshek, and Sanzhieva, *Istoria Ust'-Ordynskogo Buriatskogo Avtonomogo Okruga*, 84.
11. Rupen, "Cyben Zamcaranovic Zamcarano."
12. Tarmakhanov, Dameshek, and Sanzhieva, *Istoria Ust'-Ordynskogo Buriatskogo Avtonomogo Okruga*, 89–91.
13. Tarmakhanov, Dameshek, and Sanzhieva, 91–92.

14. Montgomery, *Late Tsarist and Early Soviet Nationality and Cultural Policy: The Buryats and Their Language*, 144–49.

15. Ibid.

16. Badiev, *Kul'turnoe Stroitel'stvo v Buriatskoi ASSR: Dokumenty i Materialy*.

17. Smith, "The Soviet State and Nationalities Policy"; Hirsch, *Empire of Nations*.

18. Renner, "State and Nation."

19. Martin, *The Affirmative Action Empire*, 32.

20. Stalin, "Marxism and the National Question."

21. Martin, *The Affirmative Action Empire*, 12; Smith, "The Soviet State and Nationalities Policy," 6–8.

22. Erbanov, "Tezisy Po Dokladu M. N. Erbanova 'Kul''turno-Natsioanalhoe Stroitelstvo BMASSR,'" 81–91.

23. Babueva, *Materialhaia i Dukhovnaia Kul'tura Buriat*.

24. Newyear, "'Our Primitive Customs' and 'Lord Kalym.'"

25. Badiev, *Kul'turnoe Stroitel'stvo v Buriatskoi ASSR: Dokumenty i Materialy*, 177.

26. Goffman, *Frame Analysis: An Essay on the Organization of Experience*, 123–55.

27. Donahoe and Habeck, *Reconstructing the House of Culture*; Anderson, "Bringing Civil Society to an Uncivilised Place"; Humphrey, "Ideology in Infrastructure."

28. Badiev, *Kul'turnoe Stroitel'stvo v Buriatskoi ASSR*, 135.

29. Donahoe and Habeck, *Reconstructing the House of Culture*.

30. Erbanov, "Tezisy Po Dokladu," 83–84.

31. Ibid.

32. Hosking, *A History of the Soviet Union 1917–1991*.

33. Rupen, "The Buriat Intelligentsia."

34. Chakars, *The Socialist Way of Life in Siberia*, 71–6; Forsyth, *A History of the Peoples of Siberia*, 334.

35. Badiev, *Kul'turnoe Stroitel'stvo v Buriatskoi ASSR*, 95, 99.

36. Balzer, "Dilemmas of Federalism in Siberia"; Chakars, *The Socialist Way of Life in Siberia*, 76–78.

37. Martin, *The Affirmative Action Empire: Nations and Nationalism in the Soviet Union, 1923–1939*, 372–92.

38. Naidakova, "Teatr," 531; Frolova, "Narodnaia Myzikal'naia Kul'tura," 553; Badiev, *Kul'turnoe Stroitel'stvo v Buriatskoi ASSR: Dokumenty i Materialy*, 201.

39. Frolova, "Narodnaia Myzikal'naia Kul'tura," 553.
40. Baldaev, *Buriatskie Narodnye Pesni (Sovetskii Period)*; Sharakshinova, *Buriatskogo Narodnoe Poeticheskoe Tvorchestvo*.
41. Shoolbraid, *The Oral Epic of Siberia and Central Asia*.
42. Krist, "Where Going Back Is a Step Forward"; Humphrey, *Marx Went Away—But Karl Stayed Behind: Updated Edition of Karl Marx Collective: Economy, Society and Religion in a Siberian Collective Farm*, 380–82.
43. Binns, "The Changing Face of Power: Revolution and Accommodation in the Development of the Soviet Ceremonial System: Part I."
44. Khamutaev, *Buriatskoe Natsionalhoe Dvizhenie 1980–2000-3 Gg.*, 156; Palkhaeva, "Razdel Buriat-Mongol'skoi ASSR v 1927g," 236.
45. Ibid., 156.
46. Stroganova, *Buriatskoe Natsionalno-Kulturnoe Vozrozhdenie*, 60.
47. Khamutaev, *Buriatskoe Natsionalhoe Dvizhenie 1980–2000-3 Gg.*, 230–37.
48. Ibid., 133.
49. Ibid., 134.
50. Ibid., 245–46.
51. Stroganova, 63–64.
52. Ibid., 55.
53. Ibid., 75, 99.
54. Khamutaev, 154.
55. Khamutaev, 155; Stroganova, 65.
56. Khamutaev, 154.
57. Ibid.
58. Vereshchagina, "Pesni Rodnoi Zemli."
59. Oshirova, "Razvitie Kul'tura v Ust'-Ordynskom Buriatskom Avtonomnom Okruge."
60. Ibid., 126.
61. Anderson, *Identity and Ecology in Arctic Siberia*; Balzer, *The Tenacity of Ethnicity*.
62. Vitebsky, *Reindeer People*.
63. Goffman, *Frame Analysis* 139–40.
64. Humphrey, *Marx Went Away—But Karl Stayed Behind*.

FIVE

TERRITORIAL UNIFICATION AND NATIONAL CULTURAL AUTONOMY IN CISBAIKALIA

ON FEBRUARY 22, 2006, I made my way to the central square in Ust'-Orda settlement. The temperature was more than twenty degrees below zero Celsius, but the sky was bright and clear and the square was a hive of activity. A large banner wished everyone a happy *Sagaalgan*, the festival of the lunar new year. Around the Lenin statue, six yurts had been erected, each one representing one of the raions of Ust'-Orda Buryat Autonomous Okrug. Smoke billowed from the chimneys as delegations cooked freshly butchered meat for guests. TV and print media were in attendance as the governor of Irkutsk Oblast, Alexander Tishanin, was escorted around the square by the okrug's chief administrator, Valeri Maleev, and other local dignitaries. At each yurt, representatives wearing the traditional Buryat *degel* welcomed the governor, presenting him with a *khadag*, the silk scarf traditionally given to honored guests. The governor was shown formal hospitality in each yurt—given a little food and drink—and outside each tent he joined hands with delegation members before being whisked around for a few verses of the Buryat circle dance, the *yokhor*.

The governor's much-publicized visit clearly sought to demonstrate harmonious relations between oblast and okrug. Tishanin's careful show of respect for Buryat culture was matched by the traditional welcome given by local Buryats. Such spectacles became common in the spring of that year in the run up to the April referendum on the unification of Irkutsk Oblast and Ust'-Orda Buryat Autonomous Okrug. The campaign not only featured numerous public displays of Buryat culture but also a revival by Russian authorities of the long-dormant ideology of National Cultural Autonomy. The change marked a radical rethinking of the relationship between culture and territory in Russian policy.

RETHINKING THE FEDERATION

From the USSR, Russia inherited a complex federal system in which subject territories enjoyed varied levels of autonomy and comprised a mixture of designated national territories and purely administrative regions. When the Russian Soviet Federative Socialist Republic became the Russian Federation in 1991, there were eighty-nine subject territories.

The national republics within the Russian Federation are the largest of the national territories and enjoy the greatest autonomy. Most, like the Republic of Buryatia, were formerly Autonomous Soviet Socialist Republics (ASSRs). National republics have their own elected presidents and constitutions. Oblasts and krais are generally administrative territories, usually taking the name of their biggest city. Of the five national autonomous oblasts that existed in 1991, four became national republics in the early post-Soviet years and only the Birobidjan Jewish Autonomous Oblast remains today. The autonomous okrugs, known as national okrugs until 1978, were mostly located within larger oblasts or krais, as with Ust'-Orda Buryat Autonomous Okrug in Irkutsk Oblast and Aga Buryat Autonomous Okrug in Chita Oblast.

The most senior partners within the USSR had been the union republics; Russia, the Baltic countries, the Caucasian and Central Asian Republics, Ukraine, Belarus, and Moldova. Following the secession of the union republics and consequent collapse of the USSR, the early post-Soviet years were characterized by a trend toward greater national autonomy within the Russian Federation. The elevation of four autonomous oblasts to Republic status was symptomatic of this early trend, as was Article 5 of the 1993 constitution, which granted the autonomous okrugs equal status with larger subject territories. From that point onward, each autonomous okrug had budgetary autonomy, their own assembly (*duma*), and their own representative in the Russian federal *duma*.

Despite moves to devolve power in the 1990s, territorial restructuring in the 2000s was symptomatic of renewed political centralization in Russia. Talk of reducing the number of administrative regions of the Russian Federation began under President Boris Yeltsin in the 1990s. The task of reorganizing the federation began in earnest with Vladimir Putin's first administration and with the aim of streamlining what Putin called the *power vertical*.[1] In 2001 the federal law "On the Process of Accession to the Russian Federation and Foundation of a New Constituent Unit of the Russian Federation" made the merger of subject territories possible in order to further simplify power structures.[2] The law immediately prompted discussions in the Baikal region as to the possibility of merging the Buryat okrugs with the larger oblasts.

Centralization of power was further evident in the law of 2005 that decreed that oblast and krai governors would be nominated by the president and approved by local legislatures rather than be elected.[3] Alexander Tishanin was one of the first oblast governors to be directly appointed in this way. Tishanin became governor of Irkutsk Oblast in September 2005 after proving himself as a regional railway manager.

Valeri Maleev, the chief administrator of Ust'-Orda Buryat Autonomous Okrug, pledged his support for the unification of the okrug with Irkutsk Oblast as early as April 2001, when the federal law was first discussed.[4] In April 2002 a working group was formed by the legislature of Irkutsk Oblast to consider a merger.[5] Although Maleev was in favor, he did not have the support of local deputies, and in November of that year, the *duma* of Ust'-Orda Buryat Autonomous Okrug issued a declaration against the okrug's absorption by Irkutsk Oblast.[6] In June 2003, the previously nonpolitical All-Buryat Association for the Development of Culture (*VARK*) and the Congress of the Buryat People held a congress in Ust'-Orda to address the proposed merger. In his address D. S. Sanditov, then president of VARK, argued against the federal reorganization of Russia: "There is an alternative choice, known as national-territorial autonomy," he argued, suggesting that aiming for an American model of territorial federalism would "liquidate the nations of Russia, including the Buryat nation."[7] At the same congress, the political scientist Vladimir Khamutaev argued, in line with many of the Buryat intelligentsia at the time, that the possibility of reuniting the okrugs with the Republic of Buryatia should be given to Buryats. Attempts to push this idea were met with state authorities responding that the 2001 federal law only allowed for neighboring regions to merge and stating that a reunited Buryatia with its pre-1937 borders would be "unconstitutional."[8]

Though local opposition stalled the merger of okrug and oblast for a time, the idea was rekindled in 2005. An amendment to the original federal law on unification in that year placed the responsibility on regional governors to initiate public votes on territorial mergers. This move made referendums appear to be locally initiated rather than top-down decisions. Sure enough, on October 11, 2005, the newly appointed Tishanin, Maleev, and chairmen of the oblast and okrug legislative assemblies composed a letter to the president requesting initiation of a unification process. The letter, widely published in the local press, emphasized the pooling of economic resources and the desire to raise the standard of living for all inhabitants of the region.[9]

By the time a referendum was initiated in Irkutsk Oblast and Ust-Orda Buryat Autonomous Okrug, four autonomous okrugs in Russia had already voted to merge with neighboring or surrounding oblasts.[10] The date for the Cisbaikal referendum was set for April 16, 2006.

THE REFERENDUM CAMPAIGN IN CISBAIKALIA

As the referendum approached, the pro-unification cause dominated public discourse. Banners, posters, special newspapers, and television adverts were financed by a group named For a New Pribaikal'e. The group comprised prominent local politicians, including the oblast governor and business leaders. A logo of two figures in Buryat and Russian national costume with their arms around each other appeared on the group's publicity material, most of which was emblazoned with the slogans "Together we're stronger!" (*Vmeste my sil'nee!*) and "We will be together!" (*Budem vmeste!*). The logo could be seen everywhere in the spring of 2006. On Defence of the Fatherland Day, February 23, I was given a greeting card by volunteers on the street wishing me a happy day. The photo on the front showed Russian and Buryat soldiers marching together and featured the campaign logo on the rear. Ubiquitous posters distributed by the campaign bore slogans urging voters to "Unify Russia!" and "Think about Siberia!"

Of this material, little was concerned with questions of Buryat political autonomy. In Irkutsk, television advertisements focused on the increased budget that Irkutsk Oblast was to receive because of unification and its potential to be the leading economic region of eastern Siberia. Municipal regeneration was a major theme of the referendum campaign in Irkutsk. At a televised meeting of local leaders with Putin, the Russian president chided Tishanin and his colleagues for the run-down appearance of the city: "Clean Irkutsk!" he told them. "Clear the streets and repair the facades!" His instructions were accompanied by a pledge of money for such municipal works.[11] Putin further promised that if voters agreed to unification, he would provide funds to complete a road bridge

"16th April—For Unification" banner in Irkutsk city, April 2016.

over the Angara River, which had been started six years previously but had continually run out of funding. The completion of the bridge became a major motif of the campaign. Outside the state technical university in Irkutsk, I was given a card depicting a jigsaw puzzle of the Angara bridge with a piece missing, waiting to be slotted into place. A television advert in favor of unification showed a scene from "summer 2007," when someone arriving in Irkutsk and being taken across the new bridge by taxi was so thrilled to see it finished that he spontaneously burst into song with the driver, belting out a nostalgic chorus about the Angara River.

In Ust'-Orda okrug, a flyer posted to every house emphasized the poor state of agriculture in the territory and the need for social and economic development from an increased budget. Another outlined how 1.5 billion rubles, promised by Putin, would be spent on the development of the territory. This included the construction of a new antenatal center, three new hospitals, two polyclinics, a children's center, six new schools, and the completion of a sports center in Ust'-Orda settlement that had been started years before but, like the Angara bridge, had run out of funding several times. Calendars bearing the slogan "Always Together!" featured photographs of Buryats in traditional clothing undertaking traditional sports and folklore performances alongside Russians in their own national dress.

The pro-unification campaign's emphasis on regenerating infrastructure is significant. In the previous chapter, I described the way cultural development in the Soviet Union was explicitly linked to infrastructure in national territories. The assertion that infrastructural regeneration was now in the gift of central government marked a step away from national territorial autonomy, even if it was not explicitly articulated as such. Opposition to unification was muted in Cisbaikalia. Those employed by the local administration were on message in favor of unification or quiet throughout. A group of opponents of unification complained that while forty-two organizations were registered in favor, they had not been allowed to register an organization opposing the merger.[12] A single website in Ust'-Orda became the mouthpiece of dissenting voices locally.

The most prominent opposition came from the Buryat intelligentsia in the Republic of Buryatia. The Congress of the Buryat People facilitated roundtables in Ulan-Ude, and VARK published several articles in which unification was openly questioned.[13] In March 2006 I attended a demonstration against unification in the central square of Ulan-Ude. Speeches were not permitted, but banners on display proclaimed that protesters were "defending the sacred land of Ust'-Orda" and that "a strong Buryatia means a strong Russia." Alongside these posters, flags bearing the logo of the opposition party, *Yabloko*, were flown and a number of attendees wore orange armbands, making a visual reference to Ukraine's Orange Revolution. During the same week, I heard

"The referendum is everyone's business—that's what the polytechnic thinks." Poster in Irkutsk, featuring the pro-unification campaign logo: an image of harmony between Russians and Buryats, April 2006.

that a *tailgan* had been planned in Ulan-Ude, where offerings would be made for the preservation of Ust'-Orda Buryat Autonomous Okrug. In the end, however, I was told that the rite was cancelled after the shaman due to preside had been warned off by the secret service. Certainly the FSB were in conspicuous attendance at the silent demonstration as large vans and men in black surrounded the square. A visiting American scholar who attended the meeting and chanted political slogans had her visa cancelled and was told to leave the country the following week.

In Irkutsk, Buryat cultural activists were vocal in favor of unification and clearly saw the campaign as a chance to garner state support for their activities in a city not previously acknowledged as Buryat territory. In pamphlets distributed in the city, Irkutsk was pushed as the logical center of Buryat culture in the region.

As the referendum neared, publicity took on a solemn tone emphasizing the duty of everyone to vote and vote in favor of unification. The rector of the university where I was based made a speech to students urging them to do so. Giant placards were affixed to the front of the university and the hall of residence where I was staying. The placards proclaimed that "the referendum is the business of everyone—that's what the polytechnic thinks!" Further signs around the city pointed out that "the future's in your hands!" or simply proclaimed themselves "for unification!" (*za obedinenie!*).

It is notable that the pro-unification campaign group and government discourse increasingly chose to refer to the combined territory of oblast and okrug as *Pribaikal'e*. The term denotes a region "next to Baikal" whereas *Predbaikal'e* would be the literal equivalent of Cisbaikalia. Some expected this to mean that the newly unified territory would be known as *Pribaikalskii Krai*, with the proposed unification of Aga Buryat Autonomous Okrug and Chita Oblast to be named *Zabaikalskii Krai* (Transbaikal Krai). More suspicious minds wondered if the broader implication of Pribaikal'e might even presage an eventual unification with Buryatia as a single Baikal region, though this was not suggested in any official discourse at the time.

CONSPICUOUS CULTURE

As the referendum campaign intensified, Buryat cultural events gained regular media coverage in Irkutsk. On February 11, I attended a large *Sagaalgan* concert at the city's musical theater organized by the Center for Buryat Culture. Proceedings began when

Valentin Khagdaev, a well-known shaman from Ol'khon Raion made offerings to a fire in front of the assembled crowd. The auditorium was thick with incense as Buddhist monks recited prayers while the audience took their seats. Yet the tone moved from spirituality to politics when Tishanin, the Irkutsk governor, and Maleev, representing Ust'-Orda okrug took the stage to make official speeches of congratulations to the Buryat community on the lunar new year. The deputy governor of the oblast and the mayor of Irkutsk were also conspicuously present. Ensembles from the Irkutsk and Angarsk cultural centers performed, and a star turn was taken by Stepnye Napevy from Ust'-Orda.

Üür, the publication of the Centre for Buryat Culture in Irkutsk, increased from an occasionally printed newsletter to a broadsheet issuing several editions that spring thanks to an injection of funding from the oblast government. On the front page of a special *Sagaalgan* issue, politicians again congratulated their "fellow countrymen" on the lunar New Year.[14] High-profile events continued throughout the spring. In February Stepnye Napevy and ensembles from the culture center in Irkutsk traversed the region as "Artists for Unification" in a concert tour titled "The Baikal Express." In March, a festival of Buryat wrestling was organized at the Palace of Sport in Irkutsk flanked by okrug and oblast flags hanging together. During this period a news bulletin was even broadcast in Buryat language on the local television station. The implicit message from local authorities that Buryat culture would be safe in a unified region was clear.

One issue of *Üür* made the message explicit. The editor expressed gratitude for state support in producing several issues of the paper that year, and a large photo of Tishanin graced the front cover with the enlarged quote, "We'll do everything necessary in the united federal subject to guarantee the preservation and development of Buryat culture and language."[15] In the same issue, a prominent cultural activist and committee member of the Irkutsk Buryat culture center argued against a "purely emotional

"Yes? The future is in our hands." Pro-unification poster in Irkutsk, April 2006.

approach" to unification. In an extensive interview, he lauded the concentration of financial resources that unification would allow.[16]

In the context of the referendum, the public framing of Buryat culture gave significance to performances beyond the conventional symbolism of national identity. The newspaper reports, speeches, and participation of performers from both Irkutsk and Ust'-Orda meant that these events were more than just celebrations of *Sagaalgan* or expressions of national belonging; they also demonstrated solidarity between oblast and okrug and implied support for territorial unification by those taking part.

THE PATH TO UNIFICATION

While state employees spoke publicly in favor of unification, rumors circulated on internet forums that voters in the okrug had been encouraged to show their loyalty to the pro-unification cause by writing their names on their ballot slips. After the vote I heard rumors that pensioners had been warned to vote "correctly" to guarantee an increase in their pensions and that state employees had been warned similarly to ensure preservation of their jobs. It was also reported to me in the city that students in university halls of residence were warned to vote in favor of unification to ensure they kept their subsidized accommodation. Opponents of unification also pointed to news reports that independent observers had been barred from entering polling stations on the day of the referendum.[17]

I should be clear that I did not investigate these rumors vigorously, or push anyone to talk about this issue for fear of creating a difficult situation for my interlocutors. None of the people who shared these rumors are identifiable in this book. For those who did speak to me, there was a mood of frustrated resignation rather than scandal. The situation was shrugged off by one person I spoke to who stressed "we're used to it." The readiness of okrug inhabitants to go along with the vote despite the private reservations of many and the willingness of cultural activists to stand on platforms for unification recalled the Soviet experience of outward complicity with state doctrines whatever someone's personal views, a point that my interlocutor made readily.

The official results reported 89.76 percent of Irkutsk Oblast voters as being in favor of unification and 9.43 percent against, on a turnout of 68.94 percent of eligible voters. In the okrug, turnout was given as 99.45 percent, with 97.79 percent of the voters in favor of unification and just 1.55 percent against.[18] On December 15, a federal constitutional law was passed with the unwieldy title *On the foundation within the composition of the Russian federation of a new subject of the Russian federation as a result of the unification of Irkutsk Oblast and Ust'-Orda Buryat Autonomous Okrug.*[19]

Unification ultimately to took place on January 1, 2008. Article 5 allowed the territory of the okrug to remain an "administrative-territorial unit with special status" simply titled "Ust'-Orda Buryat Okrug." The law further decreed that the new oblast *duma* was to be made up of fifty deputies: twenty-five elected from the whole of the united territory according to proportional representation from party lists, twenty-one directly elected from the previous oblast territory, and four from the special administrative unit of the former okrug.

In December 2006, the chief administrator of the okrug, Maleev, who had spoken out continually in favor of unification, was elected as one of the region's new representatives in the Russian federal parliament from the pro-Putin United Russia party list. A decree from the president in January 2007 allowed Tishanin, the governor of Irkutsk, to perform the dual role of oblast governor and okrug chief administrator in advance of unification. In March 2007 Chita Oblast and Aga Buryat Autonomous Okrug voted in a referendum on a merger that followed a similar campaign and achieved the same result as the vote held in Cisbaikalia a year earlier.[20] Those territories merged in March 2008 under the new name of Zabaikal (Transbaikal) Krai while, despite the speculation as to the title of the unified territory west of Baikal, the new federal subject simply retained the name Irkutsk Oblast.

THE RESURRECTION OF NATIONAL CULTURAL AUTONOMY

Government pledges to support Buryat culture cited National Cultural Autonomy as the proposed paradigm for managing cultural institutions after unification. Policymakers referred to the 1996 federal law, *On National-Cultural Autonomy*, as providing a framework for cultural activities. The Buryat cultural centers in Irkutsk, Angarsk, and Ol'khon Raion were accordingly renamed as *national autonomies* in the spring of 2006. In the pages of *Üür*, the director of the Irkutsk center emphasized the mandate for the new organizations to cooperate in preserving Buryat language and culture across the oblast.[21]

The resurrection of Renner's vision of cultural autonomy in place of the territorial autonomy inherited from Soviet policy was presented as the key to squaring a more streamlined federation while recognizing Russia's multinational composition. When the law *On National-Cultural Autonomy* was passed in 1996, it allowed Russia to sign the Council of Europe's Framework Convention for the Protection of National Minorities.[22] Russia's 2000 report to the Council of Europe stresses the formation of a number of national cultural associations titled *autonomies* under the law. Of the seven formed at federal level by that time, five were nationalities without a given territory in Russia (the Belarussians, Koreans, Lezgins, Germans, and Serbians), four of which had a nominal homeland elsewhere.[23] The report noted that the Jewish, German, and Tatar autonomies were the most active at that time. The formation of autonomies by nationalities with their own designated territories inside Russia was considerably less popular.[24] The shift to National Cultural Autonomy in a region containing a former national territory was something of a test case in Cisbaikalia.

One Buryat cultural activist argued in an interview that this may be a way of revitalizing language and culture preservation, lamenting Buryats' reliance on state institutions to preserve culture as a reason for the decline of many customs and practices: "We got used to the fact that for many years the state decided for us what language to speak, what to believe—we don't want to understand that we now live in a different state . . . this proposes citizens' responsibility."[25] On the other hand, opponents such as the Regional Union of Young Scholars in Buryatia argued that "preservation of Buryat language in the absence of conditions of national-state autonomy is practically impossible."[26] Others expressed to me privately their doubts as to whether the support for the Irkutsk center would continue once the momentum of the referendum died down.

AFTER THE REFERENDUM

Following unification a new "Center for the Preservation and Development of the Buryat Ethnos" (*Tsentr Sokhraneniia i Razvitiia Buriatskogo Etnosa—TsSRBE*) was founded in Irkutsk to allocate funding for Buryat cultural activities and initiatives in the newly unified oblast. Its management was drawn primarily from the urban intelligentsia—activists of the Irkutsk center who were on message during the referendum campaign. The director of the Irkutsk Center for Buryat Culture became the new center's director on its inception.

The choice of the word *ethnos* (*etnos*) was significant. Most notably adopted and developed in the ethnographic works of Shirokogoroff in the 1920s, Anderson and Arzyutov's examination of the term suggests that it has a more primordialist, even *biosocial*, connotation than contemporary Western understandings of ethnicity, which are centered on cultural elements of social differentiation.[27] Ethnos theory gained currency in Soviet social sciences from the 1960s onward, in particular due to the work of Iulian Bromlei.[28] Its utility came in accounting for the tenacity of national identities in spite of the initial assumptions of Marxism-Leninism that such affinities would eventually give way to proletarian consciousness. To account for those tenacious symbolic and linguistic elements of culture, the term *ethnos* was invoked to suggest that elements of identity persist through the stages of a Marxist schema of history. An ethnos was identified by cultural diacritics, such as language, but it was assumed that every person belonged to one from birth.

The naming of the Irkutsk Centre in this way was the first time I had seen its application in Buryat institutions—I had more often seen Buryats described as a *narod* (a "people" or "folk") or as a *natsional'nost'* (nationality). Some of my interlocutors privately expressed quite a visceral disdain for this apparent downgrading of their nationhood. The idea of Buryats as an ethnos was, however, clearly agreeable to the Russian government. The word did not carry the weight of the term *nation* (*natsiia*) that organizations such as VARK and the nationalist parties of Buryatia regularly used in their discourse. This terminological shift was particularly salient given the centrality of territory to the Soviet definition of nationhood.

The shift from Ust'-Orda to Irkutsk as the center for Buryat cultural activities in Cisbaikalia continued the momentum it gained during the referendum campaign for several months after the vote, driven by the activities of the new center. A Buryat language course was founded at Irkutsk State Linguistic University, a youth magazine, *Buryat-Land*, was founded by young people working at the new center, and Irkutsk Oblast was named host of the biannual all-Buryat *Altargana* festival to be held in 2008. In summer 2006, I traveled with the Novonikolaevsk folklore ensemble to the Irkutsk city *Sur-kharban*, even though the ensemble did not attend the raion event that year. One member of the ensemble explained to me that attendance was "political," in that they needed to show their faces in Irkutsk, where power over funding for cultural activities was soon to be held.

The switch of power to Irkutsk caused frustration among some cultural activists in the okrug who resented the control and funding moving to the city. In Irkutsk, meanwhile, the publicity afforded by the referendum campaign, gained a profile for Buryat culture in the city not seen in the past. Activists emphasized to me their role of promoting Buryat culture in all corners of the new oblast, not just in the territory of the former okrug. I heard a telling comment in Irkutsk that critics "are not real patriots. They think that Buryats live only in the okrug!"

SHIFTING TERRAIN

Tishanin's inclusion in renditions of the *yokhor* in Ust'-Orda resembled a physical embodiment of the logo used by the campaign for unification: Russians and Buryats arm in arm, harmonious and united. These images aligned with the central messaging of the campaign that "together we're stronger." Yet the relations and shifts at play below the surface of the campaign were more complex than binary interethnic relations.

The shift of political power from Ust'-Orda to Irkutsk was paralleled within the Buryat population by a shift of leadership in the institutions of national culture from the okrug to the city of Irkutsk. Resentful comments in Ust'-Orda okrug at the time of the referendum were tempered by a pragmatic need to engage with those now leading the agenda. The referendum campaign showed that while cultural institutions might form part of an apparently blossoming civil society in post-Soviet Russia—initiated and led by volunteer activists in cities like Angarsk and Irkutsk—public culture could still be mobilized and appropriated for the purposes of the state. While the content of the well-publicized performances of 2006 was much the same as those that heralded a Buryat cultural renaissance in the 1990s—national song, dance, and theatricalized customs—their public framing provided a new narrative. The newspaper articles endorsing unification, the congratulations and assurances of political leaders, and the speeches that accompanied public concerts all heralded support for the project of unifying Ust'-Orda okrug and Irkutsk Oblast. In this respect these events could be seen as performances of complicity with that state agenda. On the other hand, urban activists can be seen as leveraging visibility for Buryat culture never seen before in the cities of Cisbaikalia.

The most fundamental shift at play, however, was the move from national territorial autonomy for Western Buryats to the paradigm of National Cultural Autonomy. Some Buryats in the okrug held genuine fears for the future of local cultural institutions after unification. As I walked across the square in Ust'-Orda settlement while local ensembles cleared away their yurts following Tishanin's visit in February 2006, one local man lamented to me, "That will be the last *Sagaalgan* you see here." Moreover, as I discuss in subsequent chapters, the idea of culture divorced from land is anathema to a Buryat sense of belonging that is firmly rooted in the ancestral homeland.

NOTES

1. Gel'man, "Leviathan's Return: The Policy of Recentralization in Contemporary Russia."
2. Oracheva, "Unification as a Political Project: The Case of Permskii Krai," 83.
3. Sakwa, *Russian Politics and Society*, 277.
4. Radio Free Europe / Radio Liberty, "Another Autonomous Okrug Leader Calls for Merger."
5. Radio Free Europe / Radio Liberty, "Preparations Underway for Merger of Siberian Regions as Irkutsk Legislators Study Possible Expansion of Their Region."
6. Ubeev, *Buriatskoi Avtonomii: Byt' Ili Ne Byt'?*, 121.
7. Ibid., 100.
8. Ibid., 19–23.
9. Tishanin et al., "Ob Obrazovanii Novogo Sub'ekta Rossiskoi Federatsii."
10. These were the Komi-Permiak, Evenki, Taimyr, and Koryak Autonomous Okrugs.
11. Kolesnikov, "Sobiratel' Zemel' Irkutskikh."
12. Ubeev, *Buriatskoi Avtonomii: Byt' Ili Ne Byt'?*, 105.
13. Ibid.
14. Üür no. 1 (February 2006): 1.
15. Üür no. 3 (April 2006): 1.
16. Bolotova, "Otvetstvennost' Za Sokhranenie Buriatskogo Iazyka i Kul'tury- Na Kazhdom Iz Nas."
17. Ubeev, *Buriatskoi Avtonomii: Byt' Ili Ne Byt'?*, 103–4.
18. Petrova, "Vybor Sdelan. Oblast' i Okrug Progolosovali Za Obedinenie."
19. Russian Federal Law No. 6–FK3, 2006: "Ob obrazovanii v sostave Rossiiskoi Federatsii novogo subekta Rossiiskoi Federatsii v rezultate ob"edineniia Irkutskoi oblasti i Ust'-Ordinskogo Buryatskogo avtonomnogo okruga'"[On the foundation within the composition of the Russian

federation of a new subject of the Russian federation as a result of the unification of Irkutsk Oblast and Ust'-Orda Buryat Autonomus Okrug].

20. Graber and Long, "The Dissolution of the Buryat Autonomous Okrugs in Siberia."

21. Alsaev, "ERKHÜÜtskie Buriaty Obreli Novyi Status."

22. Bowring, "Burial and Resurrection: Karl Renner's Controversial Influence on the 'National Question' in Russia."

23. Torode, "National Cultural Autonomy in the Russian Federation: Implementation and Impact."

24. Bowring, 203.

25. Bolotova, "Otvetstvennost' Za Sokhranenie Buriatskogo Iazyka i Kul'tury-Na Kazhdom Iz Nas."

26. Ubeev, 95.

27. Anderson and Arzyutov, "The Etnos Archipelago: Sergei M. Shirokogoroff and the Life History of a Controversial Anthropological Concept."

28. Banks, *Ethnicity: Anthropological Constructions*; Bromlei, "The Object and Subject Matter of Ethnography," 17–23; Dragadzhe, "The Place of Ethnos Theory in Soviet Anthropology."

SIX

BURYAT DANCE AND THE AESTHETICS OF BELONGING

BURYAT DANCE PROVIDES AN INSTRUCTIVE medium through which to consider how performative media express and reconstitute feelings of belonging. Modern Buryat dance typifies the Soviet project of shaping performance genres according to European conventions. However, analysis of an older form—the circle dance known as the *yokhor*—illustrates some of the paradoxes and possibilities of meaning-making that occur when a dance is removed from its ritual context and framed on stage.

BURYAT NATIONAL DANCE

In Spring 2006, I sat in on dance rehearsals with the Stepnye Napevy ensemble in Ust'-Orda. On the occasion that I recounted in the introduction, I watched the performers go through their moves in the rehearsal room of the Erdem theater. Misha sat alongside me interpreting the dances. He emphasized that "to understand our dances you have to understand the steppe." Bair, the ensemble's choreographer and another graduate of the East Siberian State Academy of Culture in Ulan-Ude, then demonstrated a catalogue of moments to illustrate this. He showed me how a stalking hunter's movements were smooth and slow, yet determined, and emphasized the same quality in Buryat dances. He demonstrated with impressive dexterity how dancers evoking a horsemen moved their legs to the rhythm of a horse's trot while keeping their upper body rigid to depict the rider, arms held straight as though holding a set of reins.

On another occasion I interviewed Natalya, the choreographer of a local youth ensemble based at the house of culture in Ust'-Orda settlement. Natalya demonstrated to me how sweeping movements of a dancer's arms define the undulating horizons of the steppe landscape. She explained: "The Buryats are a steppe people... with our hands we express the beauty of nature—every movement has that kind of foundation. We express the beauty of nature, the gallop of horses. The horses for us are the first among our friends; they are always alongside a person. We are cattle herders and hunters so there's even elements of dance that show the dance of hunters... how they round up their animals."

The development of this modern Buryat national dance began in the 1920s and was pioneered by choreographer Gombo Tsydynzhapov. Tsydynzhapov's template for both adapting traditional forms and depicting scenes from traditional steppe life defined the genre for decades. In the 1930s he incorporated elements of Uzbek and Kalmyk dance into the Buryat circle dance.[1] As well as evoking the nature and landscape of the steppe, modern dance features choreographic representations of Buryat myths and traditions. In the theaters of Buryatia and Cisbaikalia, I have watched balletic depictions of horse riders, hunters, birds and animals; dances that portray the three traditional Mongol sports of horse racing, wrestling, and archery; and seen those Buryat legends recorded by ethnographers set to music. The origin myth of the Khori clan is a perennial favorite, in which a swan maiden from Baikal is forced to marry a hunter after he steals her magical clothes. The graceful dance of the swan maidens, in distinctive headdresses and flowing white dresses, features in many repertoires.

The most famous practitioners of Buryat national dance are the Baikal ensemble, the professional state company of the Buryat republic. Baikal's performances draw large crowds, and the group regularly tours overseas. As the professional ensemble of Ust'-Orda Buryat Autonomous Okrug, Stepnye Napevy also employed dancers trained in the institutions of Ulan-Ude. The performance of modern national dance by amateur and youth ensembles has been greatly aided by a choreographic manual written by T. E. Gergesova in 1974 and republished in 2002 amid the renaissance of Buryat national culture.[2]

While modern national dance consists of spectacular displays and choreographed depictions of Buryat life, the work of folklore ensembles is centered on the preservation of pre-Soviet forms, such as the oral epic (*uliger*), the traditional praise song (*magtaal*), and the *yokhor*. However, in an interview with me in March 2006, Dandar Badluev, then recently appointed director of the Baikal ensemble, stressed his desire to infuse more folkloric elements into the repertoire of modern national culture. Badluev lamented that musical and vocal styles in Buryat national song and dance had become too influenced by European conventions. He saw one of the main challenges of the ensemble as rediscovering the old styles of singing from local folklore groups and bringing the traditional style into a broader public arena. He particularly emphasized a need to continue training dancers once they had come to the ensembles from the academies. He felt that while graduates were technically accomplished, they did not always have a feel for traditional culture.

Later that Spring I witnessed this desired shift in Baikal's self-styled *ethno-show* named "Spirit of the Ancestors" (*Bur. Ugaim Sülde*). The show combined mythological themes and elements of folkloric forms. Scenes included a dance battle between Bukha Noyon, the bull-lord ancestor of the Bulagat clan, and his rival, the blue bull lord; the story of the Khori swan maidens; and a stylized dance in which Buryat women sprinkled milk products for the spirits. The ancestral spirits depicted were summoned in

A modern variant of the Buryat *yokhor*, Ulan-Ude, June 2011.

the narrative of the show by a shaman in full costume beating his drum and leaping around the stage. The show culminated in a joyful celebration featuring a fast-paced swirling *yokhor*. Unlike the folkloric performances of the *yohkor* I had witnessed, this presentation was not sung by the performers but accompanied by a lively orchestral soundtrack.

Incorporating a pre-Soviet dance such as the *yokhor* into modern Buryat dance transforms it into a striking spectacle. Such a presentation represents a considerable change from the historical context in which the *yokhor* was danced as a participatory, rather than spectacular, form. Tracing the different contexts in which the *yokhor* has been danced and the way it has evolved illustrates the multifarious ways that performance genres mediate social relations.

THE BURYAT *YOKHOR*

In the 2000s the *yokhor* was a staple of every Buryat folklore ensemble. It seemed that no Buryat cultural event took place without a performance. Over several years of fieldwork in Cisbaikalia, I saw versions of the dance performed often: at the *Sur-kharban* traditional sports competitions, at *Sagaalgan* concerts marking the lunar New Year, and at the *Altargana* festival of Buryat culture. Folklore competitions invariably stipulate the inclusion of the *yokhor* in performances and the pan-Buryat *Altargana* festival included a competition devoted to the dance when I attended in 2006 in Ulan-Ude.

The *yokhor* is not danced by other Mongols, but variants of the form are found among other indigenous peoples in Siberia. A circle dance known as the *ohuakhai* is performed among the Turkic-speaking Sakha to the northeast, who are thought to have originated in Cisbaikalia.[3] Tungusic-speaking Evenki and Dolgan peoples also perform a variant of the *yokhor*.[4]

Historically danced by Western Buryats and referred to as *khatarkha* (trotting), the dance became an important emblem of Buryat national identity in the early Soviet period and is now performed in communities across the Baikal region. Roberte Hamayon has recorded the shift to using the term *yokhor* in the same period, as an onomatopoeic reference to breathing during the dance.[5] Like *khatarkha* the word appears often in the accompanying song texts and is repeated over and over during some variants.

When it is performed by folklore ensembles, the *yokhor* is accompanied only by the singing of the dancers. Participants form a circle with their hands joined. During the first, slow phase of the dance, the arms are bent at the elbow, the forearms are held at a right angle to the body, and the dancers' interlinked hands swing steadily left and right. Their hands move in time with the slow steps that dancers begin to take to the left as the whole circle starts to move. The dance always moves in the same sunwise direction, like shamanist ritual practices. The first steps consist of a short pace sideways with the left feet. The right feet are then drawn to meet them.

A folklore ensemble perform the *yokhor* at the Altargana festival in Ulan-Ude, June 2006.

The singing begins quietly at first, and the steps are slow and steady. Often an older member present will begin singing a couplet before all the dancers sing the same couplet back. At other times the leader will sing different verses while the rest of the dancers sing back a common refrain. The *yokhor* consists of a progression of different sections, each with its own set of lyrics and melody. The version performed by Bayan Tala, the folklore ensemble in Novonikolaevsk, consisted of fifteen such sections.

As the *yokhor* progresses, the singing and movements become steadily faster. The final sections are often quite frenzied. The simple leftward steps of the opening section are replaced by backward and forward movements into the circle while still moving in a sunwise direction. The singing becomes louder and dancers' hands, still clasped together, make a thrusting motion into the circle as the dance reaches its frenetic climax. The full rendition of the *yokhor* can take fifteen to twenty minutes, and performers are exhausted by the end.

The gestures, melodies, and lyrics vary from district to district and even between one village and the next. Verses usually refer to the places from which dancers have come, the geographical features of their homelands, the beautiful jewelry and costumes adorning the dancers, and the joy of dancing:

Yookhortoo yereebdi	We came to [dance] the *yokhor*.
Yokhorlokhoyoo oroldoobdi!	We will try to dance the *yokhor!*
Ekhe Zygaada yereebdi	We came to make merry.
Zygaalkhayaa oroldoobdi!	We will try to make merry![6]

The *yokhor* was only danced in Western Buryat communities until the twentieth century. It was introduced into Transbaikalia when the Soviet leadership adopted the dance as a centerpiece of Buryat national culture in the 1920s.[7] The dance epitomizes the homogenization of cultural practices across the Buryat national territories that was undertaken by the Soviet leadership.

Most of the *yokhor* texts performed today retain Sovietized lyrics that were developed under communism. These include praise of Lenin, the communist youth league (*Komsomol*), the communist party, and the USSR. As such, T. Skrynnikova and her colleagues have suggested that Lenin has taken the place of ancestors in the texts, the *Komsomol* the place of the clan:[8]

Übgen Lenin Ükheeshaa	Although our old Lenin is dead,
Soyuz molodyozh' zalguuzha	The youth of the union continue [his work].[9]

Aside from the symbolic significance of Soviet ancestors, it is important to note that today's *yokhor* texts refer to civic territorial divisions. Two lines from the Novonikolaevsk *yokhor* exemplify this:

Ene aimagta Ekhirit-Bulagadhaa bayar asaraab	To this region we bring joy from Ekhirit-Bulagat [Raion].
Ust'-Orda daidahaa bayar asaraab	From the rich Ust'-Orda territory we bring joy.

This content is significant when considering the context for dancing the *yokhor* in the Soviet and post-Soviet periods. As people were moved from clan communities to collective farms and Buryat folklore became institutionalized as an activity of state ensembles, it was divorced from its ceremonial context. Now accommodated within the state houses of culture, the *yokhor* represents and refers to civic communities. Moreover, the public occasions where the *yokhor* is commonly danced today are state-sponsored events. In folklore competitions, as in sporting competitions, the collectives represented are civic ones.

Within the frame of public culture, staging the *yokhor* has established the dance as a symbol of Buryat national identity and a medium for expressing civic belonging. However, most scholarship on the *yokhor* has focused on the pre-Soviet period, analyzing the symbolism of the dance in references to the pastoral shamanist milieu. Understanding the ritual origins of the *yokhor* can elucidate the dance's relationship to the Western Buryat ethos described in chapters 2 and 3, but it is also important to recognize the polysemic qualities of the *yokhor* for performers in the twenty-first century.

INTERPRETING THE *YOKHOR*

Russophone scholarship on the *yokhor* is largely taken up with piecing together the dance's origins or decoding its form. Buryat ethnographer Matvei Khangalov, working at the turn of the twentieth century, surmised that the circle dance was historically danced after large communal hunts and later at gatherings for cattle herding. At these times the initiation of shamans, weddings, and sporting events would take place, and Khangalov situates the *yokhor* as part of these events.[10] Writing during the mid-twentieth century S. P. Baldaev, another eminent Buryat scholar, drew on oral accounts from the pre-Soviet era to describe the role of the *yokhor* in wedding rites, where young people from the bride's *ulus* would dance through the night before feasting, making offerings to the ancestors of the natal clan, and sending the young woman away to her marital home. In Baldaev's analysis of the song texts, he remarks on the use of toponyms to evoke the journey from one *ulus* community to another.[11]

In more recent times, Buryat scholar D. S. Dugarov has cited records of the *yokhor* as part of shamans' initiation ceremonies in the first half of the eighteenth century and also posited that the dance formed part of clan *tailgan* ceremonies.[12] Skrynnikova et al. have described the prevalence of the *yokhor* at offering rites for water spirits and have drawn on Baldaev's work to discuss the role of the dance at weddings.[13] These scholars describe a form embedded within a pre-Soviet Buryat culture where kinship and social solidarity were underpinned by shamanist practice and belief.

Situating the *yokhor* in its historical milieu often features attempts to interpret the formal elements of the dance. Several scholars have pointed to the imitative nature of the dancer's movement. Use of the term *khatarkha*, or "trotting," to describe the dancing is said to reference the likeness of the *yokhor*'s rhythms to the motions of horse or deer.[14] I. A. Manzhigeev has therefore suggested that the dance is a sophisticated variant of games played by children that mimic hunting, echoing the graceful moves of hunters and the trotting of horse.[15] Roberte Hamayon similarly emphasized the ludic quality of the dance and imitation of animals but associated this more closely with sexual play and analogies to animals mating.[16] Dugarov's rather speculative account argues that the rhythms of the *yokhor* resonate with the use of the shaman's drum, surmising that the dance may have been used to aid the soul of a shaman in a trance in his journey to the sky, home of the deities.[17]

The circular form of the *yokhor* has attracted a wide array of interpretations. Khangalov posited the *yokhor* as imitative of hunting parties where chains of hunters encircled their prey.[18] Others have looked for deeper symbolism. Skrynnikova et al. suggest that on occasions the *yokhor* was danced around the ceremonial tethering post, the *serge*, as a phallic symbol. As such, they contend, the *yokhor* evoked an act of coitus with the circle representing a vagina, a metaphor enhanced by the climactic nature of the dance.[19] The dance, in these authors' view, is rooted in cults of fertility. The authors also highlight the womb-like qualities of the *yokhor*'s circle, connoting social and individual death and rebirth: in *tailgan* rites the social group is reborn; in rites of passage, such as a shaman's initiation rites or wedding rites, the *yokhor* marks the change in status of the protagonists as they are reborn into new lives. To these individual and social rebirths is added the rebirth of the cosmos and the circular form of the *yokhor* is linked to a cult of the sun.

Anglophone anthropologists have variously sought to place dance forms in wider cultural contexts of body movement and gesture. Some, such as Drid Williams, have examined dance movement as a "lexicon of gestures," likening dance to language as a sequence of signs.[20] This approach would elucidate the choreographed contemporary Buryat dances explained by my interlocutors above; it might also explain some of the mimetic and symbolic elements of the *yokhor* explored in the Russophone literature. However, to recognize dance as a performative medium requires understanding of the experiential elements of bodily movement and identification of the pragmatic inferences that might occur in a given enactment. All of these approaches to the *yokhor* require sensitivity to context and the spatial and bodily practices of Buryat ritual. In combination these perspectives can account for semantic, aesthetic, and pragmatic ways of making meaning.

REFERENCE, SYMBOLISM, AND FORM

In the language of semiotics, developed by Charles Peirce and used by many anthropologists, the analyses described above would be understood as detailing the *iconic* and *symbolic* elements of dance.[21] The former is used to describe those elements of signification that reference the world through likeness—such as physical imitation. In contemporary Buryat dance, as described by Bair and Natalya, this is evident in gestures referring to the steppe landscape or imitating hunting and horsemanship. The analyses of the *yokhor* cited here identify reference to animal movements through imitation and, in the circular form of the dance, references to the sun, the womb, or the vagina. The symbolic element of semiotic analysis lies in identifying conventional meanings to certain signs or actions. This mode of meaning is evident in identifying the representation of the sun as symbolic of shamanic cosmology or the circle as a likeness of a vagina, which in turn symbolizes collective rebirth.

These analyses provide insight into the historical context, but the symbolism and meaning of the dance for contemporary participants often lies beyond these direct semantic references found in the gestural or lyrical content. Taken as a whole, for example, the dance conventionally symbolizes national belonging. Yet to understand *how* the *yokhor* creates a powerful sense of belonging among participants and to understand contemporary resonances of the *yokhor*, exploring the relationship between form and experience is helpful.

In the historical context of Buryat weddings, Skrynnikova and her colleagues note that the dance's circular form emphasized the bride's transition from one clan to another, included and then excluded from the circle at her natal home. This leads the authors to categorize the dance as a "spatial code." Dancing the *yokhor* in a range of ritual contexts must have defined, through inclusion in the circle, who belonged to a given collective. The ways in which a closed, circular form can effectively include and exclude people, defining who are members of a given social group and who are not, is an important key to understanding the dance in the context of Buryat sociality and ritual practice that makes a clear distinction between one's own and others.

The way that the circular form of the *yokhor* includes and excludes is at least as important for understanding the form as whether dance references animal movements through imitation or symbolizes renewal and rebirth through reference to wombs, vaginas, and suns. Furthermore, attention to the experience of participation is key. This requires understanding the aesthetic and pragmatic ways that the dance becomes meaningful.

AESTHETICS AND EXPERIENCE

In previous chapters I have described the sense of *communitas* evinced though commensality and ritual participation. The *yokhor* provides a particularly intense experience of collective activity. Khangalov noted of the circle dance that "when it is danced a state of excitement is reached, much like a kind of ecstasy."[22] Natalya, the youth ensemble director in Ust'- Orda, made similar observations on the uplifting and transcendental sensation possible when dancing the *yokhor*: "If a person is in a bad way—a bad mood—and they are invited into the circle of the *yokhor*, the energy of every person concentrated in the circle cleans like soap—the identical movement, the common mood—this movement creates a higher mood."

Dancers I interviewed in both Irkutsk and Ust'-Orda described powerful feelings of collective joy when performing the *yokhor*. Two lines from the Novonikolaevsk *yokhor* emphasize this collective experience:

Kholshoroo negedeed zugaalaya!	We are unified in our happiness. Let's celebrate!
Zurkhoo negedeed zuugaalaya!	Let's unify our hearts and celebrate!

In my Buryat language class at the Irkutsk cultural center, we learned two regional versions of the *yokhor*. Most of the time our amateur efforts were clumsy and ill-timed, but on just one or two occasions when our singing and movement coincided, I can attest to a very powerful sensation from singing at full volume and moving in unison.

Dandar Badluev, of the Baikal ensemble, emphasized to me that traditional dances are "deeper than professional dance." He went on: "It has a complex internal feeling, a sensation like meditation. At first glance it looks simple to dance like that ... to move and sing—but the root is shamanic, you have to preserve the internal feeling."

The collective joy that is both described and experienced in dancing the *yokhor* cannot be accounted for by semantic analyses of the dance's gestures. Certain media—be they visual, material, or performative—create their effects through sensory, embodied, and emotive responses, as much as through the conscious deployment of referential symbols.

A number of thinkers have wrestled with ways to describe those visceral ways that ritual and performing arts create meaning for participants. Suzanne Langer famously distinguished between "discursive" and "presentational" modes of meaning making. In Langer's schema discursive symbols, such as language, form ordered chains of meanings, while presentational symbols resonate with emotional experience in a pre-reflective or visceral way.[23] While the first type aligns with the idea of dance as a lexicon of intentional gestures, the second is closer to a description of aesthetics in performance.

While the field of aesthetics was first developed by philosophers to describe the visceral, sensory effects of European art, anthropologists have looked to explore aesthetics as a cross-cultural category. This entails looking at the way that practices and sensibilities found in a particular cultural context might inform artistic and performance genres and the way that people respond to them. For Angela Hobart and Bruce Kapferer, who have explored aesthetics in relation to performance, attention to aesthetic process is attention to "compositional forms and forces in which life is shaped and comes to discover its direction and meaning."[24] This formulation has considerable purchase here.

Such a cross-cultural approach to aesthetics means that discussion of forms and practices cannot be restricted to a bounded domain of art, nor the qualities of their effects to terms like *beauty* or *the sublime*, which dominate European philosophical literature. A truly cross-cultural approach to aesthetics seeks contextually meaningful notions of value that find form in artistic and performative practices. In the case of the *yokhor*, this requires thinking about formal analogies with other aspects of Buryat practice and the relationship between cultural and social forms in Cisbaikalia.

In analyzing Kuranko dance in Sierra Leone, anthropologist Michael Jackson drew on the notion of the *habitus*—used to great effect by Pierre Bourdieu—to better understand how dancers drew on a repertoire of gestures rooted in everyday practice and transposed them to the domain of ritual dancing.[25] This notion of bodily movement and habit as being culturally specific was part of an anthropological tradition that dated back to Marcel Mauss, who coined the notion of the *habitus*, and has spawned a broad literature on embodiment in anthropology, including the work of Jackson.[26] Identifying the ways that habitual practice and the use of space reveal social sensibilities and dispositions is highly pertinent to the analogies of form found across different domains of Buryat practice.

The circular movement of the *yokhor* may be uniquely stylized and rhythmic, but the sunwise motion of the dance relates directly to the circling of the fire, the *obo* or *serge* during offering rites. The same circular motion is evident when smoking goods to be offered and when a vodka glass is passed around during everyday hospitality practices. Just as ritual participants line up to face the fire at offering rites so the dancers in the *yokhor* fall into line in the most literal example of an inward-facing form in the Buryat repertoire.

To analogy of form I would add analogy of experience. In this book I have argued that analysis of offering rites needs to consider elements of communion, or *communitas*, found in ritual practice, eating together, and collective labor. In the case of dance, those sensations of *communitas* come about through the powerful experience of moving and singing in unison. As such I think we might suggest *communitas*, or indeed social belonging, as an aesthetic quality experienced by dancers of the *yokhor* and informed by the sensibilities engendered in ritual practice and everyday sociality.

Influential anthropologist Marilyn Strathern identifies the aesthetic as the process by which valued social relations are objectified and visually apprehended in certain forms. In the Melanesian context described by Strathern, this key social form is the person, and aesthetically valued objects encapsulate the social relations involved in making a person.[27] This attribution of aesthetic qualities to social values and sensibilities is highly pertinent to a cross-cultural understanding of aesthetics. Yet beyond visual impact, the aesthetic should also be understood as noteworthy for the *way* value is apprehended—through powerful, emotive experience. Aesthetic processes make the social not just visible but also *felt*. Such feelings may be evoked by material objects, visual or aural phenomenon, but also by mediums of performance in which bodies move within space in particular ways. In the *yokhor* it is not the individual person that is seen as an embodiment of social relations but the collective made corporeal in the form of the *yokhor*.

As well as its symbolic or referential qualities, the form of the *yokhor* thus creates effects in its own right. In its historical context of weddings and clan rituals, the *yokhor* does not just *stand for* the social group but *is* the social group in action. If there is a powerful response to the *yokhor* that is engendered in the dance's form, then rather than beauty or the sublime, *belonging* itself could be considered such an aesthetic quality.

PERFORMANCE, PRAGMATICS, AND POLYSEMY

An important contribution of performance paradigms to the study of ritual and collective events has been the understanding that performances are temporally unique events. Each enactment of a dance, play, or oral poem can elicit a new significance to performers and audience members. Ritual theorists in particular have noted that practices that retain apparently unchanging forms and semantic structures send different signals at different moments in time according to their framing, scale, and perceived audiences.[28]

In this vein linguistic scholars invoke a difference between semantic references and pragmatic elements to communicative acts.[29] Where the former denotes the ways that particular signs and symbols convey meaning, the latter relates to meanings that are specific to the context in which an act takes place. Anthropologists have drawn on these theories of pragmatics and performance to analyze the historicized, contextual meanings that certain ritual enactments evoke.[30]

I do not propose to give a detailed pragmatic analysis of individual *yokhor* performances in the manner that linguistic anthropologists undertake piece-by-piece deconstructions of individual speech acts. However, some attention to the way that *yokhor* performances were framed publicly during my field research and the kinds of discourses that performers used to describe the dance tell of the changing and personalized meanings of the *yokhor* in twenty-first-century Cisbaikalia.

As the 2006 referendum in Cisbaikalia approached, performances of the *yokhor* took on new significance. As described in the previous chapter, the inclusion of the Irkutsk governor in a few verses of the dance in Ust'-Orda reinforced the message of a harmonious and reciprocal relationship between oblast and okrug, Buryats and Russians. The performances at *Sagaalgan* concerts in Irkutsk and Ust'-Orda and the Baikal Express tour were all prefaced with political speeches and visibly supported by the local state institutions. As documented in the previous chapter, this framing implicitly signaled support for a territorial merger from the local Buryat intelligentsia and made a display of state support for Buryat culture even after the dissolution of Buryat political autonomy.

Yet the polysemic nature of the form and the personal significance for performers gave rise to further considerations. In October 2006, I interviewed members of the Ayanga and Ulaalzai ensembles, affiliated with the Centre for Buryat Culture in Irkutsk. The former consisted mainly of performers in their sixties and seventies, the latter were the center's youth ensemble. While Ulaalzai performed contemporary Buryat dance and pop music, the two ensembles often joined together for folklore competitions. Dancing seemed, for members of both groups, to be important to a sense of self. But the process of dancing and its relationship to identity, was conceptualized in different ways between the two generations.

The members of the older generation whom I interviewed had grown up in the villages of Ust'-Orda Buryat Autonomous Okrug and danced the *yokhor* in their youth before moving to the city to study and work. However, when I asked one man, now seventy, where he had learned the *yokhor*, I got a shrugged answer. "We just danced when we gathered together—parties, celebrations, weddings." For the generation growing up in the okrug between 1937, when it was severed from the Buryat Republic, and the 1970s, when Buryat culture went through a revival in the territory, Buryat folklore had known little state support and was not learned through the institutions of ensembles. The *yokhor* was danced at this time but rarely in the context of public events. The man in question seemed particularly befuddled when I asked about the circumstances of his learning the *yokhor* as he had never really thought about formally learning it—it had just been something that he had picked up through doing it. Another lady, now in her seventies, also remembered dancing in her youth but never in formal ensembles. Moreover, older performers did not objectify the *yokhor* in quite the same way as the younger dancers. All used *yokhor* as a verb, conjugated with a Russian verbal ending. Hence the older generation talked not of *performing* or *presenting* the *yokhor* but simply of *yokhoring*. "My sobiralis, yokhorili"—"we gathered and we yokhored"—one older lady recounted. Ayanga members nonetheless saw the dance as important for a sense of self-identity. "In the Soviet times, the *yokhor* was forgotten," another septuagenarian told me. "For half a century, I didn't yokhor. I thought that I had forgotten everything but then we old folk got together, it turned out we hadn't forgotten anything!" When I asked her what the sensation of dancing the *yokhor* meant to her, she answered: "Pleasure—that I didn't forget, pleasure in remembering my youth, when everything was joyful." Older performers also saw the preservation of forms for younger generations as an important role. As one performer remarked to me: "Our language, our songs and dance are being forgotten. This is very offensive—therefore when I found out there was this ensemble, I joined with pleasure, to teach the young people, to pass on what I know."

A more politicized desire to assert their national identity seemed evident among the younger generation. One young performer told me, "We must show that we have songs, dance, a beautiful language." Another explained: "When we perform in Irkutsk, we must show that here on this land live the Buryat people, an amicable people, that we will continue to exist. We show our love for our homeland, our dance, culture, customs. I'm a Buryat. To me it's important I must know the language, know the dances. We are a unique people."

Baira Nikolaeva, the director and choreographer of Ulaalzai ensemble, made similar assertions for the presentation of Buryat forms in public life: "We are the native population, and our culture should be present at every public event. We must show our culture, even greet guests who will see that you're *our* guests.

Every person who lives on the land of Irkutsk Oblast should know that Buryats are the native population and know the national dance and songs."

It is particularly striking that Baira related idioms of hospitality to Buryat cultural performance in Cisbaikalia. In earlier chapters I described the hierarchy and ritual precedence of the host or *khoziain* in hospitality practices. In asserting that visitors to the okrug were *our* guests, Baira made an assertion not just of Buryat indigeneity but of a perceived status to the indigenous population in a putative hierarchy of belonging, a phenomenon I return to in chapter 8. Idioms of hospitality are a common feature of civic events in the Republic of Buryatia, where the image and practice of gifting the ceremonial scarf—the *khadag*—are ubiquitous.[31] However, it was novel to hear the positioning of Buryats as *hosts* in the city of Irkutsk, which had never been formally identified as Buryat territory.

While the younger generation seemed more attuned than their seniors to the outward projection of identity, dancers of all ages noted a qualitative difference between performing the *yokhor* and performing modern national dance. The comments of one young dancer from Ulaalzai captured nicely the simultaneously aesthetic experience of the dance and conscious presentation of identity when I asked him if the *yokhor* held a different sensation to dancing modern dance: "Of course! How to put it . . . I don't even know how to express it—when you sing you feel your national spirit. It's not simply a dance—other national dance is simply movement. You could say [the *yokhor*] is your spirit, your life. It's the spirit of your homeland that you are dancing."

For these younger dancers, the aesthetic of belonging that inheres in the *yokhor* is attributed to national belonging and not just to the immediate circle of dancers. Much as the *tailgan* is a kind of representative communion among designated clan members, contemporary *yokhor* performances could be understood as a representative *communitas*, a feeling of national belonging engendered among performers during the dance.

In my analysis of *tailgan* rites, I noted that undertaking significant practices can be understood as a form of placemaking, embedding belonging in key sites in the landscape, while staged national culture resides primarily in the houses of culture, theaters, and museums that make up state infrastructure in the national territories. It is also possible to understand performing Buryat culture in the civic arenas of Irkutsk as a kind of placemaking for Buryats. The city had no institutions of Buryat national culture prior to 1990 and was never designated as Buryat national territory. At the same time as making an outward show of complicity in the process of unification, dancing the *yokhor* played an important role for Buryats in demarcating civic places in Irkutsk as part of the Buryat homeland. Performing in the theaters, horse racing stadiums, and city squares embedded Buryat belonging in that urban milieu in a way that had never been possible in Soviet times. Moreover, it did so in a way that avoided the overt nationalist discourse that was repressed at the time. In such a context, this Buryatization of civic sites carried undertones of resistance, or at least defiant expression of belonging, in response to the dissolution of Buryat political autonomy. A member of the Ayanga ensemble, then in her sixties, recalled to me how as a student in Irkutsk in the 1960s, she and her friends had been dancing the *yokhor* in the park only to have it broken up by the police. The experience of dancing in Irkutsk today was particularly resonant for a generation for whom the city and countryside were, in the past, such different spaces: one a Soviet and largely Russian city, the other an autonomous homeland where the places and districts to which the *yokhor* texts refer are located.

A JANUS-LIKE FORM

The Buryat *yokhor* encapsulates multiple layers of meaning and multiple modes of *making* meaning. At an embodied, experiential level an aesthetic of social belonging is discernable, analogous across ritual and artistic forms, and present in collective, transcendent experiences. In the theatrical staging of the form at civic events, the dance provides a conventional symbol of national and civic belonging within the repertoire of official culture. In the wider public framing of the form, pragmatic, context-specific meanings are mobilized—for instance, support for territorial unification or commitment to Buryat culture during the 2006 referendum. As the narratives of dancers attest, there are also personal significances born of individual experience and historically constituted.

The Buryat *yokhor* could be said to have a Janus-like character—simultaneously inward and outward facing.[32] For performers, the dance provides an embodied experience of social belonging that resonates with the circular forms and collective experience of Buryat ritual. At the same time, the dance projects a symbol of nationality and civic belonging outward into the public sphere. This formal quality speaks to the multiple roles, relations to others, and relations to place through which Western Buryats move and which coexist at times in complementarity, at others in tension. These multiple meanings, and ways of meaning, are manifested in unique, intense moments as bodies move together on stage.

NOTES

1. Babueva, *Materialhaia i Dukhovnaia Kul'tura Buriat*, 182.
2. Gergesova, *Buriatskie Narodnye Tantsy*.
3. Crate, "Ohuokhai: Sakhas' Unique Integration of Social Meaning and Movement." This paper documents the parallel trajectory of the *ohuokhai* to the *yokhor* from ritual dance to emblem of Soviet nationality and later post-Soviet cultural revival.
4. Babueva, *Materialhaia i Dukhovnaia Kul'tura Buriat*, suggests the word is of Tungusic origin.
5. Hamayon, *Why We Play*.
6. Manzhigeev, *Buriatskii Ekhor*, 12.

7. Dugarov, *Istoricheskie Korni Belogo Shamanstva*, 85.
8. Skrynnikova et al., *Obriady v Traditsionnoi Kul'ture Buriat*, 169.
9. Dugarov, 100.
10. Khangalov, *Sobranie Sochinenii, Vol. 1*, 233.
11. Baldaev, *Buriatskie Svadebnye Obriady*.
12. Dugarov.
13. Skrynnikova et al., 174–79.
14. Manzhigeev, *Buriatskii Ekhor*, 6; Dugarov, *Istoricheskie Korni Belogo Shamanstva*, 95.
15. Manzhigeev, *Buriatskii Ekhor*, 21.
16. Hamayon, "Game and Games, Fortune and Dualism in Siberian Shamanism"; Hamayon *Why We Play*.
17. Dugarov, 95–98.
18. Khangalov, *Sobranie Sochinenii, Vol. 1*, 233–34.
19. Skrynnikova et al., 169.
20. Williams, *Anthropology and the Dance*, 216.
21. Peirce, "What Is a Sign?"
22. Khangalov, 233.
23. Langer, *Philosophy in a New Key*, 79–103; Langer, *Feeling and Form*.
24. Hobart and Kapferer, *Aesthetics in Performance*, 5.
25. Jackson, "Knowledge of the Body"; Bourdieu, *Outline of a Theory of Practice*.
26. Jackson, "Knowledge of the Body"; Csordas, "Embodiment as a Paradigm for Anthropology"; Mauss, "Techniques of the Body."
27. Strathern, *The Gender of the Gift*, 176–82; Leach, "Drum and Voice."
28. Bloch, *From Blessing to Violence*; Tambiah, "A Performative Approach to Ritual."
29. Silverstein, "Shifters, Linguistic Categories, and Cultural Description."
30. Tambiah, "A Performative Approach to Ritual"; Keane, *Signs of Recognition*.
31. Quijada, *Buddhists, Shamans, and Soviets*.
32. Humphrey, "Janus-Faced Signs," uses this metaphor in a discussion of political discourse in twentieth-century Buryatia.

SEVEN

INSTITUTIONALIZED SHAMANISM AND RITUAL CHANGE

THE POST-SOVIET DECADES HAVE SEEN shamanism regain a place in public life across Siberia and Inner Asia. Alongside local ritual practitioners, professional shamans' associations have enjoyed increasing visibility in the Republic of Buryatia, particularly in the capital city of Ulan-Ude, since the 1990s. By the mid-2000s the influence and presence of these associations could be observed in Cisbaikalia.

Caroline Humphrey characterizes North Asian shamanism as a dispersed and segmentary phenomenon. Shamanism is *dispersed* insofar as it is not a religion with a central authority, scripture, or homogeneous practice but includes a heterogeneous range of beliefs, practices, and ritual practitioners. In this account of shamanism, changes in social circumstances can lead to *segmentation*, where a new set of ritual practices and practitioners appear in order to meet the needs of a changing social milieu, taking their place alongside existing domains of practice.[1] This analysis could well describe contemporary Buryat shamanism: while longstanding household and kin-based rites provided a model for reciprocity and mutual support, public and professionalized shamanism has often been linked by theorists to a revival in national consciousness.[2]

During my field research, the increasing presence of Ulan-Ude shamans' associations in Cisbaikalia led to tensions with local shamans and to discourses and critiques that highlighted some fundamental differences in their modes of practice. However, local ritual practice was not without its own innovations and responses to social change.

MARKING SHAMANIST TOPOGRAPHY

In July 2006 I joined Diadia Vitia and around forty of his relatives for a *tailgan* in Khuty. The ceremony was held for two families, descendants of two brothers who had settled in the *ulus* around one hundred years earlier. The younger of these two brothers was the great grandfather of Diadia Vitia and Nikolai. As those brothers were only four generations removed from Diadia Vitia's generation, the two families constitute one lineage, defined as all relatives within eight generations of a common ancestor. No one knows the ancestry of these two families prior to their arrival in Khuty.

As well as following the conventions described in chapter 3, the *tailgan* served as the dedication of a ceremonial tethering post, or *serge*, at the lineage's clan hearth. The dedication of *serge* posts was a growing trend in Cisbaikalia at that time, with more and more posts appearing in the landscape every summer.

Among Eastern Buryats in Transbaikalia, a clan's designated offering place is usually known as an *obo* and marked by a stone cairn, a phenomenon found across the wider Mongolian region and known as an *ovoo* in other Mongol dialects. In many instances, *obo* ceremonies are syncretized with Buddhist practice. In Cisbaikalia, the *serge* is a more-prevalent means of marking ritual sites. Ritual tethering posts are common to several of the indigenous peoples of Siberia, particularly the Turkic-speaking communities in northeastern and southern Siberia.

A *serge* usually stands about five feet tall with a pointed top and two or three horizontal grooves cut into it. Some ethnographers have identified the *serge* as a phallic symbol, while others have likened it to a "tree of heaven" reaching from the earth to the sky.[3] The posts were traditionally erected by Western Buryats at the time of marriage to constitute the formation of a new household.[4] Anathema to Soviet values of civic identity over kinship, and markers of a belief system that was illegal under communism, *serge* posts were mostly cleared away in the antireligious drives of the midtwentieth century. Their reappearance in the post-Soviet decades serves as a visible reminder of a shamanist topography that remains significant for Buryats. On the Cisbaikal steppe today, *serge* posts generally stand apart from extant houses and mark the sites of former *ulus* settlements or family homes. As well as making ritual hearths, the posts have been erected to demarcate *bar'sa* sites in some instances.

Decorative versions of the *serge* became a national symbol for the Buryats in the early post-Soviet years, erected on district borders and in public spaces. As noted in chapter 4, a circle of *serge* posts was dedicated in 1995 at a site above Goose Lake in Buryatia as an offering place to the epic hero Geser Khan.[5] The boundary between Ust'-Orda okrug and Irkutsk Oblast was marked by a concrete representation. A little farther along the road that takes tourists to Baikal, a picnic place was created in 1996 with large decorative *serge* posts and a sign explaining to travelers the need to make offerings when crossing the okrug territory.

The Khuty dedication ceremony was mostly organized by city dwellers, and in the run up to the event, Vitia, not contactable by telephone, knew few details. The prime mover in the organization of the rite, it turned out, was a man named Andrei, one of the leading activists at the Buryat culture center in Irkutsk, though I was unaware of his connection with Khuty (and he of mine) until the ceremony. I returned to Khuty for the *tailgan* after a few days in Irkutsk in a minibus full of Diadia Vitia's relatives. On the way, I chatted with half a dozen students and young professionals in their twenties, most of whom had not been to the village since

INSTITUTIONALIZED SHAMANISM AND RITUAL CHANGE

Decorative *serge* (tethering posts) on the road into Ust'-Orda Buryat Autonomous Okrug from Irkutsk.

childhood. Two of them had never been at all. As we and other vehicles arrived, it felt very strange to see so many people and feel such a buzz of excitement in a place that I knew as tranquil and quiet, with its usual population of twelve people.

The rite took place at the site of the first house inhabited by the lineage, where the elder of the two brothers had built his home. The first task, as with so many sprinkling rites, was to find the place where the *serge* was to be erected. While Andrei's father found the correct spot, a work team headed off in a truck to cut down a selection of birch branches from the woods around Khuty. The women present gathered in the kitchen of Vitia's house while the men began preparing for the rite.

Activities were directed by Leonid Stepanov, a shaman from nearby Baiandai settlement. Under Stepanov's energetic lead, a team of men constructed a small, fenced enclosure where they placed blacksmith tools: an anvil, hammer, tongs, and bellows. Another group stripped a thick birch trunk of its bark, fashioned it into the tethering post, and set it into the ground. At the same time, kinsmen lit the ritual fire that was to burn throughout the rite. A shelter was set up to provide shade a short distance from the offering place, and the women came and joined the group soon after. Unlike the Khertoi *tailgan* described in chapter 3, women were present throughout the rite, though they remained largely in the shelter—set back from the pyres and *serge*—during the prayers, the sprinkling of vodka, and the slaughtering of the animals. In this case offerings comprised a ram, a ewe, and a billy goat.

As a commonly found symbol, Andrei found it easy to explain to me the significance of the *serge*. In the future, he explained, he would call his ancestral spirits to the post when he made offerings. The exact significance of the blacksmith's tools seemed less clear to participants when asked, and Andrei simply stated that the Ekhirit, and his clan, were blacksmiths. Ethnographic literature attests that blacksmiths (*Bur. darkhan*) were revered figures across northern Eurasia and blacksmith shamans are found in many shamanist communities in the Mongolian region. Blacksmith cults and the dedication of tools are described in historical ethnographies of the Buryats.[6] Diadia Vitia referred to the shaman Leonid Stepanov as someone well-read on shamanism. I wondered, given the apparent novelty of these aspects of the rite compared with regular *tailgan* ceremonies, how far the dedication of both the *serge* and blacksmith's tools might have been recreated from ethnographic material.

Before offerings began the men cleansed their feet in the smoke of the ritual fire and women smoked their hands. The men then fell into a line facing the *serge*, lining up in order of seniority. First in line were the descendants of the eldest brother, followed by descendants of the second. A number of relatives were present whose mothers had come from the lineage. These men were thus

INSTITUTIONALIZED SHAMANISM AND RITUAL CHANGE

Dedication of a *serge* (ceremonial tethering post), Khuty, July 2006.

classified as *zee* (affines) and attended as guests. They took their place at the end of the line before myself and two neighbors who also held guest status. Initial sprinkling of vodka and milk was undertaken by the eldest male of each family to prayers made by Stepanov. A glass of vodka was then passed along the male line for each person to drink.

After sprinkling, the whole party, including women, assembled in a circle around the *serge*. The shaman initially poured vodka over the tethering post while calling the lineage spirits. Each man present then took a glass of vodka and drank a little before pouring it over the post. After each male had done so, everybody present stood in a circle around the *serge*. The eldest lady from the lineage was directed to pour vodka onto the *serge* before each woman tied a ribbon to the post, starting with the youngest.

The slaughter of the three animals and cooking of the meat were carried out in the same way as the *tailgan* rituals described in chapter 3. Women stayed away during the slaughter but joined in with preparing and cleaning the meat once it had been carried out. After the construction of three offering pyres, the women retreated and the men fell back into line. As the pyres were set alight, the shaman sprinkled vodka on each one and all the men once again shared a glass of vodka passed along the line. All of the men, and then all of the women present, were separately called on to circle the *serge* three times in the direction of the sun, completing its dedication.

Finally, nine men of the two paternal lines entered the blacksmith's enclosure as the blacksmith's tools were dedicated. These items also form a permanent marker of the lineage's offering place. A second ritual fire was lit inside the enclosure. Each of the nine sprinkled onto the fire and the blacksmith's tools, and each was called on to make several blows to the anvil with the hammer. The nine were entirely made of up those related through the male line and only after the dedication of the tools were in-laws, neighbors, and guests invited into the enclosure to drink from the remaining vodka. Rather than distribute meat by household, the whole clan joined in a feast that evening in Vitia's yard.

The atmosphere throughout the ritual was joyful and festive. The sense of *communitas* felt when erecting the *serge*, butchering the animals, circling the *serge*, and sharing meat during the feast was palpable. The day remains one of my fondest memories of fieldwork for this reason. Children and teenagers who had never met before became acquainted and played with one another; adults who had not seen each other for years enjoyed catching up and drinking together. The feast continued through the night. I was told by many people with visible excitement that this was a "once in a generation" rite and that even Andrei's father, the oldest man present, could not remember such a ceremony being held before.

Whatever the historical or scholarly interpretations of the *serge* or the blacksmith's tools, they play a significant role as markers of the ancestral homeland today. For those who have left the countryside, physical markers of belonging, like the *serge*, are not only symptomatic of the religious freedoms of the post-Soviet era but also illustrate the need for a sense of belonging among kin groups that are increasingly atomized. For those living in an impersonal urban milieu, *serge* posts are a material anchor for kinship in the ancestral homeland. Dedication rites constitute placemaking in a very literal sense: *serge* posts provide a tribute to the tenacity of the kin groups that associate themselves with these places and serve as a reminder of the ancestral spirits that populate those landscapes. The posts make the Buryat shamanist topography concrete and visible on the Cisbaikal steppe.

Andrei stressed to me the need for somewhere his children and grandchildren would be able to come in order to understand that this was their *rodina* and tied this in very closely with his sense of national identity: "My grandchildren must be proud that they live around Baikal; if we don't do such things [as the dedication of the *serge*], they won't be able to say that their clan, and my ancestors, lived around Baikal."

Anthropologist Justine Quijada records that a lack of genealogical knowledge among the contemporary urban Buryats with whom she worked was often a source of anxiety.[7] Such anxiety seemed to be informing Andrei's desire to reestablish his lineage as a social group. Andrei was of the first generation to have grown up away from Khuty. Though he sprinkled there every year, the recent births of his grandchildren were something of a catalyst for wanting his family hearth marked. Referring to his broken genealogy and the expectation that he should know eight generations along the paternal line, he told me: "We only know three generations. We must know and will know more," he said, emphasizing his resolve to provide genealogical knowledge for future generations.

As practices that took place among a closed group, the clan *tailgan* and *serge* dedication were important in reconstituting kinship and belonging to a clan. That the *serge* is also an established national symbol added a further layer of social belonging reaffirmed in this process. As symbols of Buryat national identity and belonging, the appearance of *serge* posts on the landscape at a time when Buryat territorial autonomy was being dissolved added to their resonance.

Contemporaneous with this trend was a growing public presence for shamanism in Cisbaikalia. I was struck when, at the end of the *tailgan* in Khuty, Stepanov made an appeal to participants to make a donation to the Ust'-Orda okrug's association of shamans, *Sakhilgaan*. I knew about shamans' associations in the Republic of Buryatia and their public rituals, but until this point, I had not known of an okrug association. Stepanov, in his baseball cap and flannel shirt had clearly been directing the rite but did not resemble the professional shamans I had seen pictured in Buryatia with their brightly colored costumes and drums.

The influence of Ulan-Ude shamans on local practice and the presentation of ritual in the public realm in Cisbaikalia seemed to grow over the course of my fieldwork, however, but it was also contested and questioned by local shamanists.

INSTITUTIONALIZED SHAMANISM IN THE REPUBLIC OF BURYATIA

In the Republic of Buryatia, and particularly in the capital city of Ulan-Ude, the role of the professional shaman has been reinvigorated since the fall of communism. The contemporary form of shamanism that has emerged is often termed *neoshamanism* by scholars. Russian ethnographer Natalia Zhukovskaya has characterized the phenomenon as comprising the rise of shamans' associations; the ties of newly initiated shamans with the academy and scholarship on shamanism; and a public profile gained through engagement with the media. Zhukovskaya has contextualized neo-shamanism as part of the renaissance of Buryat national consciousness in the 1990s.[8]

At the time of my field research, two shamans' associations dominated the scene in Ulan-Ude: the Association of Buryat Shamans, then known as *Böö Mürgel*, and *Tengeri*, a self-styled *association of modern shamans*. Both associations reconstructed shamanic practice from a combination of scholarly knowledge of shamanist history, and the apprenticeship of leading members with Buryat shamans in Mongolia, where it was felt that shamanic practice was better preserved in the communist era. Both associations carry out rituals of initiation (*Bur. shanar*) to nine levels of seniority as recorded in historical ethnographies.[9]

Böö Mürgel was the older of the two organizations. Founded in 1993 as "the Thundering Drum," this association was active in the 1990s in reconsecrating important sacred places across the region and dedicating new ritual sites. The association was initially led by Nadia Stepanova, who became a well-known public figure and has lectured all over the world on shamanism. Both Stepanova and Boris Bazarov, the chair of the association at the time of my research, have published extensively on shamanist practice.[10]

Tengeri was founded in 2002. Its first chairman came from Aga Buryat Autonomous Okrug to the east of Buryatia. The association particularly advocated the use of trance techniques, and on a number of occasions, I saw shamans undertaking trance in both private consultations and public events. In each instance spirits took possession of shamans' bodies and ritual participants were able to address questions directly to those spirits. Tengeri held public spring and autumn *tailgan* ceremonies at the horse racing ground (known as the hippodrome) in Ulan-Ude, where they began and ended the ritual season. These rites were addressed to the ninety-nine *tengeri*—the forty-four spirits of the eastern sky and fifty-five spirits of the west—that form part of a pre-Soviet pantheon of deities described in ethnographic literature.[11] Tengeri also held a large public *tailgan* every summer on Ol'khon Island addressed to thirteen master spirits historically recorded as part of Western Buryat cosmology.[12]

The practices of both associations exemplified neoshamanism as it is commonly described. Though Zhukovskaya has been careful to stress this phenomena as a natural evolution of shamanic practice appropriate for contemporary Buryat society, I prefer to avoid neoshamanism as an analytic device as it has since come to connote illegitimacy or inauthenticity in some circles, as I describe below.[13] Finding an alternative term is not straightforward: to write of urban or rural shamanism would gloss over the rural ceremonies undertaken by the shamans' associations—particularly initiation rites that take place in shamans' ancestral homelands. Similarly, a label of *contemporary* or *modern* shamanism might suggest that practices in the villages of Cisbaikalia have never changed or evolved. Noting that shamans' associations that are registered public organizations, with largely homogenized practices, and some level of professionalization, I opt for the term *institutionalized shamanism*.[14] Crucially, this institutionalized shamanism resembles official Buryat national culture in ways that contrast local practice in Cisbaikalia.

INSTITUTIONALIZATION IN UST'-ORDA BURYAT AUTONOMOUS OKRUG

Compared with Buryatia, shamanist practice initially had a limited public profile in post-Soviet Cisbaikalia. However, in 1997 an association for the revival of shamanism named Sakhilgaan was founded in Ust'-Orda Buryat Autonomous Okrug after local practitioners attended a landmark conference held by academics and shamans from Buryatia in 1996.[15] Leonid Stepanov, who conducted the *serge* dedication ritual in Khuty, was chairman of the association in 2006. Sakhilgaan at that time comprised a fairly loose conglomeration of shamans, as the term was understood locally, and people interested in promoting the revival of shamanism and the preservation of ritual knowledge. It was not a professional organization and did not train or initiate members. Local shamans did not wear costumes or practice drumming, and their work up until 2007 largely comprised of reinvigorating large-scale *tailgan* ceremonies.

The organization began to organize large-scale *tailgan* ceremonies in the 1990s. These rituals followed the form of clan and family ceremonies and usually took place at important local sacred sites. The ceremonies included participants of different clans, and one member of the organization explained to me how prominent local shamans lined up behind those shamans most closely related to the sacred place in question, who took precedence. Offerings at Baitag would be led by local Ekhirit descended from Bura, those on the hill of Bulen by Bulagats, and so on.

From spring 2007 I noticed Sakhilgaan taking a more prominent role in public discourse in Irkutsk. In May of that year, it was announced that Sakhilgaan would organize a special offering rite for the protection of Irkutsk Airport. In July 2006, an Airbus passenger plane had crashed on landing at the airport killing 125 people, including fifty schoolchildren, on a trip to Baikal. The disaster was just the latest in a series of crashes at the airport. The association had decided that neglected offerings to the spirits of the region had been to blame. Leonid Stepanov stated in a newspaper interview that the shamans felt guilt at what had happened due to their neglect. He promised that offerings would be made regularly to prevent air catastrophes. He also asserted that offerings would be made on behalf of all the residents of the region, not just Buryats.[16]

As well as the airport ritual, the association announced that a *tailgan* dedicated to the master spirits of the Angara and Irkut Rivers would be held on behalf of all residents of Cisbaikalia. Significantly, these rivers meet in the city of Irkutsk, the administrative heart of the soon-to-be-unified territory. Initially I heard that the event, in which two horses and two rams were to be slaughtered, would be held in Irkutsk's Stadium of Labor in the heart of the city, though it was ultimately held at a site outside of the city, close to Lake Baikal.

In addition to these events, Sakhilgaan stipulated that if such a large-scale territorial ritual were to be undertaken, local *tailgan* ceremonies would need to be held first. Thus for the first time in several years, a big *tailgan* was organized by the association on Baitag.[17] At this *tailgan*, two horses and two rams were offered with attendant clans responsible for collecting financial contributions for the animals. I was told by friends in Novonikolaevsk that around three hundred people were present. That events were linked in this way is highly significant. Much as household sprinkling has to be carried out before a clan *tailgan*, those rites had to be held before the big *tailgan*. The Baikal rite was thus placed at the head of a layered hierarchy of ritual events.

Within the Buryat communities of Cisbaikalia, these rituals met with mixed responses. In Novonikolaevsk, where I spent much of summer 2007, the Baitag *tailgan* was widely attended, while only a small group of representatives went to the ritual near Baikal. Some people I spoke to were very supportive of the Baikal event, another suggested to me that "of course no one really wants to go—it's just theater." Even some whom I knew to be skeptical of the second event were, however, keen to attend the first. I am sure that this had much to do with the fact that Baitag, an established sacred place in the local shamanist topography, was the setting for this rite.

In 2008, Sakhilgaan did not repeat the rite on behalf of all the oblast but instead drew media attention toward another big *tailgan* in Ust'-Orda. The ceremony took place on the sacred hill of Bulen, to the north of Ust'-Orda settlement. I attended the rite, where two horses were slaughtered. Attendance was high: approximately four hundred people turned out. The ceremony was framed as a significant event in the life of the region through the

A pyre containing meat from a slaughtered horse burns at a Sakhilgaan *tailgan*, June 2008.

invitation of print and broadcast media who covered the *tailgan* in regional news.[18] I was struck by one piece of oratory: as Leonid Stepanov made his final prayers, he turned to the long, semicircular line of attendees and broke off from Buryat to declare in Russian (perhaps for the benefit of the media, perhaps to be clear to all attendees): "We have united because we have strength!" The large gathering was a striking show of social solidarity in the year that oblast and okrug had formally merged. In this respect, the rite took on similar qualities to the *yokhor* when the dance was framed on the stage. It remained an inward-facing form and served as a communion for the clans present, but it also projected a show of strength and a relationship with the land outward into the public domain.

The work of Sakhilgaan constituted a step toward the institutionalization of shamanism in Cisbaikalia. The organization of rituals on behalf of large territorial populations, publication activities, and the use of news media to publicize the association's work gave local shamanism in Cisbaikalia an increasingly public profile.

SHAMANS' ASSOCIATIONS IN WESTERN BURYAT SPACE

The two large shamans' associations from Buryatia had a growing presence of their own in Cisbaikalia at this time. In summer 2006, I was present at the first-level initiation ceremony of a shaman by Böö Mürgel. The ritual was held at the site of the former *ulus* of Khara-Nur, between Khuty and Muromtsovka. The novice was a local man who had been advised to become a shaman after suffering long-term illness. This was recognized as shaman sickness, often the first sign of shamanic calling, by one of Böö Mürgel's members who was related to him by marriage. This was the first initiation by the association locally and was carried out by Edward Makhutov, a senior shaman of Western Buryat origin who was well known in Buryatia. During the ceremony the shamans addressed prayers to the novice's ancestors, while his relatives slaughtered a ram and made offerings of milk and vodka. The visiting shamans wore colorful cloaks and hats and used drums and bells to summon the spirits.

The initiation was met with a mixed response locally. Relatives of the novice shaman were, of course, proud. Others were more bemused. One local man expressed surprise, stating that "it is not our tradition to initiate shamans—someone's either a shaman or they're not." Another recounted hearing that two Buddhist lamas had conducted the ceremony, telling me, "They were from Ulan-Ude—there they have Buddhism, here shamanism, right?" While this was a clear misconception of religion in Buryatia, it does betray an underlying feeling of difference between Eastern and Western Buryats.

While Böö Mürgel's initiation bemused some locals in the Novonikolaevsk area, the Tengeri association seemed to wield increasing influence within official institutions in Cisbaikalia. The chair of the organization made a high-profile visit to Ust'-Orda in January 2007 to meet with Sakhilgaan, and Tengeri began working closely with the *TsSRBE* in Irkutsk at that time. Particularly instrumental in facilitating this relationship was Andrei, who brokered a number of these meetings. The growing presence of Tengeri in Cisbaikalia reflected the evangelism for shamanic practice professed by the association. In my discussions with Tengeri shamans, it was clear that they saw part of their mission as educating the public about shamanic practice. In September 2007, I interviewed Viktor Tsydypov, one of the association's senior shamans. Viktor particularly stressed "the art of trance" as important to revive and his view that Tengeri were going beyond neoshamanism.

Like Böö Mürgel, Tengeri had begun initiating shamans from Cisbaikalia at this time, and Viktor told me that five shamans from Cisbaikalia were in training from the association. He was respectful of the differences in Cisbaikal shamanism, but he also suggested that an exchange of knowledge was necessary: "We show our practice, our school. We hold master classes on how to call the gods. Irkutsk shamans watch. They can't do it, but they have their own methodology. It's an exchange," he told me. One such exchange took place when members of Sakhilgaan and Tengeri met on an island on Lake Baikal in July 2007.

A *TAILGAN* ON OL'KHON ISLAND

In July 2007 I was invited by Andrei to join him at a *tailgan* ceremony led by Tengeri on Ol'khon Island, off the western shore of Lake Baikal. The *TsSRBE* had hoped to build a festival of shamanist culture around the event, including a conference and performances of the *yokhor* by the Irkutsk ensembles. A lack of funding and logistical problems had prevented the full event going ahead. However, Andrei did successfully broker a meeting between a group of the Sakhilgaan shamans from Ust'-Orda and members of the Tengeri association.

On the eve of the *tailgan*, I joined a meeting between the Ust'-Orda delegation and representatives of Tengeri in a yurt on the lakeshore. The delegation was greeted by Viktor Tsydypov, before Budazhab Shireterov, another Tengeri shaman, then vice-chair of the association, demonstrated his trance technique to them. Trance was a well-known feature of the Tengeri association's work but had not been used in Western Buryat practice for a long time.

On this occasion the local shamans were asked to write down their names and clans on pieces of paper along with questions that they might wish to ask the spirits. Shireterov, already wearing a traditional Buryat *degel*, donned an elaborate headdress, his face covered by a veil. After drumming himself into a trance, he jumped up as he was possessed by a spirit. As the possessed shaman walked up and down with a stooped, sauntering gait, the spirit was identified as an old woman before the shaman settled down and helped onto a cushion by his assistant. Members of the delegation were asked to approach on their knees one at a time with their questions and warned not to make eye contact with the spirit. The spirit answered their questions in a low, rasping tone, sung in a repeating melody. Eventually the shaman jumped up again, convulsing as the spirit left his body. He was once again sat down by his shaman assistant and fed tea as he came out of the trance. Afterward the shaman told us that he could not remember what had taken place.

Addressing the group after the rite, Viktor emphasized the need to revive lost elements shamanic practice in Cisbaikalia, quoting Khangalov's ethnographic descriptions of Western Buryat shamanism in the late nineteenth century. He was particularly keen to persuade the Sakhilgaan shamans of the power of trance as a means of communicating with spirits.

On the following day, I joined friends from Irkutsk in purchasing sweets and vodka for offering before finding a good spot to place their deck chairs and watch the proceedings. The ritual site was across the bay from Ol'khon's famous Shaman Rock, the most sacred place on the island. The site consisted of

Tengeri's vice-chair introduces a *tailgan* ceremony to attendees, Ol'khon Island, July 2007.

a cordoned-off area where thirteen birch branches stood decorated with ribbons, one for each of the thirteen master spirits to be summoned. The shamans' drums and headdresses hung on a large rack, and tables were set up facing the rock, packed with tea and vodka for offerings. Burning incense billowed clouds of scented smoke. Local television news, newspapers, and photographers were in attendance along with tourists, local people, and those who had come to the island especially for the ceremony. Food stalls served hot *buuzy* (meat dumplings), drinks, and snacks throughout the day.

At the beginning of the ceremony, Shireterov—in his role as deputy chairman of Tengeri—explained the ritual to those who had gathered and introduced the shamans who would be taking part, all of whom were standing alongside in their costumes. In the manner of a civic event, speeches of welcome were made by Andrei on behalf of the *TsSRBE*, a representative of the Ust'-Orda

A Tengeri shaman in costume.

shamans spoke, and a response was made by Shireterov. Schedules were handed out that outlined the sequence of the rite to come. The delegation of Ust'-Orda shamans were invited inside the ritual area to observe and assist. Dressed in their day-to-day clothes, they were easily distinguishable from the Tengeri shamans in their bright costumes.

The ritual began with the shamans drumming and offering vodka to summon up their own ancestral spirits and protectors. The sound of these drums beating in unison accompanied by the low chanting of the shamans created a powerful sound. While this took place, a single ram was slaughtered, and the meat was placed on a platform in the middle of the birch branches as an offering to the spirits that would be summoned during the rite.

During the trance section of the *tailgan*, each of thirteen master spirits from the Western Buryat pantheon was called to possess each of thirteen shamans in turn. The shamans drummed themselves into a trance while running around the birch branches, usually with one or two fellow shamans in tow to communicate with the spirit in possession of the shaman's body. Once each spirit had made itself known, attendees were allowed to cross into the ritual space and approach them with questions. Some questions related to health, some people asked advice on important decisions, others asked about the future. People wanted to find out when members of their family would be married, for example, or if they would have grandchildren. All of the spirits answered questions in the same low, rasping tones as the old woman's spirit I had witnessed in the yurt the night before. All followed the same repeating melody before eventually leaving the shamans' bodies in a series of convulsions.

The master spirit of the island, Hoton Babai, took particular effort to summon and provided a climax to the session. All of the shamans gathered around Bayar Tsyrendorzhevich, the chairman of Tengeri, singing in unison for the spirit to come forward as the shaman drummed himself into a trance. As his body was possessed, he leaped up. The spirit shouted into the gathered crowd in a booming voice, shook his head—clanking the metal bells attached to his headdress—and demanded to know who had called him to the ritual site and why. The spirit was placated by the other shamans before being settled down to answer questions for attendees as before.

Following the lengthy period of trance sessions, attendees returned to their places around the ritual site and placed vodka and sweets on the ground to be blessed. The spirits then departed to the accompaniment of the Tengeri shamans' drums. We were instructed to take these sweets home to share, as with *tailgan* meat at local rites. As the farewell was drummed to the departing spirits, the birch branches were paraded around the ritual site, some carried by the Ust'-Orda shamans, before being burned. Finally attendees were invited to come forward, strip to the waist, and be beaten with the last few remaining branches that had been dipped in hot water. This was explained as a way of ensuring future physical health for attendees.

I was struck by the involvement of Andrei in the Tengeri association's ritual on Baikal. He facilitated the meeting with local shamans, rushed around encouraging people to put questions to the spirits, and evangelized about both the practice and public role of the Tengeri shamans. On a personal level, he talked in an interview with me about the help of Tengeri shamans in finding out about his own genealogy: "I know who my grandfather was, my grandmother, who my great-grandfather was, but I want to know five or six generations and when I know I will be spiritually rich. A shaman can tell me where, who, what kind [of people] up to twenty-five or twenty-six generations back, the story of our lineage."

For Andrei, engagement with the practice of Tengeri was, like the dedication of the *serge* at Khuty, a means of reestablishing his lineage identity. Andrei agreed with Tengeri shamans that too much shamanist knowledge had been lost in Cisbaikalia. He not only stressed his own faith but the need for the promotion of shamanism because of a perceived encroachment by Buddhism in Cisbaikalia as competition for the hearts and minds of local Buryats. Andrei stressed to me that he felt it important to preserve shamanism as the genuinely indigenous faith of the Buryats. For someone used to publicizing Buryat national culture, collaboration with the evangelizing Tengeri shamans was a logical means to achieving just that.

SHAMANSHIP, PERFORMATIVITY, AND AUTHORITY

Jane Atkinson's landmark study of Wana ritual in Indonesia describes performance as a central part of shamanship. She posits that the efficacy of the shaman relies on a convincing demonstration of skill.[19] In their analysis of Daur Mongol rituals of the early twentieth century, Humphrey and Onon draw on the work of Atkinson to emphasize the difference between the attention demanded by clan offering rites and the séances of specialist shamans that they refer to as performances. The former, they suggest, were less intense occasions and attention could wander at times, the latter required great focus on the actions of the shaman, suspending disbelief and following the journey narrated or acted out in a state of trance.[20]

These reflections on performance and authority align with my own observations in Cisbaikalia: while both kin *tailgan* rites and the Tengeri Ol'khon ceremony had moments of relaxation and moments in which attention was demanded of participants, I think a distinction can be made between the collective action of the clan *tailgan* and rites in which specialist shamans entered trances and summoned up spirits by drumming. The practices of Tengeri are recognizable as the performative shamanship described by Atkinson and Humphrey. The shamans' drumming and singing and their entering and leaving trance, all demand attention and set the shamans apart from lay attendees. Their actions seemed a far cry from the half-whispered offerings made by Diadia Vitia or Dmitri at their hearths or the prayers led by senior clan members at Baitag and Khertoi.

In taking ritual and performance as modes of action, I suggested in previous chapters that local rites were ritualized but not greatly performative, whereas rites theatricalized by folklore ensembles were entirely performative but professed no ritual intent. The Tengeri rite was simultaneously ritualized *and* performative. The shamans' ritual purpose lay in offering to the spirits of the region for the well-being of all residents and the facilitation of direct communication with spirits by participants. Yet the costumes, drums, and stylized gesture framed the rite as a spectacle to assembled participants. The conspicuous display of skill, a performance of shamanic knowledge and authority, marked out professional Buryat shamans as cultural specialists.

The spatial organization of the Tengeri *tailgan* resembled a theatrically staged event. For periods of the rite, attendees were roped off from the shamans in the manner of an audience, watching the demonstration of ritual knowledge and shamanic technique before them. The framing conventions of public cultural events were also evident in the speeches made at the start, highly reminiscent of the *Sagaalgan* concerts or *Sur-kharban* festivals where local dignitaries made their addresses to attendees.[21] The presence of broadcast and print media took this process of framing beyond the immediate dynamics of the event by representing the rite to a broader public. These Soviet and civic presentational frames, along with the *TsSRBE*'s attempts to place ritual activities within a festival of shamanist culture, brought ritual into the public domain and into line with the conventions of Buryat national culture.

In chapter 4, I recounted how the Soviet state of the 1920s and 1930s created alternative cultural specialists to those that existed before the revolution. While state agents dismissed, denounced, and even executed shamans and Buddhist monks, the state publicly honored those artists and scholars who excelled themselves within the parameters of official Buryat culture. Research on the early years of shamanist revival in Siberia has documented the link between emergent high-profile shamans and institutions of the arts and academia.[22] Scholarly knowledge of ethnography and shamanic history proudly demonstrated by contemporary shamans taps into notions of authority rooted in Soviet and civic ideals. This is evident not only in Viktor's quoting of Khangalov and Leonid Stepanov's reputation for being well-read but in the publication work undertaken by shamans such as Boris Bazarov and Nadia Stepanova. The presentational conventions of Buryat national culture, particularly performance frames, also asserted shamans' claims to cultural specialism and authority.

AUTHENTICITY AND RELATEDNESS

The practices of the two Ulan-Ude associations met with mixed responses in Cisbaikalia. One Western Buryat whom I knew to be very involved in civic cultural activities felt there to be a qualitative difference between the shamanism of the big organizations and local practice: "The real *tailgan* rites are here [Ust'-Orda]," he told me. "There [Buryatia] they eat sweets. Women are there. It's not real shamanism." On the other hand, a Khertoi friend told me enthusiastically of a Böö Mürgel ritual on Ol'khon Island that he had attended: "You should have come—the shaman there used a drum! Come next year, and you can film it!" The two forms of practice are not mutually exclusive domains, then, for all local people.

I did gather a strong sense from some local shamans that they felt the presence of the large shamans' associations to be an incursion into their space. Aleksei, whom I introduced at the beginning of this book, was highly critical of shamans who undertook offering rites beyond their own clans and communities, a practice that he felt counter to traditional practice. Aleksei is extremely well-versed in local traditions and history. He has been involved in projects mapping sacred places; he has attended conferences on shamanism with Native Americans and Amerindians; and he is not averse to advocating shamanist tradition in public media. He was, however, reluctant to resurrect lost practices and felt that contemporary shamans should not try to equate their knowledge or spiritual powers with those of the great shamans of that past. Aleksei disliked what he referred to pejoratively as neoshamanism. "They come here with their drums," he complained. "It's just theatricalization," making explicit an equivalence between performing arts and public rituals. In the same vein, another local shamanist described the practices of the associations as "theatre" and a "big show."

The professional nature of the associations was also somewhat frowned on. One Buryat academic expressed to me that she saw cynicism in the motives of the associations, suggesting that "it's not tradition; they *use* tradition to earn money." Without naming any specific organizations or individuals, Aleksei put this in stronger terms still when I interviewed him:

> The biggest threat is commercialization. Our country has many problems of the social type—unemployment... that kind of thing. With such complications people seek some kind of way out. And they turn to gods. They have their needs, and they are, unfortunately, ready to pay money to some supposed shamans—charlatans. People don't know and out of ignorance go to someone who says, "I can do this." And this charlatan might demand five thousand, ten thousand, twenty five thousand, half a million [rubles]. They understand psychology, and they play with peoples' complications. It's a big danger to contemporary shamanic practice.

Aleksei impressed on me that while it was traditional to pay a shaman for their work—a token payment known in Buryat as *mense*—this should not be demanded by the shamans. Aleksei insisted that individuals should pay according to what they could afford and that shamans should not profit from their work. Yet Aleksei had faith in local people to discern authentic practice as he saw it: "They know who is genuine and who is playing," he assured me.

The presence of institutionalized shamanism in Cisbaikalia has, however, occasionally had the reverse effect and caused the authenticity of local practice to be questioned. Some local scholars of Buryat culture whom I knew asserted that the local ritual practitioners were really *elders* rather than shamans. Others repeated the narrative of the large shamans' associations that shamanic practice had been lost and needed to be recovered. Diadia Vitia, who was highly respected as a shaman by Khuty kin, was usually reticent to talk about shamanist cosmology and practice. When I finally did get him talking about the subject he asserted—"I'm just a dilettante. If you really want to know about shamanism, go and speak to Stepanov. He has lots of books." The systematized spread of institutionalized knowledge about ritual practice, often rooted in ethnographic texts, seemed to sow some self-doubt for Vitia about his own.

The more dominant tone I heard was one of skepticism, however, and local cultural politics also informed this view. The increasing prominence of Tengeri in Cisbaikalia is in no small part due to the evangelism of Andrei and the *TsSRBE* for their style of rite. With his own profound belief in shamanism, Andrei clearly saw public ritual as a way of asserting the place of shamanism as the indigenous faith of the region. Others were less enthusiastic, and concerns over commercialization and authenticity were exacerbated by a feeling of impotence at the shift in leadership of cultural activities from Ust'-Orda to Irkutsk. Indeed, there was even a concern that local shamanist practice would be eclipsed or supplanted. One activist friend invoked those possessive adjectives noted in my earlier observations on belonging: "We are worried that in the future there will be shamans here—but that they won't be *ours*."

My friend's distinction between Eastern Buryat shamans as *others* and locals as *ours* is reflected in a cosmological distinction between the kinds of spirits to whom rituals were addressed. Public rites of the Ulan-Ude associations were largely dedicated to deities from a pantheon recorded in pre-Soviet literature. Tengeri's rite to Hoton Babai and the thirteen master spirits of the region exemplify this practice. Such deities are useful in building a national constituency of belonging and situating shamanism as a national religion for the Buryats. However, I rarely knew of these deities being cited in local ritual practice. In Ekhirit-Bulagat Raion, I have only known ancestors and spirits closely tied with the local shamanist topography to be named in ritual offerings. So while canonical deities may be faithfully revered, there is a perceived kinship with local spirits—whether adopted *ulus* master spirits or direct ancestors—that differentiates local rites from public ritual.

In chapters 2 and 3, I suggested that named spirits participate in ongoing cycles of reciprocity and that relatedness is established through commensality. If the deities named in public rites appeared less established in local consciousness, it was perhaps because there were no such established cycles of reciprocity and communion. At the Tengeri *tailgan*, sweets were brought to the rite, blessed, and then taken away. More significantly, the *tailgan* meat was not shared among participants. This marks a fundamental difference between both the symbolism of public and kin rites and the experience of attendance. Moreover, while being an audience member at a performance event can be understood as a form of participation, the division of space between shamans and attendees at public rituals led to a very different experience from the kind of *communitas* experienced in collective labor and offering.

SEGMENTATION, FRAMING, AND CULTURAL POLITICS

The dispersed and segmentary nature of Buryat shamanism meant that an array of practitioners and practices could be found across the Baikal region in the mid-2000s. Following Humphrey's argument that different forms of shamanist practice meet different societal needs, it is possible to see two processes at work here. On the one hand, local shamans mediated a particular Western Buryat notion of social belonging and maintained relationships with spirits in the landscape in the face of rapid out-migration from the countryside. On the other, the institutionalized shamanism developed in Ulan-Ude provided an intersection with official national culture and public assertions of Buryat identity. It would be wrong, however, to present local practice as entirely representative of continuity and professional shamanism of novelty. As this chapter has shown, local practice also evolved and changed to meet the demands of the time. While writing of segmentation might imply a clear delineation between the role of each set of practitioners, there was a clear influence from institutionalized shamanism on aspects of local practice and tensions between forms of shamanism operating in the same space. *Tailgan* ceremonies, whether led by Tengeri or Sakhilgaan, held a common function as rituals of offering to powerful spirits. However, the framing strategies described here differed substantially—one type of ritual was inherently performative, public, and outward facing, the other used public media to frame ostensibly inward-facing ritual forms, giving them a Janus-like character comparable to the *yokhor* performances discussed in chapter 6.

In a period where Buryat territorial autonomy was dissolved, the work of local shamans was crucial in demarcating shamanist topography in Cisbaikalia and asserting links to powerful local spirits. The Sakhilgaan *tailgan* rites simultaneously constituted and asserted in public media the sense of belonging that local Buryats held to the landscapes of Cisbaikalia. It is striking that such assertions of belonging became public at exactly the time that Buryat territorial autonomy had been abandoned.

The work of Ulan-Ude shamans' associations, promoted by newly powerful Irkutsk institutions, brought shamanist practice into the domain of national culture. The work bolstered those institutions' efforts to maintain a public presence for Buryat culture across the newly unified territory of Irkutsk Oblast. Planning a festival of shamanist culture, the presence of shamans at public concerts, and the public rituals of Tengeri all formed part of this shift.

Either form of public framing would have been unthinkable in Soviet times. In the Putin era, this framing of ritual practice made an assertion of belonging to land in a way that avoided explicit political discourse but nonetheless articulated in public the notion of Cisbaikalia as Buryat cultural space. However, the differences in approach reflected the different cosmologies that each ritual form appealed to. Where Tengeri appealed to powerful deities and evangelized for Buryat shamanism, Sakhilgaan's work, addressed to local spirits of place, appealed more directly to the Buryat ethos of reciprocity and mutual obligation over time.

In relating shamanism to national renaissance in the wider Siberian context, ethnographers have noted the tendency toward homogenization and expansion among professional movements, sometimes in conflict with local practitioners. A similar tension between institutionalized religion and local shamanist practice has been observed among Telengits in the Altai, for example.[23] The appeal of institutionalized shamanism for this end was evident in the work of Irkutsk cultural organizations that sought to link shamanist practice to a wider Buryat culture in Cisbaikalia, an agenda aligned with Tengeri's mission to promote revived shamanic practice in places where they felt it had been forgotten. Concern at these developments was audible in the discourse of local shamans who saw the presence of Ulan-Ude organizations as an incursion into their own space by people who were not *theirs* and who they described as "neoshamans" practicing "theater." The discourses between the different shamans' associations reflect the cultural politics of the time, a milieu where Irkutsk organizations sought to keep Buryat national culture in the public eye but where local Buryats in Ust'-Orda sought to maintain their own autonomy and way of doing things. In a context where shamans were increasingly positioned as cultural specialists and leaders, and in which the relationship between culture and land was being reconfigured, these were important debates and claims about where authority should lie.

NOTES

1. C. Humphrey and U. Onon, "Shamans and Elders," 320.
2. Zhukovskaya, "Neo-Shamanism in the Context of the Contemporary Ethno-Cultural Situation in the Republic of Buryatia"; Zhukovskaya, "Religion and Ethnicity in Eastern Russia, Republic of Buryatia: A Panorama of the 1990s"; Hamayon, "Shamanism, Buddhism and Epic Heroism."

3. Skrynnikova et al., *Obriady v Traditsionnoi Kul'ture Buriat*; Zhambalova, *Profannyi i Sakral'nyi Miry Ol'khonskikh Buriat (XIX–XX Vv.)*.

4. Zhambalova, *Profannyi i Sakral'nyi Miry Ol'khonskikh Buriat*, 262–74.

5. E. A. Stroganova, *Buriatskoe Natsional'no-Kul'turnoe Vozrozhdenie*, 99–112.

6. T. M. Mikhailov, *Buriatskii Shamanizm*.

7. Quijada, "What If We Don't Know Our Clan? The City Tailgan as New Ritual Form in Buriatiia."

8. Zhukovskaya, "Neo-Shamanism in the Context of the Contemporary Ethno-Cultural Situation in the Republic of Buryatia."

9. Mikhailov, *Buriatskii Shamanizm*, 101.

10. Zhukovskaya, "Neo-Shamanism in the Context of the Contemporary Ethno-Cultural Situation in the Republic of Buryatia"; Hurelbaatar, "The Creation and Revitalization of Ethnic Sacred Sites in Ulan-Ude"; Humphrey, "Shamans in the City."

11. Mikhailov, *Buriatskii Shamanizm*, 13.

12. For more in-depth work on the Tengeri organization see Quijada, "What If We Don't Know Our Clan? The City Tailgan as New Ritual Form in Buriatiia" and her book *Buddhists, Shamans, and Soviets: Rituals of History in Post-Soviet Buryatia*.

13. Zhukovskaia, "Buriatskii Shamanizm Segodnia: Vozrozhdenie Ili Evolutsiia?."

14. For a comparable use of "institutionalization," see Quijada, Graber, and Stephen, "Finding 'Their Own.'"

15. Mikhakhanova-Baliueva, *Ekhered-Bulgadai Baabai*.

16. Kork, "Shamany Provedut Obriad Zashchity Aeroporta."

17. Ibid.

18. Kork, "Rodovoi Obriad Vozle Sviashchennoi Gory."

19. Atkinson, *The Art and Politics of Wana Shamanship*.

20. Humphrey and Onon, 227–37.

21. For comparable observations on a Tengeri event, see Quijada and Stephen, "Performing 'Culture': Diverse Audiences at the International Shaman's Conference and Tailgan on Ol'khon Island."

22. Balzer, "Two Urban Shamans: Unmasking Leadership in Fin-de-Soviet Siberia"; Zhukovskaya, "Neo-Shamanism in the Context of the Contemporary Ethno-Cultural Situation in the Republic of Buryatia."

23. Halemba, *The Telengits of Southern Siberia: Landscape, Religion and Knowledge in Motion*.

EIGHT

MANKHAI REVISITED
Placemaking and Precedence after Territorial Autonomy

I BEGAN THIS BOOK BY recounting a trip to the sacred hill of Mankhai in late 2005 with Aleksei, a shaman whose voice has surfaced at different points and who became an important guide in my understanding of shamanism. As my research in the area progressed, I came to understand that when Aleksei had spoken emotionally of Mankhai as his homeland, he had been alluding to the mountain as his *malaia rodina*.

Aleksei's *ulus*, the Kharazargai, conduct their *tailgan* rites on a hillock known as Ukir, which faces Mankhai from across the Kuda River. I had the privilege of attending one of these rites at Aleksei's invitation during a return visit in the summer of 2008. When I joined the Kharazargai *tailgan*, I traveled with Aleksei's kinsmen from the present-day village—the former *ulus* winter site—along the clan's pastoral migration route. We stopped to make offerings at a *bar'sa* in the woods before reaching Ukir, which once formed part of the clan's summer pastures. The birch altars and offering pyres all faced Mankhai, to whose spirit the rite was addressed.

Mankhai is a revered, sacred site for many of the Ashabagat and Bulagat *ulus* communities that live in the Kuda Valley. The American ethnographer Jeremiah Curtin described a *tailgan* ceremony on the site in 1900, and his photographs and descriptions record fifteen stone cairns on the hillock, which have long been cleared away. Curtin records that Ashabagat clans addressed their offerings to the master spirit of Mankhai, whom he names as Malan Noyon.[1]

Aleksei and I got to know each other well over the course of my research from 2005–7. I often called in at his home in Ust'-Orda settlement *en route* from Irkutsk to the countryside, and Aleksei seemed to be impressed that I had spent time living in villages in the north of the raion. There was a sense of symmetry to my research when he asked me to return to Mankhai during my last weeks in the area in October 2007.

That September, Aleksei and Nikolai came to visit me in Irkutsk. Over the summer it had been discovered that illegal quarrying for stone had been taking place on Mankhai, and almost all the remaining petroglyphs had been destroyed by the excavations. Aleksei blamed the country's nouveau riche, who were demanding attractive stone mantelpieces for their newly built homes. As Mankhai still fell within the territory of Ust'-Orda Buryat Autonomous Okrug at the time, Aleksei and Nikolai had gained funding from the okrug administration to mount an expedition in order to assess the damage and make proposals for the preservation of the site. Despite having reservations about archaeology on sacred sites, they were keen that my archaeologist colleagues at the University in Irkutsk should be involved. With my contacts in the academy, it was time for me to fulfill my reciprocal obligations in return for the support that I had been given.

Aleksei and Nikolai's aim for the expedition was to propose that Mankhai be made an area of conservation and that an education center be set up to inform people about both the archaeological and spiritual significance of the site. They also wanted to argue for the repatriation of archaeological objects taken from the mountain in the twentieth century.

PETROGLYPHS AND PREDECESSORS

The petroglyphs on Mankhai have long made it a site of archaeological interest. Over the course of the twentieth century, several excavations took place on the mountain. The Russian archaeologist Khoroshikh led expeditions to Mankhai in the 1920s, 1930s, and 1940s. He was followed in the 1950s by the famous scholar Okladnikov, who excavated grave sites on the hilltop.[2] Many of the petroglyphs on Mankhai were removed by Khoroshikh during his excavations. Twenty-three are kept in the Ust'-Orda Regional Museum and a further six are held in store at the Irkutsk Museum of Art. Human remains taken from graves at the site are held at Novosibirsk University hundreds of miles away to the west.

Dating the petroglyphs has been a speculative business. This has been achieved chiefly through excavating nearby grave sites and comparing both graves and petroglyphs to others in the region. Okladnikov identified graves and petroglyphs as belonging to the Kurumchinsk culture, thought to be Turkic speakers of the eighth or ninth centuries CE. Khoroshikh speculated that a few of the images might have been created later, from the twelfth to fourteenth centuries, by Mongolic speakers who later became known as Buryats. More recent theories divide the petroglyphs into two stylistic groups, identifying one group with each period.[3]

Though archaeologists today do not excavate identifiably Buryat graves, only those identified with earlier archaeological cultures, digs are a source of vexation for some local shamanists who believe that the spirits of the deceased will be disturbed. As Nikolai emphasized to me, "It's not important whether they're our ancestors our not. They're alive!" To underscore his point, Nikolai invoked the famous example of the *Altai princess* in southwestern Siberia. The anger of this noblewoman at the excavation of her ancient burial site and removal of items, such as her jewelry, was cited by people in Altai as the cause of environmental and economic disasters that subsequently blighted their province.

There is a clear obligation in Western Buryat practice to honor the spirits of predecessors on the Cisbaikal steppe. As recounted in chapter 2, the *mongol* spirits addressed in household rites were once understood as the spirits of those who lived on the land before the present inhabitants. This explains Nikolai's comments about spirits being alive, whoever they are, and Aleksei's reverence for the petroglyphs at Mankhai, whoever created them. The ambiguous identities of masters of place, often beyond genealogical memory but revered nonetheless, does not preclude duties of reciprocity into which local Buryats are ritually bound. If the master spirit of Mankhai was bound to protect Aleksei and his clan, then in the spirit of reciprocity cemented in offering rites, Aleksei was also obliged to protect their dwelling place.

AN EXPEDITION AND ANOTHER RITE

The expedition was convened with some urgency in order to take quick measures to save the remaining petroglyphs. My friends were also cognizant of wider pressures. First, the prospect of an oil pipeline joining Angarsk to pipelines north of Baikal were being investigated by oil companies at the time. The Kuda Valley was earmarked as a possible route. Like excavations and illegal quarrying, prospective pipelines were a source of trepidation locally as something that might disturb the sprits in the landscape, with negative consequences for local communities. Measures to recognize and conserve sacred places might serve to mitigate this threat. Second, this urgency was compounded by the political situation in the region at the time. Ust'-Orda Buryat Autonomous Okrug was due to merge with Irkutsk Oblast the following January. The organizers of the expedition sought a resolution to protect Mankhai by the okrug *duma* before it was dissolved. This way, a case could consequently be made to the oblast *duma* in Irkutsk to honor the resolution after the merger.

My archaeologist colleagues agreed to join the expedition. Although excavations in sacred places is a cause for concern for Aleksei, I had found most contemporary archaeologists, some of whom are Buryats themselves, to be respectful of local customs and beliefs. When I had accompanied archaeologist colleagues on trips in the region, I found them to be extremely methodical about making offerings at local sacred places and before starting work. Despite any reservations that Aleksei may have had, he recognized both the value of prominent scholars arguing for the protection of Mankhai, and that the current generation of archaeologists, with their greater sensitivity to local beliefs, might be engaged over issues of repatriation. At our initial meeting in Irkutsk, my archaeologist colleagues agreed to both arguments.

The expedition was sponsored by two deputies of the okrug *duma* who made office space available to the organizers and gained funding to support it. When the expedition convened on September 12, 2007, the core team consisted of two scholars of the National Institute of the Humanities at Buryat State University in Ulan-Ude; Aleksei and Nikolai; the two members of the *duma* who had facilitated the expedition; myself; the director of the Ust'-Orda Centre for Cultural Heritage; and two of my archaeologist colleagues from Irkutsk State Technical University who joined us later.

After a meeting at the expedition's offices on the morning of September 12, we went to the okrug administration building. In the *duma* chamber, we met with the okrug's deputy chief administrator and several members of the *duma* to outline the goals of the project. Our task was to assess the damage to Mankhai, to raise awareness of sacred sites among local schoolchildren, and to make recommendations for the preservation of the mountain. Following this meeting, a delegation that included representatives of the okrug administration made its way to the top of Mankhai, along with a local photographer and journalist who filmed the proceedings. On top of the hill, Aleksei led an offering rite much like the

Surveying damage to Mankhai, October 2007.

one we had carried out two years earlier. He lit a fire, cleansed the ritual site with smoke, and led prayers to the spirits of Mankhai for success in the expedition and in preserving the site. The representatives of the state *duma*, local officials, and scholars all joined in the rite and in the form of commensality by now familiar to me, drank, and sprinkled vodka and milk on the fire.

We proceeded to the site of the petroglyphs, where I was shocked to see the extent of the damage. Were it not for the familiar view of the Kuda Valley, I would barely have recognized the place. The large flat-faced rocks once emblazoned with the pictures of horses were all but gone, leaving gaping craters of loose stone. The damage had been carried out by industrial diggers. The shapes of just two horses were now discernible among the loose rock.

That evening the team developed a position statement proposing that Mankhai become a "specially protected natural-cultural territory for the development of tourism." By emphasizing the place of Mankhai on the tourist route from Irkutsk to Baikal, the expedition members hoped to gain funding for the education center on the site. The purpose of the park was emphasized as "the preservation of historical-cultural heritage of the indigenous population of Irkutsk Oblast and Ust'-Orda Buryat Okrug." The statement further emphasized that the institution of a park would be "the best method of protecting the natural and cultural complex and biological diversity," stressing a ban on building and digging on the territory and limiting use of resources in the park to "organic" and "traditional" methods. The position statement also emphasized an onus on the state to provide funding for the park via the Ekhirit-Bulagat Raion administration.[4]

When the expedition reconvened at the okrug administration, the deputy chief administrator and members of the *duma* were present, along with a representative of the Irkutsk Oblast tourist board, the chief of the Gakhan rural administration where Mankhai is located, and members of the regional press and media. The film of the offering rite and the damage to the rocks was shown, and members of the expedition took turns speaking. Aleksei explained the significance of Mankhai as a sacred place for his clan; my archaeologist colleagues discussed the uniqueness and importance of the petroglyphs; and the professors from Ulan-Ude emphasized that damage to Mankhai signified too little emphasis on Buryat national traditions and culture within okrug schools. I felt that I had little expertise to offer, but I was asked to talk about my impressions at seeing the damage to Mankhai compared with two years before and to talk a little about British models for preserving cultural heritage. I soon realized that in this context my role was to illustrate that if a European anthropologist was interested enough to be there, preserving Mankhai must be important. Finally, the representative of the oblast tourist board was consulted about how a visitor center might be promoted as part of the tourist route from Irkutsk to Baikal. The meeting ended with the okrug's deputy chief administrator agreeing to fit a resolution on Mankhai into the legislative schedule before the dissolution of the okrug *duma* in December that year.

Throughout this book I have contrasted a local notion of belonging, focused on significant places such as clan hearths and sacred hills, with a state-sponsored conception of land as civic and national territory. In anthropological literature, state agencies are frequently described treating land as uniform *space*, apportioned into administrative territories and managed as though from above, through the process of mapping.[5] As this book has shown, the Soviet state typified this approach, obviating shamanist placemaking in favor of sanctioned cultural activities identified with the titular populations of national territories. In the post-Soviet era, however, the okrug as a national territory at least gave Buryats a space within which shamanist topographies and local ritual practices could be reestablished. Damage to Mankhai in 2007 was felt acutely in a context where the broader national territory in which local practice could thrive was soon to be dissolved.

Mankhai was, for Aleksei and his colleagues, primarily a sacred place and a part of the shamanist topography of the Kuda Valley. Its meaning was constituted through ritual practice and a relationship with the spirits there. The expedition demonstrated once again how ritual practice might be framed to assert a local sense of belonging in the public domain. With the end of national territorial autonomy, Aleksei and his colleagues had to find alternative placemaking strategies to conceptualize and protect Mankhai. In the expedition's report, Mankhai was presented simultaneously as a sacred place to the indigenous people of the region, an archaeological monument, a tourist destination, and a site for nature conservation.

MOBILIZING INDIGENEITY

Central to the expedition's report and recommendations was the appeal to protect "the indigenous population's historical cultural heritage."[6] Discourses of indigeneity have been an increasing feature of identity politics in Siberia in the post-Soviet decades.[7] Working in indigenous Siberian communities throughout the 1990s and 2000s, David Anderson observed the change of gear in Siberian discourses of autonomy from the late Soviet period. Then, in local discourse, "aboriginality" connoted backwardness, so there were "no aboriginal peoples in Russia (only Siberian nationalities)."[8] In recent years, however, activists have increasingly used the term *korennoi* ("indigenous" or "native") to negotiate rights and express solidarity among ethnic groups.

Kathryn Graber has noted a reluctance of some Buryats in the republic to identify as a native or indigenous people. The groups officially recognized as such in Russia have historically been those categorized under Soviet policy as "small-numbered peoples of the North, Siberia and the Far East,"[9] while notable Buryat activists in Ulan-Ude have seen Buryatia as a nation, with their own republic, on par with the other large nations of the Soviet Union and Russian Federation. Some also emphasize their connection with the wider Mongol world over other Siberian peoples.[10] I saw no such hesitancy from Nikolai, who has long explored international connections with other indigenous peoples, or from his colleagues. It is notable that in the context of Cisbaikalia, where a titular territory was soon to be dissolved, the trope of indigeneity became an important one in making claims of authority over land use.

Some anthropologists have critiqued the concept of indigeneity as essentialist, eschewing use of the term. As the principle has been adapted from contexts of European settler colonialism to situations of displacement and migration in Africa and Asia, its purchase has been tested.[11] In a controversial article, Adam Kuper famously argued that processes of migration have been so complex for so long that few peoples can claim to be truly indigenous.[12] Such a charge could be laid at the door of Buryats seeking to protect petroglyphs made by earlier peoples.

However, other scholars have instead stressed that indigeneity is always relational—a historically situated claim to distinguish between different actors and their rights and relationships to land, usually at moments of disenfranchisement or oppression.[13] In acknowledging this, it is imperative for anthropologists to explore why and how such claims come to be articulated and how the notion of indigeneity relates to local conceptions of territory, land, and belonging. Here the ritual element of the Mankhai expedition provides a point of departure.

In the early chapters of this book, I noted that spirits of place are honored despite being beyond genealogical memory and that some—including the *mongol* spirits—have been explicitly identified as predecessors to Buryats on the land. In chapter 2, I also documented the ways in which hospitality paradigms informed ritual offerings, recognizing the precedence of the *khoziain*. *Precedence* can be said to have two connotations—both in terms of hierarchical position in a given place and temporal priority on the land. In this respect, my interlocutors' claims to indigeneity should be understood less as a claim to absolute autochthony and more as claiming a particular place in a hierarchy of precedence.

There is no doubt that the colonization and settlement of Siberia by Slavic peoples aligns with the pattern of European imperialism found across the globe, led first by mercantile interests and then supported by military presence, state institutions, Christian proselytization, and exploitation of natural resources. The experience of Buryats mirrors that of indigenous peoples in settler states everywhere.

Seen through local shamanist cosmology, the crucial point of differentiation between Buryats and later settlers is not just one of temporal priority, however, but lies in the rupture in relations of reciprocity with spirits of the landscape and predecessors on the land. Rather than a case of simple ethnic differentiation, the underlying tension lay between those who live in reciprocity with the land and those who seek to exploit its resources. Quarrying for stone on Mankhai did not just represent a relationship of exploitation but it also damaged the material base of Buryat ritual practice—a sacred place where spirits dwell.

SPACES FOR CONSERVATION

The proposals to constitute Mankhai as a national park tapped into an established tradition in Russia, where nature conservation and traditional indigenous land use have often been related. The Baikal region has a long history of creating state reserves (*zapovedniki*) dating back to 1916. The first was at Barguzin in Transbaikalia. The park was founded to preserve stocks of fur-bearing animals and so limited hunting to indigenous methods.[14] Increased nature and heritage conservation has, moreover, gained momentum in the region in recent decades. When the Tunka Valley, a district of Buryatia to the south of Irkutsk, became a national park in 1991, Katherine Metzo documented that a "Buryat environmental ethic" was mobilized and asserted to gain the designation. In this effort, particular emphasis was paid to Buryat senses of reciprocity with the environment.[15] In the same vein, Brian Donahoe has recounted that in a campaign to designate the Oka district of Buryatia a "place of traditional inhabitancy and economic activities of indigenous small-numbered peoples of Russia," environmental preservation provided the leverage to gain state recognition of indigeneity for the Soiot people.[16] Closer to Ust'-Orda, Anya Bernstein has noted the mobilization of ecological discourses by the shaman Valentin Khagdaev in developing cultural tourism in Ol'khon Raion, a location nominally protected within the Pribaikal National Park. The Shaman Rock on Ol'khon Island has also seen the loss of petroglyphs.[17]

In the wake of the USSR's collapse, conservationist movements have gained momentum across Russia. As the environmental degradation caused by intensive industrial development has come to light, activists have forged links with international environmental movements. In 1996, Lake Baikal was designated a world heritage site by UNESCO. Traditional resource use by local indigenous people is often lauded by conservation movements and the Tahoe-Baikal Institute has included projects on Ol'khon Island to clean up sacred sites.

The conservation agenda outlined in the expedition report speaks to a wider concern voiced by exhibition members: the consultations over the routing of proposed pipelines taking place at the time. Aleksei and some of the archaeologists present had recently been working with gas and oil companies to try to avoid the proposed pipeline routes disturbing important historical and sacred sites. A year earlier a major pipeline project by Transneft, a state-owned oil company, had been rerouted under Putin's instructions after large-scale protests against its proximity to Baikal. Conservationist discourses therefore held useful currency at that moment. This was particularly salient given that the immanent unification of oblast and okrug was set to wrest any decision-making from local-level administration.

I noted above that state agencies tend to rationalize land as space, apportioning territories for economic use or as national homelands. In a context where national territories no longer provided a symbolic space where Buryat sacred sites could be protected, a proposed national park could provide an alternative form of territory that would be meaningful to policymakers.

RITUAL, RECIPROCITY, AND PRECEDENCE

Perhaps most striking about the Mankhai expedition is the way that broader political discourses of indigeneity and conservation were combined with ritual practice. Crucially, the ritual practice was not just framed in newspaper coverage and presentation to the okrug *duma* but included state representatives in offerings of shared milk and vodka, drawing those representatives into a relationship of reciprocity with the spirits of Mankhai.

In documenting ritualized hospitality in chapter 2, I suggested that offering rites make the guest-host relationship ambiguous. While the master spirits of local places are referred to as *khoziain*, rites are also referred to as *hosting* the ancestors. There I suggested that this emphasizes the relationship as one of reciprocity and mutual dependence rather than subordination and domination. I think a similar dynamic could be observed during the expedition. Expedition members could, on one level, be seen as supplicants to the state, ultimately relying on state protection for Mankhai and acknowledging the state as arbiter. The offering rite in which *duma* members participated, however, recognized the master spirit of Mankhai as a form of sovereign. Moreover, the rite gave Aleksei, with his expert knowledge, an opportunity to demonstrate custodianship over the mountain. That an expedition member could be present in his authority as shaman, rather than as a scholar or administrator, displayed recognition by the state that this was a legitimate capacity in which to act. If the creators of the petroglyphs and the master spirit of Mankhai were pre-Buryat inhabitants of the mountain, Aleksei's offerings and his explanation of the mountain's spiritual significance during the presentation made clear a relationship of reciprocity between these predecessors and the local Buryat population.

Idioms of hospitality were often used to describe interethnic relations by Aleksei, who quoted to me a well-known proverb on several occasions: "Don't enter someone else's monastery with your own rules."[18] The saying underlines the need for a guest to respect the rules and customs of their host, and it was a trope Aleksei repeated in the presentation and in later publications. In Aleksei's arguments, the obligations of hospitality were invoked to remind more recent migrants to Cisbaikalia to respect Western Buryat customs, implying their status as *guests* on the land. The incorporation of ritual placemaking in a state-funded expedition aligned with the efforts documented in the previous chapter to position shamanist ritual as a legitimate and, in this case, protected practice in Cisbaikalia. Spirits were to be recognized as true masters of the land. The expedition, like the Sakhilgaan ceremonies described in the previous chapter, positioned Buryat shamans as mediators with those spirits on behalf of the local population.

PLACEMAKING AFTER TERRITORIAL AUTONOMY

The expedition to Mankhai highlighted key themes that had emerged during my research—in particular the different ways that state regimes and shamanist practice conceive of and relate to land. The dissolution of Ust'-Orda Buryat Autonomous Okrug and the Russian government's move away from national territorial autonomy made the preservation of Mankhai less certain than it might have been previously. In the revived paradigm of National Cultural Autonomy, the state is arbiter of "economic policy and material life," while the national community takes care of "intellectual and cultural life." Yet this division between material life and culture is anathema to the worldviews of many indigenous peoples in which material places are central to cultural practice.[19] With the decoupling of culture from territory, Western Buryats had to find alternative discourses and practices through which to publicly assert attachment to place.

State policies have, at various times, threatened and negated Buryat relations to place and undermined the material basis of shamanist topography. This is exemplified in moving Buryats from their *ulus* communities, clearing away *obo* cairns and *serge* posts, allowing archaeological excavation, and undertaking resource extraction. However, some state practices have also offered regimes for the protection for local practice, either in the constitution of national homelands or in the creation of nature reserves.

In this book I have shown that Western Buryats navigate between shamanist topography, inscribed through ritual, and the infrastructure and territorial divisions of the state as they traverse the Cisbaikal landscape. My interlocutors also moved between the obligations and hierarchies of clan groups on the one hand and their civic and professional roles on the other. Likewise, Western Buryats experienced belonging to kin groups and civic and national communities through very different mediums of ritual and performance.

Much like the development of public rituals examined in the last chapter, the expedition to Mankhai demonstrates the creative ways that Buryat activists syncretized these different roles and different means of placemaking. Drawing on global discourses of indigeneity and conservationist paradigms provided a means of defining protected space in a context where national territorial autonomy no longer provided a safe space for shamanist practice.

NOTES

1. Curtin, *A Journey in Southern Siberia*.
2. Nikolaev and Melnikova, *Petroglify Kudinskoi Doliny*.
3. Ibid.
4. "Polozhenie: Ob Osobo Okhraniaemoi Prirodno-Kul'turnoi Territorii Dlia Razvitiia Turizma." Expedition report presented to the Ust-Orda duma.
5. Bourdieu, *Outline of a Theory of Practice*; Gow, "Land, People and Paper in Western Amazonia"; Scott, *Seeing Like a State*.
6. "Polozhenie: Ob Osobo Okhraniaemoi Prirodno-Kul'turnoi Territorii Dlia Razvitiia Turizma," 2.
7. Anderson, "Nationality and 'Aboriginal Rights' in Post-Soviet Siberia"; Donahoe, "On the Creation of Indigenous Subjects in the Russian Federation"; Gray, *The Predicament of Chukotka's Indigenous Movement*; Vitebsky, "The Northern Minorities."
8. Anderson, "Nationality and 'Aboriginal Rights' in Post-Soviet Siberia," 248–49.
9. Donahoe et al., "Size and Place."
10. Graber, "Mixed Messages," 30–36.
11. Shah, "The Dark Side of Indigeneity?"
12. Kuper, "The Return of the Native."

13. E. G. Merlan, "Indigeneity"; De la Cadena and Starn, *Indigenous Experience Today*, 1–30.

14. Metzo, *It Didn't Used to Be This Way*, 69–70.

15. Ibid.

16. Donahoe, "On the Creation of Indigenous Subjects in the Russian Federation."

17. Bernstein, "Remapping Sacred Landscapes: Shamanic Tourism and Cultural Production on the Olkhon Island."

18. "V chuzhoi monastyr' so svoim ustavom ne khodiat.'"

19. Patton, "National Autonomy and Indigenous Sovereignty."

CONCLUSIONS, RETURNS, AND REFLECTIONS

IN TRYING TO MAKE SENSE of Western Buryat ritual and performance in the first decade of the twenty-first century, this book has drawn on some of the classic theorists of these genres. One of the key contributions that scholars such as Victor Turner made to the wider field of anthropology was the insight that social identities, collectives, and worldviews are not given but have to be continually reconstituted and that ritual presents a vital means of achieving this. This book has focused on Buryat offering rites, particularly the clan *tailgan* ceremony, as mediums through which relationships between kin, ancestral spirits, and places are constituted. In doing so I have drawn on an anthropological tradition that recognizes the powerful experience of belonging that comes about through participation in these rites.[1] Yet in contextualizing these rites within post-Soviet Russia, I have looked to do more than restate the traditional social function of ritual within Buryat communities. Rather, I have looked to see why such forms held considerable salience in the 2000s.

The post-Soviet decades were a disorienting era for Western Buryats, as they were for minorities across the former USSR. While minority national cultures experienced a renaissance in the early 1990s, the collectives that once organized labor and provided employment had disappeared by the end of that decade. Rural communities in Cisbaikalia continued to dwindle in size, and increasing numbers of Buryats found themselves living in large cities. In that context the institution of the clan—be it a close lineage, *ulus*, or broader group—provided a stable social form in which meaningful and immediate relations of reciprocity stretched from village to city. Ritual practice provided a point of orientation that underpinned these institutions and reaffirmed a relationship with spirits of the landscape that had been suppressed in Soviet times. As this book has shown, these rituals and relationships with spirits rooted a sense of belonging firmly in the ancestral homelands of Western Buryats, even at a moment when fewer Buryats inhabited those landscapes themselves.

In showing the contemporary significance of offering rites, I have presented these practices as a counterpoint to the institutionalized and state-sanctioned forms of Buryat culture that emerged during the Soviet Union. While the former turns on communion and shared experience, reflected in the inward-facing spatial organization of these rites, the outward-facing nature of performing arts, staged in civic spaces and presented to a wider public, were developed as part of a culture that deliberately sought to downgrade kin relations and occlude religious elements of Buryat culture. However, in the Buryat circle dance—the *yokhor*—reframed as a part of this official culture, I discern a distinctive *aesthetic of belonging*, which resonates with the form of Western Buryat ritual practice. In the tradition of Bourdieu and those theorists of performance who have drawn on his work, I also find that both the *yokhor* and the *tailgan* provide analogues with habitualized, day-to-day offering practices.[2] These embodied ritual motifs engender an ethos of reciprocity in everyday life and inform the symbolism, spatial form, and experience of those larger-scale events.

The power of ritual is thus something of a paradox: much of its authority lies in its stable and constant form through time, yet, as performance and ritual theorists have shown, the framing of ritual in changing political circumstances provides pragmatic meanings and inferences specific to those contexts.[3] The dissolution of Ust'-Orda Buryat Autonomous Okrug and the move away from national territorial autonomy by the Putin government of the mid-2000s created a context in which Buryat culture was made highly visible for a time. While the presentation of performing arts made a public show of support for merging Ust-Orda Buryat Autonomous Okrug with Irkutsk Oblast, performers made their own interpretations of dances, such as the *yokhor*, stressing the value of displaying indigenous culture in places where it had hitherto lacked visibility and drawing on the aesthetics of belonging to inform the meanings that they attached to the dance. At the same time, shamanist rituals were mobilized according to the conventions of Buryat national culture. The increasing publicization of rituals by the local shamans association in Ust'-Orda, Sakhilgaan, represented a concerted effort to bring relations of reciprocity with the spirits and a connectedness with the Cisbaikal landscape into public discourse. These Janus-like events, facing both inward and outward, asserted a relationship to the land in spite of a model of extraterritorial National Cultural Autonomy, which split culture from place, departing from Soviet models of national autonomy and running contrary to indigenous understandings of relationships to the land. These local rites have been openly contrasted by some Buryats with the more performative practices of other shamans' associations, which appear less like a communion with local spirits and closer to the outward-facing theatrical practices of public culture. These debates over authenticity recall the dilemmas and tensions navigated by indigenous peoples around the globe who seek recognition for their own worldviews and practices while adopting, often through necessity, the presentational conventions and institutions of post-imperial states in order to do so.

RETURN TO SIBERIA

In 2011 and 2012, I returned to Siberia for postdoctoral research and had the opportunity to reconnect with my friends and acquaintances in Cisbaikalia. Ust'-Orda Buryat Okrug, with *autonomous* now removed from its title, remained as a nominal entity within Irkutsk Oblast. A deputy governor of the oblast was based at the okrug administration. However, I learned from friends that several jobs within the administration had either been moved to Irkutsk or lost. There were no signs of the better infrastructure, improved roads, or completed sports center promised during the campaign to unify oblast and okrug. The condition of Mankhai was still a concern for Aleksei and his colleagues, with no sign yet of national park status being granted. Stepnye Napevy remained in residence within the settlement but were taking on an increasing number of engagements in Irkutsk itself, often organized by the Buryat cultural institutions there, which held the funding for such events.

Buryat culture in Irkutsk continued to grow in visibility. The former Center for Buryat Culture continued as Erkhüü Buryat Cultural Autonomy, while the Center for the Development of the Buryat Ethnos was renamed as the Center for the Indigenous Peoples of Pribaikal'e in 2011. Indigenous Evenki activists from the north of Irkutsk Oblast were keen to gain visibility for their own culture and had been successful in securing the support of the oblast government through the institutions set up in the wake of the referendum. The increased center staff had relocated from their offices in the center of Irkutsk to a new building close to the railway station with larger office space and an adjoining café selling traditional *buuzi*. The space was abuzz with activity, as ever, with ensemble members, artists, and activists coming in and out to meet colleagues, organize events, and contribute to an ever-growing calendar of activities. I found as warm a welcome as ever from the team and called in on many occasions when passing through.

In June 2011 I traveled with a delegation including key members of the center, Evenki activists, and guests from the Republic of Sakha (Yakutia) in northeastern Siberia to the Ërde games. The event took place at the foot of the sacred hill of Ërde in Ol'khon Raion, on the western shore of Baikal. The games had been revived in the post-Soviet decades as a reconstruction of the historical gatherings of Buryat clans for traditional games and ritual events. The Irkutsk center was central to the organization of the event. That year, the event had been branded as an *international ethnocultural festival*. The festival featured all the traditional games of the *Sur-kharban*; folklore competitions with delegations from across the Baikal region; a beauty contest; and rows of stalls selling Buryat traditional food. The Irkutsk center had taken on much of the organization. The games were accompanied by a conference on indigenous culture held at a nearby tourist base, where I presented alongside colleagues from Sakhilgaan on local shamanism. Tengeri, a renamed *Böö-Mürgel* (now *Böö-Darkhan*) and Sakhilgaan all led offering rites, as did invited shamans from the Sakha Republic in northeastern Siberia. Local shaman Valentin Khagdaev drummed at the top of Ërde while dancers encircled the hill in a giant *yokhor* to close the event. The games perhaps represent most clearly the way shamanist heritage has been rehabilitated and absorbed into public forms of Buryat national culture. The success of the Irkutsk Centre at organizing events and cultural activities was such that the team was increasingly called on by the oblast administration to provide organizational support for cultural events of other national minorities.

I was able to spend a good deal of time with Sakhilgaan members in Ust'-Orda in the summer of 2011. A change in leadership of the organization had seen Aleksei and Nikolai become far more involved in their work, including brokering several cultural exchanges through Nikolai's international networks. The group had traveled to meet other indigenous Siberian shamans and make offerings together in the Altai republic and had traveled to Lake

Sakhilgaan shamans lead a *tailgan* for Bubain Toodei, July 2011.

Tahoe in the United States to exchange indigenous approaches to ecology and conservation through the Tahoe-Baikal Institute. Thanks to Aleksei and Nikolai's introductions, I was fortunate that the new chair, Semien Bubaev, embraced my interest and invited me to accompany him and his colleagues to a number of events.

The focus of that year's collective *tailgan* was the sacred place known as Bubain Toodei, close to the village of Kor'sik, from where Semien hailed. As a Buryat *toodei*, or grandmother spirit, after whom the site is named, Bubain Toodei's story was significant to her status. Like many revered *toodei* spirits, Bubain Toodei was explained to me as an important matriarch for the clan she had married into and a carrier of shamanic *utkha*. Her natal clan was in the northwest of the okrug, and I learned that a number of sacred places were dedicated to her on the route that she had traveled from her natal clan to her ultimate home in the Kuda Valley. As such, she was described to me by one shaman as a "federal spirit"—her biography and her trajectory including places across the territory of the okrug.

That rite was marked by a continued engagement with the public framing and institutionalization of practice seen a few years earlier. Again the event was trailed in the local press. For the first time, and to my surprise, some of the Sakhilgaan shamans opted to wear traditional *degel* robes to the ceremony, distinguishing them, by appearance at least, from other participants. While some had clearly invested in their costumes, which I saw them wearing on a number occasions, another that I had spoken to had borrowed his from the local folklore ensemble, underscoring the link with performative elements of national culture.

Efforts to make the local shamanist topography more visible were also underway. In chapter 2, I noted that tourists and travelers entering the okrug from Irkutsk formerly stopped at a picnic site with artistically decorated *serge* posts, while local Buryats stopped at unmarked *bar'sa* sites. In 2011 Nikolai had gained funding from the center in Irkutsk to erect dedicated offering enclosures on the road through Ust'-Orda to Baikal. The enclosures marked recognized *bar'sa* sites for the sacred hill of Kapsal and the site of Bubain Toodei. Shelters had been built and *serge* tethering posts had been erected and dedicated by Sakhilgaan so that travelers could make offerings to local spirits at the correct places.

I joined Semien when, for the first time, Sakhilgaan shamans greeted German travelers who were interested in shamanism on an organized tour. My friends demonstrated their practice, explained local shamanist cosmology, and made offerings for the tourists at the newly marked *bar'sa* site for safe travels. I had seen Misha demonstrating local custom in this way to tourists at the ethnographic museum while dressed in a historical shaman's costume, but this was a first for Sakhilgaan. Semien told me that he felt this was necessary as custodians of local culture because if Sakhilgaan didn't welcome guests to the area, travelers would turn to shamans from elsewhere. While attempts to establish Mankhai as a national park had stalled, the organization had obtained land to build a center for shamanism in Ust'-Orda to educate more people about local shamanist practice.

Yet while Sakhilgaan's practice may have superficially borne greater resemblance to the work of the Ulan-Ude associations—in wearing costumes, greeting tourists, and publicizing their work—the organization was more vociferous than ever in its mission to defend local practice. Tengeri shamans had been undertaking trance ceremonies and consultations in venues around the okrug in intervening years, much to the consternation of my friends, who remained skeptical about reviving elements of practice that had been lost or forgotten locally in case it was incorrectly practiced. While public framing and colorful costumes were evident in Sakhilgaan's practice, local rites retained their essentially inward-facing form, dedicated to local spirits. Curiously, while local shamans remained critical of the work of other shamans' organizations, the dedication of a Buddhist temple in Ust'-Orda that year was seen as less of an incursion: Sakhilgaan enjoyed good relations with the local Buddhist monk, who was respectful of their practice. At the opening ceremony, representatives of Sakhilgaan presented gifts to the Buddhist clergy present.

Sakhilgaan seemed to be assertive and confident about promoting their own practice and that summer even saw the organization's activities moving beyond the landscapes of Cisbaikalia. The principle of female *toodei* spirits as unifying figures was further evident at a *tailgan* held in Ivolginskii Raion of the Republic of Buryatia. The previous year, Sakhilgaan shamans had traveled to lead a *tailgan* rite at the white rock in Buryatia's Tunka Valley, a sacred place commemorating Bukha Noyon—founding ancestor of the Bulagat clan. The 2011 *tailgan* brought activities into the heart of the republic, close to the capital of Ulan-Ude. One of Sakhilgaan's leading figures lived in Ulan-Ude himself and explained to me that Western Buryats living in the city needed someone to offer to. The spirit of Emneg Toodei was discovered as a Western Buryat woman who had traveled from her natal home in Cisbaikalia and settled in the region. An important and powerful spirit for local Buryats, she was identified by Sakhilgaan as a precursor to the mass migration of Western Buryats to Ulan-Ude in the Soviet period and a suitable protector for the many Western Buryats living in the city today.

When Sakhilgaan visited the Emneg Toodei ritual site ahead of their *tailgan*, I joined them in a press conference at Buryat State University in Ulan-Ude to engage the local media there. Both the rector of the university and the chairman of VARK in Ulan-Ude at the time were Western Buryats supportive of Sakhilgaan's work. The event was popular, and I counted around four hundred people present when I attended the ceremony in August 2011. While in 2007 local shamans had been concerned about the presence of Ulan-Ude shamans in their space, by 2011 Sakhilgaan seemed more confident about legitimizing their own presence—for *their* people and *their* ancestors—on the home turf of others. If this book characterizes shamanism as focusing on place rather than territory, it is notable that female kin—as people who have moved—increasingly offer exemplars for broadening spatial relations and extending the linked network of places that constitute the shamanist topography of Western Buryats.

That same summer saw a remarkable civic festival organized in Ulan-Ude to mark 350 years since the voluntary accession of Buryatia into the Russian state. The name of the celebration could have been challenged in almost every aspect—the incorporation of the lands around Baikal were part of a steady process over decades, the allegiances of indigenous peoples were not, in all cases, voluntary and at times quite violent, and there was no unified Buryat territory nor a unified group using the ethnonym *Buryat* in the region at the time. The anniversary date was chosen to commemorate a year when several Buryat clans came under the protection of Russian forts along the Irkut River. An academic conference establishing this dating as a legitimate one and publishing the theory formed a substantial part of the celebration.[4]

"Together through Time." Poster celebrating "350 years since the voluntary accession of Buryatia into the Russian state."

The festival also featured performances of Buryat, Russian, and *Semeiskii* (Orthodox "old believer") culture on a stage in the city square and a spectacular concert in the city's sport stadium. The festival's logo—Russian and Buryat figures in national dress, accompanied by the slogan "Together through Time" bore remarkable resemblance to the iconography of the referendum campaign in Cisbaikalia five years earlier. Some people expressed cynicism regarding the festival to me, with one shaman telling me that he would not be attending as it would be offensive to his ancestors. Others enthusiastically joined in, with delegations from Irkutsk coming to Ulan-Ude to perform in the central square and attend the gala concert in the city's sports stadium.

The significance of the festival was heightened by the attendance of Vladimir Putin, then serving as prime minister. In the weeks preceding the event, the route from the airport was carefully tidied, public buildings were painted, and large cloths employed to mask any buildings undergoing building work or

Performers in traditional Slavic and Buryat dress carry the *khadag* at a concert attended by Putin, July 2011.

renovation. On the day of the largest events, rumors swirled as to whether or not Putin was really attending.

On a warm summer evening, I attended the stadium concert featuring famous Russian and Buryat pop stars; acrobats; fireworks; and choreographed displays of Buryat national culture on a grand scale, featuring hundreds of dancers and singers. Excitement built as Putin appeared in the middle of the show, walked to a microphone in the center of the stadium, and delivered a speech congratulating the people of Buryatia on "this beautiful celebration."

The juxtaposition of Sakhilgaan's *tailgan* for Emneg Toodei and the stadium concert in Ulan-Ude seemed to exemplify, and take to a new level, the trends I had seen in Cisbaikalia five years previously. Here were Western Buryat shamans publicly framing their own form of practice with a growing confidence and an expanding conception of their own shamanist topography. At the same time, the festival's branding—an image of Russians and

Buryats hand in hand—resonated strongly with the imagery of the 2006 referendum campaign in promoting a state-sanctioned historiography of Buryats within Russian statehood.

LOCAL TRENDS AND GLOBAL DISCOURSES

Most of this book deals with a particular moment in time and analyzes the way that Buryat ritual and performance practices were understood and employed in the context of the mid-2000s. My return in 2011–12 saw many of the same social dynamics at play. Yet subtle developments and changes also underlined the insights that performance theory brought to the study of ritual in social collectives—that the unique circumstances of any given performance will provide context-specific meaning and elements of even the most longstanding ritual practice morph and are reframed over time. The increasing performativity and spectacle evident in Sakhilgaan's practice illustrate this point very well. Yet the fundamental elements of communion, reciprocity, and relation to the spirits of the landscape were as evident as before, retaining what seemed to me a qualitative difference from the more institutionalized shamanism practiced by the larger organizations.

The strategy of maintaining visibility and recognition for Buryat culture through official channels remained the approach of Buryat cultural institutions in Irkutsk, whose energetic team remained as active as ever in organizing performances and events across the unified oblast. The questions of complicity with state agendas remained a point of critique for those who shunned the festival celebrating Buryats within the Russian state, reflecting the balancing act undertaken by those practicing Buryat culture in the public sphere.

In chapter 8, I described how assertions of indigeneity were combined with discourses of environmental conservation by a small group of Western Buryats in the protection of the sacred site of Mankhai in 2007. Embracing this paradigm not only revealed the resonance of Western Buryat experience with that of other indigenous peoples but the need to find new, globally recognized discourses for expressing the rights of Buryats in a political context where a turn to National Cultural Autonomy meant that the old Soviet paradigm of territorial autonomy no longer had purchase.

The increasing turn of Buryat interlocutors to discourses of indigeneity remained salient in the framing of cultural practice on my return to the region. The contact and exchanges of *Sakhilgaan* with other indigenous shamans and Native Americans mirrored the official renaming of the Irkutsk Centre for Buryat Culture as one for "Indigenous Peoples of Pribaikal'e." Tropes of indigeneity continued to grow in importance as a means of articulating the value of Buryat culture in the public sphere, and Buryat experience continued to resonate with that of indigenous peoples everywhere. The Janus-like nature of Buryat ritual and dance can equally be found in ethnographic descriptions of Inupiaq dancing in Alaska, Yolungu pre-burial ceremonies in Australia, or shamanic education initiatives among Turkanoans in Columbia.[5] These performances carry the same high stakes of preserving indigenous knowledge, cosmologies, and social relations while asserting those worldviews in the public realm of post-imperial states that wield considerable power over allocation of resources, land, and the means to self-determination.

THE VIEW FROM THE 2020S

In a recent survey of political currents in the Buryat Republic, Marjorie Balzer reports rumors of further territorial merger and growing concern at the potential erosion of Buryat cultural identity and sovereignty. Public assertions of discontent have apparently been met with more active repression and harassment of outspoken activists and scholars, with some notable figures fleeing Russia.[6] Irkutsk Oblast and Ust'-Orda do not appear to have been such noticeable crucibles of political foment, despite the fact that many of the promises of economic prosperity and improved infrastructure made in the mid-2000s remain unfulfilled.

Revisiting the material in this book for publication in the early 2020s, it is difficult not to view the events of the mid-2000s through the prism of Putin's war in Ukraine. The dissolution of indigenous regions in Siberia hardly made military aggression beyond Russia's borders inevitable, and few could have foreseen the extent of the violence that would be visited on a former Soviet neighbor. Yet the dismantling of autonomous okrugs, little remarked in international or even national media at the time, does represent a significant step along the path to ever more centralized power in the Russian Federation since Putin's accession to the presidency in 2000. The effective stifling of political debate and the submission of local media to government narratives can, in perspective, be seen as part of an increasingly emboldened Kremlin leadership wielding both ideological and political power to exercise its will.

The events recounted in this book can therefore be seen as part of a process of consolidating power that has grown in intensity and ambition. While undertaking military action beyond Russia's borders in Georgia in 2008 and in the east of Ukraine and Crimea since 2014, Putin has, as both president and prime minister, variously invoked nostalgic visions of medieval Rus, Imperial Russia, and Stalinist power as justification for territorial expansion and models for statehood while openly repressing political opposition.

It is notable that the terminology of *ethnos* theory, reviled by some of my interlocutors in relation to the initial naming of the Irkutsk culture center, has since been adopted in right-wing intellectual discourse in Russia and used by Putin himself as Russia seeks to reassert its place in the world through increasingly violent means.[7] The flirtation with ethnos theory suggests that the challenge of reconciling a culturally heterogeneous territory with an idea of Russia that can unite and command the loyalty of such a diverse population, particularly in the circumstances of violent conflict, remains as salient as ever.

I have seen diverse viewpoints among Buryats on social media. Some younger, urban commentators have voiced their opposition to the war, informed by international media and engagement with political opposition movements. Several have expressed exasperation at their own parents and elders who follow the official line on state television that the "special military operation" is a response to Western-backed fascism in Ukraine and still see in Putin the "strong leader" that Russia needs. Others post patriotic memes, Russian flags, and government speeches as the conflict escalates.

The tragedy experienced by Ukrainians at the present time is unfathomable for many of us. Pictures appear daily of bombing, violent assaults on citizens, and refugees fleeing through devastated infrastructure. Following the invasion, scenes also circulated on social media showing the "mass mobilization" of Russian citizens to be deployed on the Ukrainian front. On one post, students from Buryat State University, where I had been based for much of 2011–12, were shown apparently being rounded up and conscripted for service. Reports online suggest that the mobilization efforts were disproportionately targeting indigenous and rural communities in areas where political opposition to Putin was less strong than in cosmopolitan settings such as Moscow. Watching these scenes, I remembered stories I had been told by Buryat friends of their fathers or grandfathers fighting on the eastern front of World War II, proud that native Siberians were revered as soldiers because they were hunters and therefore good marksmen. I recalled an older Buryat man in Ust'-Orda who had recounted the stress of being on the frontlines in Hungary during the uprisings of the 1960s while undertaking national service. The war memorials found in even the smallest Buryat villages, inscribed with the names of local men, stand testament to the reach of these wars.

Historic parallels abound: soldiers from the British colonies rallying to fight on the European fronts of two World Wars, or Native Americans fighting in Vietnam for the United States only to experience discrimination and marginalization on their return. While not all my interlocutors might see it this way, the ironic tragedy of indigenous peoples mobilized to fight for territory thousands of miles away, when their own relationship to land has been radically altered by the states that they serve, seems to me to be achingly familiar.

NOTES

1. Smith, *Lectures on the Religion of the Semites*; Durkheim, *The Elementary Forms of the Religious Life*; Turner, *The Ritual Process*.

2. Bourdieu, "Outline of a Theory of Practice"; Jackson, "Knowledge of the Body."

3. Tambiah, "A Performative Approach to Ritual"; Bloch, *From Blessing to Violence*.

4. Khalsaraev, *Vremia, Sobitiia, Liudi*.

5. Ikuta, "Embodied Knowledge, Relations with the Environment, and Political Negotiation"; Morphy, "Extended Lives in Global Spaces"; Jackson "Preserving Indian Culture."

6. Balzer, *Galvanizing Nostalgia?*.

7. Anderson and Arzyutov, "The Etnos Archipelago."

BIBLIOGRAPHY

Alsaev, B. "ERKHUUtskie Buriaty Obreli Novyi Status." *Üür* (February 2006a).

Anderson, David G. "Bringing Civil Society to an Uncivilised Place: Citizenship Regimes in Russia's Arctic Frontier." In *Civil Society: Challenging Western Models*, edited by Chris Hann and Elizabeth Dunn, 99–120. London: Routledge, 1996.

———. *Identity and Ecology in Arctic Siberia: The Number One Reindeer Brigade*. New York: Oxford University Press, 2000.

———. "Nationality and 'Aboriginal Rights' in Post-Soviet Siberia." *Senri Ethnological Studies* 66 (2004): 247–67.

Anderson, David G., and Dmitry V. Arzyutov. "The Etnos Archipelago: Sergei M. Shirokogoroff and the Life History of a Controversial Anthropological Concept." *Current Anthropology* 60, no. 6 (2019): 741–73.

Atkinson, Jane Monnig. *The Art and Politics of Wana Shamanship*. Berkeley: University of California Press, 1989.

———. "Shamanisms Today." *Annual Review of Anthropology* 21 (1992): 307–30.

Atwood, Christopher. *Encyclopedia of Mongolia and the Mongol Empire*. New York: Facts on File, 2004.

Austin, John Langshaw. *How to Do Things with Words*. New York: Oxford University Press, 1975.

Babueva, V. D. *Materialhaia i Dukhovnaia Kul'tura Buriat*. Ulan-Ude: Tsentr Sokhraneniia i Razvitiia i Kul'turnogo Naslediia Buriatii, 2004.

Badiev, A. A. *Kul'turnoe Stroitel'stvo v Buriatskoi ASSR: Dokumenty i Materialy*. Ulan-Ude: Buriatskoe Knizhnoe Izdatel'stvo, 1983.

Baldaev, S. P. *Buriatskie Narodnye Pesni (Sovetskii Period)*. Vol. 3. Ulan-Ude: Buriatskoe Knizhnoe Izdatel'stvo, 1970.

———. *Buriatskie Svadebnye Obriady*. Ulan-Ude: Buriatskoe Knizhnoe Izd-vo, 1959.

———. *Rodoslovnye Predaniia i Legendy Buriat*. Vol. 1. Izd-vo Buriatskogo Gosuniversiteta, 2009.

Balzer, M. M. "Dilemmas of Federalism in Siberia." In *Center-Periphery Conflict in Post-Soviet Russia*, edited by Mihkail A. Alekseev, 131–66. Basingstoke, England: Macmillan, 1999.

———. *Galvanizing Nostalgia?: Indigeneity and Sovereignty in Siberia*. Ithaca, NY: Cornell University Press, 2022.

———. *The Tenacity of Ethnicity: A Siberian Saga in Global Perspective*. Princeton University Press, 2021.

———. "Two Urban Shamans: Unmasking Leadership in Fin-de-Soviet Siberia." In *Perilous States: Conversations on Culture, Politics and Nation*, edited by George E. Marcus. University of Chicago Press, 1993.

Bamford, S., and J. Leach, eds. *Kinship and Beyond: The Genealogical Model Reconsidered*. Oxford: Berghahn, 2009.

Bamford, Sandra. "'Family Trees' among the Kamea of Papua New Guinea: A Non-Genealogical Approach to Imagining Relatedness." In *Kinship and Beyond: The Genealogical Method Reconsidered*, edited by Sandra C. Bamford and James Leach, 159–74. Oxford: Berghahn, 2009.

Banks, Marcus. *Ethnicity: Anthropological Constructions*. London: Routledge, 1996.

Bateson, Gregory. "A Theory of Play and Fantasy." In *Steps to an Ecology of Mind*. 177–93. New York: Ballantine. 1972.

Bauman, Richard. *Verbal Art as Performance*. Prospect Heights, IL: Waveland, 1984.

Bauman, Richard, and Joel Sherzer. *Explorations in the Ethnography of Speaking*. New York: Cambridge University Press, 1974.

Bernstein, Anya. "Remapping Sacred Landscapes: Shamanic Tourism and Cultural Production on the Olkhon Island." *Sibirica* 7, no. 2 (2008): 23–46.

Binns, Christopher A. P. "The Changing Face of Power: Revolution and Accommodation in the Development of the Soviet Ceremonial System: Part I." *Man*, 1979: 585–606.

Bloch, Maurice. *From Blessing to Violence: History and Ideology in the Circumcision Ritual of the Merina of Madagascar*. Cambridge: Cambridge University Press, 1987.

———. *Prey into Hunter: The Politics of Religious Experience*. Cambridge: Cambridge University Press, 1992.
Bolkhosoev, S. B. "K Voprosy ob Obshikh Istokakh Proiskhozhdeniia Etnonimov 'Buriat' i 'Bulagat.'" *Izvestiia Irkutskogo Gosudarstvennogo Universiteta, Seria Geoarcheologiia, Etnologiia, Antropologiia* 21 (2017): 178–96.
Bolotova, E. "Otvetstvennost' za Sokhranenie Buriatskogo Iazyka i Kul'tury—Na Kazhdom Iz Nas." *Üür*, Irkutsk. April 2006.
Bourdieu, Pierre. *Outline of a Theory of Practice*. Cambridge: Cambridge University Press, 1977.
Bowring, B. "Burial and Resurrection: Karl Renner's Controversial Influence on the 'National Question' in Russia." In *National Cultural Autonomy and Its Contemporary Critics*, edited by Ephraim Nimni, 191–203. London: Routledge, 2005.
Butler, Judith. "Performative Acts and Gender Constitution: An Essay in Phenomenology and Feminist Theory." *Theatre Journal* 40, no. 4 (December 1988).
Buyandelger, Manduhai. *Tragic Spirits: Shamanism, Memory, and Gender in Contemporary Mongolia*. Chicago: University of Chicago Press, 2013.
———. "Who 'Makes' the Shaman?: The Politics of Shamanic Practices among the Buriats in Mongolia." *Inner Asia* 1, no. 2 (1999): 221–44.
Cadena, Marisol de la, and Orin Starn, eds. "Introduction." In *Indigenous Experience Today*. 1–30. Oxford: Berg, 2007.
Carsten, J., ed. *Cultures of Relatedness: New Approaches to the Study of Kinship*. Cambridge: Cambridge University Press, 2000.
Carsten, Janet, ed. "Introduction: Cultures of Relatedness." *Cultures of Relatedness: New Approaches to the Study of Kinship*, 1–36. Cambridge University Press, 2000.
Casey, Edward S. "How to Get from Space to Place in a Fairly Short Stretch of Time: Phenomenological Prolegomena." In *Senses of Place*, edited by Fed S. and Basso, K., 14–51. Santa Fe, NM: School of American Research Press, 1996.
Castro, Eduardo Veveiros de. "Cosmological Deixis and Amerindian Perspectivism." *Journal of the Royal Anthropological Institute* 4, no. 3 (September 1998): 469–88.
Chakars, Melissa. *The Socialist Way of Life in Siberia: Transformation in Buryatia*. Budapest, New York: Central European University Press, 2014.
Chau, Adam Yuet. "Hosting as a Cultural Form." *L'Homme* 231–32, no. 3–4 (2019): 41–66.

Cocchiara, Giuseppe. *History of Folklore in Europe*. Philadelphia: Institute for the Study of Human Issues, 1981.

Conklin, Beth A. "Body Paint, Feathers, and VCRs: Aesthetics and Authenticity in Amazonian Activism." *American Ethnologist* 24, no. 4 (1997): 711–37.

Crate, Susan. "Ohuokhai: Sakhas' Unique Integration of Social Meaning and Movement." *Journal of American Folklore* 119, no. 472 (2006): 161–83.

Csordas, Thomas. "Embodiment as a Paradigm for Anthropology." In *Body/Meaning/Healing*, 58–87. New York: Palgrave Macmillan, 2002.

Curtin, Jeremiah. *A Journey in Southern Siberia: The Mongols, Their Religion and Their Myths*. Boston: Little, Brown, 1909.

De Castro, Eduardo Viveiros. "Cosmological Deixis and Amerindian Perspectivism." *Journal of the Royal Anthropological Institute* (1998): 469–88.

Dombrowski, Kirk. *Against Culture: Development, Politics, and Religion in Indian Alaska*. Vol. 1. Lincoln: University of Nebraska Press, 2001.

Donahoe, Brian. "On the Creation of Indigenous Subjects in the Russian Federation." *Citizenship Studies* 15, no. 3–4 (2011): 397–417.

Donahoe, Brian, and Joachim Otto Habeck. *Reconstructing the House of Culture: Community, Self, and the Makings of Culture in Russia and Beyond*. Oxford: Berghahn, 2011.

Donahoe, Brian, Joachim Otto Habeck, Agnieszka Halemba, and István Sántha. "Size and Place in the Construction of Indigeneity in the Russian Federation." *Current Anthropology* 49, no. 6 (2008): 993–1020.

Dugarov, D. S. *Istoricheskie korni belogo shamanstva: Na materiale obriadovogo folklora Buriat*. Moskva: Nauka, 1991.

Durkheim, Émile. *The Elementary Forms of the Religious Life*. Translated by Joseph Ward Swain. Mineola, NY: Dover, 2008.

Durkheim, Émile, and Marcel Mauss. *Primitive Classification*. London: Routledge, 2010.

Eliade, Mircea. *Shamanism: Archaic Techniques of Ecstasy*. Vol. 76. Princeton, NJ: Princeton University Press, 1972.

Empson, Rebecca. *Harnessing Fortune: Personhood, Memory, and Place in Mongolia*. Oxford: Oxford University Press, 2011.

Erbanov, M. N. "Tezisy po Dokladu M. N. Erbanova 'Kul'turno-Natsioanalnoe Stroitelstvo BMASSR' Utverzzhdenie i Pleniumom Buriat-Mongol'skogo Obkoma BKP(B)." In *Kul'turnoe Stroitel'stvo v Buriatskoi ASSR: Dokumenty i Materialy*, edited by A. A. Badiev, 81–91. Ulan-Ude: Buriatskoe Knizhnoe Izdatel'stvo, 1983.

Evans-Pritchard, E. E. "The Meaning of Sacrifice among the Nuer." *Journal of the Royal Anthropological Institute of Great Britain and Ireland* 84, no. 1/2 (December 1954): 21–33.

———. *The Nuer: A Description of the Modes of Livelihood and Political Institutions of a Nilotic People*. Oxford: Clarendon, 1940.
Feld, Steven, and Keith H. Basso. *Senses of Place. School of American Research Advanced Seminar Series*. Santa Fe, NM: School of American Research Press, 1996.
Figes, Orlando. *Natasha's Dance: A Cultural History of Russia*. London: Allen Lane, 2002.
Firth, Raymond. "Offering and Sacrifice: Problems of Organization." *Journal of the Royal Anthropological Institute of Great Britain and Ireland* 93, no. 1 (June 1963): 12–24.
Forsyth, J. *A History of the Peoples of Siberia: Russia's North Asian Colony*. Cambridge: Cambridge University Press, 1992.
Frolova, G. D. "Narodnaia Myzikal'naia Kul'tura." In *Buriaty*, edited by L. L. Abaeva and N. L. Zhukovskaia, 327–38. Moscow: Nauka, 2004.
Geertz, Clifford. *Negara*. Princeton, NJ: Princeton University Press, 1980.
Gel'man, V. "Leviathan's Return: The Policy of Recentralization in Contemporary Russia." In *Federalism and Local Politics in Russia*, edited by Cameron Ross and Adrian Campbell, 27–40 London: Routledge, 2009.
Gergesova, T. E. *Buriatskie Narodnye Tantsy*. Ulan-Ude: Buritskoe knizhnoe izdatelstvo, 2002.
Gilbert, H. "Introduction." In *In the Balance: Indigeneity, Performance, Globalization*, edited by H. Gilbert, J. D. Phillipson, and M. H. Raheja, 1–24. Liverpool: Liverpool University Press, 2017.
Goffman, Erving. *Frame Analysis: An Essay on the Organization of Experience*. Harmondsworth, England: Penguin, 1975.
———. *The Presentation of Self in Everyday Life*. London: Penguin, 1990.
GOSKOMSTAT. *Ust'-Ordynskii Buriatskii Avtonomnyi Okrug v Sifrakh i Faktakh (1990–2002)*. Ust'-Ordynskii: GOSKOMSTAT, 2004.
Gow, P. "Land, People and Paper in Western Amazonia." In *The Anthropology of Landscape Perspectives on Place and Space*, edited by Eric Hirsch and Michael O'Hanlon, 43–62. Oxford: Oxford University Press, 1995.
Graber, Kathryn E. *Mixed Messages: Mediating Native Belonging in Asian Russia*. Ithaca, NY: Cornell University Press, 2020.
Graber, Kathryn, and Joseph Long. "The Dissolution of the Buryat Autonomous Okrugs in Siberia: Notes from the Field." *Inner Asia* 11, no. 1 (June 1, 2009): 147–55.
Graeber, David. *Debt: The First 5000 Years*. Harmondsworth, UK: Penguin, 2012.
Grant, Bruce. *In the Soviet House of Culture: A Century of Perestroikas*. Princeton, NJ: Princeton University Press, 1995.

Gray, Patty Anne. *The Predicament of Chukotka's Indigenous Movement: Post-Soviet Activism in the Russian Far North*. Cambridge: Cambridge University Press, 2005.

Gregory, Chris A. *Gifts and Commodities*. London: Academic Press, 1982.

Halemba, Agnieszka. *The Telengits of Southern Siberia: Landscape, Religion and Knowledge in Motion*. London: Routledge, 2006.

Hamayon, Roberte N. "Game and Games, Fortune and Dualism in Siberian Shamanism." In *Shamanism and Northern Ecology*, edited by Juha Pentikäinen, 36–61. Berlin: De Gruyter, 1996.

———. "Shamanism, Buddhism and Epic Heroism: Which Supports the Identity of the Post-Soviet Buryats?." *Central Asian Survey* 17, no. 1 (March 1998): 51–67.

———. "Shamanism in Siberia: From Partnership in Supernature to Counter-Power in Society." In *Shamanism, History and the State*, edited by N. Thomas and C. Humphrey, 76–89. Ann Arbor: University of Michigan Press, 1994.

———. *Why We Play: An Anthropological Study*. Chicago: Hau Books, 2016.

Handelman, Don. "Introduction: Why Ritual in Its Own Right? How So?" *Social Analysis* 48, no. 2 (June 1, 2004): 1–32.

———. *Models and Mirrors: Towards an Anthropology of Public Events*. Oxford: Berghahn, 1998.

Hirsch, Eric, and Michael O'Hanlon, eds. *The Anthropology of Landscape: Perspectives on Place and Space*. New York: Oxford University Press, 1995.

Hirsch, Francine. *Empire of Nations: Ethnographic Knowledge and the Making of the Soviet Union*. Ithaca, NY: Cornell University Press, 2005.

Holy, Ladislav. *Segmentary Lineage Systems Reconsidered*. Vol. 4. Belfast, Northern Ireland: Dept. of Social Anthropology, Queen's University of Belfast, 1979.

Hosking, G. *A History of the Soviet Union 1917–1991. Final Edition*. London: Fontana, 1992.

Hubert, Henri, and Marcel Mauss. *Sacrifice: Its Nature and Functions*. University of Chicago Press, 1981.

Humphrey, Caroline. "Buryatiya and the Buryats" In *The Nationalities Question in the Post-Soviet States*, 2nd ed., edited by G. Smith, 113–25. London: Longman, 1996.

———. "The Domestic Mode of Production in Post-Soviet Siberia?" *Anthropology Today* 14, no. 3 (1998): 2–7.

———. "Hospitality and Tone: Holding Patterns for Strangeness in Rural Mongolia." *Journal of the Royal Anthropological Institute* 18 (June 1, 2012): S63–75.

———. "'Janus-Faced Signs'—The Political Language of a Soviet Minority before Glasnost." *Sociological Review* 36, no. 1_suppl (May 1, 1988): 145–75.

———. *Marx Went Away—But Karl Stayed Behind: Updated Edition of Karl Marx Collective: Economy, Society and Religion in a Siberian Collective Farm*, 2nd updated ed. Ann Arbor: University of Michigan Press, 1998.

———. "Population Trends, Ethnicity and Religion among the Buryats." In *The Development of Siberia: People and Resources*, edited by Alan Wood and R. A. French, 147–76. Basingstoke, England: Macmillan in association with the School of Slavonic and East European Studies, University of London, 1989.

———. "Shamans in the City." In *The Unmaking of Soviet Life: Everyday Economies after Socialism*, 202–22. Ithaca, NY: Cornell University Press, 2002.

———. "Some Ritual Techniques in the Bull-Cult of the Buriat-Mongols." *Proceedings of the Royal Anthropological Institute of Great Britain and Ireland* (1973): 15–28.

———. "The Uses of Genealogy: A Historical Study of the Nomadic and Sedentarised Buryat." In *Pastoral Production and Society*, 235–60. Cambridge University Press, 1979.

Humphrey, Caroline, and James Laidlaw. *The Archetypal Actions of Ritual: A Theory of Ritual Illustrated by the Jain Rite of Worship*. Oxford: Clarendon, 1994.

Humphrey, Caroline, with U. Onon. *Shamans and Elders: Experience, Knowledge and Power among the Daur Mongols*. New York: Oxford University Press, 1996.

Hundley, Helen. "Speransky and the Buryats: Administrative Reform in Nineteenth Century Russia." PhD dissertation, University of Illinois at Urbana-Champaign, 1984.

Hurelbaatar, A. "The Creation and Revitalization of Ethnic Sacred Sites in Ulan-Ude." In *Urban Life in Post-Soviet Asia*, edited by Catherine Alexander, Victor Buchli, and Caroline Humphrey, 136–56. London: UCL, 2007.

Ikuta, Hiroko. "Embodied Knowledge, Relations with the Environment, and Political Negotiation: St. Lawrence Island Yupik and Iñupiaq Dance in Alaska." *Arctic Anthropology* 48, no. 1 (2011): 54–65.

Ingold, Tim. "Ancestry, Generation, Substance, Memory, Land." In *The Perception of the Environment: Essays in Livelihood, Dwelling and Skill*, 132–51. London: Routledge, 2000.

———. *The Appropriation of Nature: Essays on Human Ecology and Social Relations*. Manchester: Manchester University Press, 1986.

———. *The Perception of the Environment: Essays in Livelihood, Dwelling and Skill*. London: Routledge, 2000.

———. "Stories against Classification: Transport, Wayfaring and the Integration of Knowledge." In *Kinship and Beyond: The Genealogical Method Reconsidered*, edited by Sandra C. Bamford and James Leach, 192–213. Oxford: Berghahn, 2009.

Jackson, Jean. "Culture, Genuine and Spurious: The Politics of Indianness in the Vaupes, Columbia." *American Ethnologist* 22, no. 1 (1995): 3–27.

———. "Preserving Indian Culture: Shaman Schools and Ethno-Education in the Vaupes, Colombia." *Cultural Anthropology* (1995): 302–29.

Jackson, Michael. "Knowledge of the Body." *Man, New Series* 18, no. 2 (1983): 327–45.

Keane, Webb. *Signs of Recognition: Powers and Hazards of Representation in an Indonesian Society*. Berkeley: University of California Press, 1997.

Kelly, C., H. Pilkington, D. Shepherd, and V. Volkov. "Introduction: Why Cultural Studies?" In *Russian Cultural Studies: An Introduction*, edited by Catriona Kelly and David Shepherd, 1–17. New York: Oxford University Press, 1998.

Khalsaraev, A. D. *Vremia, Sobitiia, Liudi: Khronologicheskii Perechen' Dat i Faktov iz Istorii Etnicheskoi Buriatii*. Ulan-Ude: Ozdatel'stvo OAO respublikanskaia Tipografiia, 2011.

Khamutaev, V. A. *Buriatskoe Natsionalhoe Dvizhenie 1980–2000-3 Gg*. Ulan-Ude: Izdatel'stvo BNTs SO RAN, 2005.

Khandagurova, Margarita Vladimirovna. *Obriadnost' Kudinskikh i Verkholenskikh Buriat vo 2 Polovine XX Veka (Basseinov Verkhnego i Srednego tTcheniiarek : Kuda, Murino i Kamenka)*. Irkutsk: Amtera, 2008.

Khangalov, Matvei Nikolaevich. *Sobranie Sochinenii*. Vol. 1. Ulan-Ude: Buriatskoe knizhnoe izd-vo, 2004.

———. *Sobranie Sochinenii*. Vol. 2. Ulan-Ude: Buriatskoe knizhnoe izd-vo, 2004.

———. *Sobranie Sochinenii*. Vol. 3. Ulan-Ude: Buriatskoe knizhnoe izd-vo, 2004.

King, Alexander D. *Living with Koryak Traditions: Playing with Culture in Siberia*. Lincoln: University of Nebraska Press, 2011.

Kolesnikov, A. "Sobiratel' Zemel' Irkutskikh." *Piatnitsa* (April 14, 2006).
Kork, B. "Rodovoi Obriad Vozle Sviashchennoi Gory." *SM Nomer Odin* (June 19, 2008).
———. "Shamany Provedut Obriad Zashchity Aeroporta." *SM Nomer Odin* (June 21, 2007).
Krader, Lawrence. "Buryat Religion and Society." *Southwestern Journal of Anthropology* 10, no. 3 (Autumn 1954): 322–51.
———. "Principles and Structures in the Organization of the Asiatic Steppe-Pastoralists." *Southwestern Journal of Anthropology* 11, no. 2 (Summer 1955): 67–92.
Krist, Stefan. "Where Going Back Is a Step Forward: The Re-Traditionalising of Sport Games in Post-Soviet Buriatiia." *Sibirica* 4, no. 1 (2004): 104–15.
Kuper, A. "The Return of the Native." *Current Anthropology* 44, no. 3 (2003): 389–402.
Lambek, Michael. "Sacrifice and the Problem of Beginning: Meditations from Sakalava Mythopraxis" *Journal of the Royal Anthropological Institute* 13, no. 1 (2007): 19–38.
Langer, Susanne K. *Feeling and Form*. Scribner's: New York, 1953.
———. *Philosophy in a New Key: A Study in the Symbolism of Reason, Rite, and Art*. Cambridge, MA: Harvard University Press, 1957.
Laufer, Berthold. "Burkhan." *Journal of the American Oriental Society* 36 (1916): 390–95.
Leach, Edmund R. *Culture & Communication: The Logic by Which Symbols Are Connected: An Introduction to the Use of Structuralist Analysis in Social Anthropology*. Cambridge, New York: Cambridge University Press, 1976.
Leach, James. "Drum and Voice: Aesthetics and Social Process on the Rai Coast of Papua New Guinea." *Journal of the Royal Anthropological Institute* 8, no. 4 (December 1, 2002): 713–34.
Lieven, Dominic. "Russia as Empire: A Comparative Perspective." In *Reinterpreting Russia*, edited by Geoffrey Hosking and Robert Service, 9–20. London: Edward Arnold, 1999.
Long, Joseph J. "Shamanist Topography and Administrative Territories in Cisbaikalia, Southern Siberia." In *Nomadic and Indigenous Spaces*, edited by Judith Miggelbrink, Joachim Otto Habeck, Nuccio Mazzullo, and Peter Koch, 181–202. Farnham, Surrey, UK: Ashgate, 2013.
Manzhigeev, I. A. *Buriatskii ekhor: Kratkii etnograficheskii ocherk*. Ulan-Ude: Buriatskoe Knizhnoe Izd-vo, 1985.
Martin, Terry. *The Affirmative Action Empire: Nations and Nationalism in the Soviet Union, 1923–1939*. Ithaca, NY: Cornell University Press, 2001.

Mauss, Marcel. *The Gift*. Translated by W. D. Halls. London: Routledge, 1990.
———. "Techniques of the Body." *Economy and Society* 2, no. 1 (1973): 70–88.
Metzo, K. *It Didn't Used to Be This Way: Household, Resources and Economic Transformation in Tunka Valley, Buriatia, Russian Federation*, PhD Dissertation, Indiana University, 2003.
Merlan, Francesca "Indigeneity: Global and Local." *Current Anthropology* 50, no. 3 (June 1, 2009): 303–33.
Mikhailov, T. M. *Buriatskii Shamanizm : Istoriia, Struktura i Sotsial'nye Funktsii*. Novosibirsk: Izd-vo 'Nauka,' Sibirskoe otd-nie, 1987.
Mikhakhanova-Baliueva, G. A. *Ekhered-Bulgadai Baabai*. Ust'-Orda: Reprotsentr A1, 2006.
Montgomery, Robert. *Buriat Language Policy, 19th c.–1928: A Case Study in Tsarist and Soviet Nationality Practices*, PhD Dissertation, Indiana University 1994.
———. *Late Tsarist and Early Soviet Nationality and Cultural Policy: The Buryats and Their Language*. Lewiston, NY: Edwin Mellen, 2005.
Morphy, Howard. "Extended Lives in Global Spaces: The Anthropology of Yolngu Pre-Burial Ceremonies." *Journal of the Royal Anthropological Institute* 22, no. 2 (2016): 332–55.
Naidakova, V. Ts. "Teatr." In *Buriaty*, edited by L. L. Abaeva and N. L. Zhukovskaia, 530–36. Moscow: Nauka, 2004.
Nanzatov, Bair Zoriktoevich. *Etnogenez Zapadnykh Buriat : VI-XIX Vv.* Irkutsk: Radian, 2005.
———. "K Voprosy o Rannei Etnicheskoi Istorii Bargu-Buriatskoi Obshnosti." *Bulletin of the Kalmyk Institute for Humanities of the Russian Academy of Sciences* 9, no. 1 (2016): 99–106.
Newyear, Tristra. "'Our Primitive Customs' and 'Lord Kalym': The Evolving Buryat Discourse on Bride Price, 1880–1930." *Inner Asia* 11, no. 1 (2009): 5–22.
Nikolaev, V. V., and L. V. Melnikova. *Petroglify Kudinskoi Doliny*. Izdatel'stvo Irkutskogo Gosudarstvennogo Tekhnicheskogo Universiteta, 2008.
Oracheva, O. "Unification as a Political Project: The Case of Permskii Krai." In *Federalism and Local Politics in Russia*, edited by Cameron Ross and Adrian Campbell, 82–105. London: Routledge, 2009.
Oshirova, L. A. "Razvitie Kul'tura v Ust'-Ordynskom Buriatskom Avtonomnom Okruge." In *Buriatskoe Neselenie Irkutskoi Oblasti (Gubernii) i Ust'-Ordynskogo Buriatskogo Avtomnogo Okruga v XX Veke*, edited by V. G. Maleev, 123–27. Irkutsk: Irkutskaia Oblastnaia Tipografiia No 1, 2002.

Palkhaeva, E. N. "Razdel Buriat-Mongol'skoi ASSR v 1927g." In *Buriatskoe Neselenie Irkutskoi Oblasti (Gubernii) I Ust'-Ordynskogo Buriatskogo Avtomnogo Okruga v XX Veke*, edited by V. G. Maleev, 123–27. Irkutsk: Irkutskaia Oblastnaia Tipografiia No 1, 2002.
Patton, Paul. "National Autonomy and Indigenous Sovereignty." In *National Cultural Autonomy and Its Contemporary Critics*, edited by Ephraim Nimni, 112–23. London: Routledge, 2005.
Pedersen, Morten Axel. *Not Quite Shamans: Spirit Worlds and Political Lives in Northern Mongolia*. Ithaca, NY: Cornell University Press, 2011.
Peirce, C. S. "What Is a Sign." In *The Essential Peirce: Selected Philosophical Writings—Volume 2 (1893–1913)*, edited by the Peirce Edition Project, 4–10. Bloomington: Indiana University Press, 1998.
Petrova, E. "Vybor Sdelan. Oblast' i Okrug Progolosovali Za Obedinenie." *Vostochno-Sibirskaia Pravda* (April 18, 2006).
Pitt-Rivers, Julian. "The Law of Hospitality." *HAU: Journal of Ethnographic Theory* 2, no. 1 (June 19, 2012): 501–17.
Povinelli, Elizabeth A. *The Cunning of Recognition: Indigenous Alterities and the Making of Australian Multiculturalism*. Durham, NC: Duke University Press, 2002.
Quijada, Justine Buck. *Buddhists, Shamans, and Soviets: Rituals of History in Post-Soviet Buryatia*. New York: Oxford University Press, 2019.
———. "What If We Don't Know Our Clan? The City Tailgan as New Ritual Form in Buriatiia." *Sibirica* 7, no. 1 (Spring 2008): 1–22.
Quijada, Justine Buck, Kathryn E. Graber, and Eric Stephen. "Finding 'Their Own': Revitalizing Buryat Culture through Shamanic Practices in Ulan-Ude." *Problems of Post-Communism* 62, no. 5 (September 3, 2015): 258–72.
Quijada, Justine, and Eric Stephen. "Performing 'Culture': Diverse Audiences at the International Shaman's Conference and Tailgan on Ol'khon Island." *Études Mongoles et Sibériennes, Centrasiatiques et Tibétaines* 46 (2015).
Radio Free Europe/Radio Liberty. "Another Autonomous Okrug Leader Calls for Merger." *Newsline—April 25, 2001*. http://www.rferl.org/content/article/1142390.html. Accessed February 20, 2009.
———. "Preparations Underway for Merger of Siberian Regions as Irkutsk Legislators Study Possible Expansion of their Region." *Newsline—April 19, 2002*. http://www.rferl.org/content/article/1142659.html. Accessed February 20, 2009.
Raeff, Marc. *Siberia and the Reforms of 1822*. Seattle: University of Washington Press, 1956.

Renner, Karl. "State and Nation (1899)." In *National-Cultural Autonomy and Its Contemporary Critics*, edited by Emphraim Nimni, 15–47. London: Routledge, 2005.
Riazanovskii, Valentin Aleksandrovich. *Customary Law of the Nomadic Tribes of Siberia*. Vol. 48. Bloomington: Indiana University Press, 1965.
ROSSTAT. *Natsionalhyi Sostav Naseleniia po Irkutskoi Oblasti, Vkliuchnaia Ust'-Ordynskii Buriatskii Avtonamnyi Okrug (Po Itogam Vserossiskoi Perepisi Naselenniia 2002g.)*. Irkutsk: ROSSTAT, 2004.
Rostas, Susanna. "From Ritualisation to Performativity: The Concheros of Mexico." In *Ritual, Performance, Media*, edited by Felicia Hughes-Freeland, 85–103. London: Routledge, 1998.
Rupen, Robert A. "The Buriat Intelligentsia." *Far Eastern Quarterly* 15, no. 3 (May 1956): 383–98.
———. "Cyben Zamcaranovic Zamcarano (1880–1940)." *Harvard Journal of Asiatic Studies* 19, no. 1/2 (June 1956): 126–45.
Sahlins, Marshall David. *Stone Age Economics*. London: Tavistock, 1974.
Sakwa, Richard. *Russian Politics and Society*. 4th ed. London: Routledge, 2008.
Sapir, Edward. *Selected Writings of Edward Sapir in Language, Culture and Personality*. Berkeley: University of California Press, 1949.
Schechner, Richard. *Between Theater and Anthropology*. University Park: University of Pennsylvania Press, 1985.
———. *Performance Theory*. 2nd ed. London: Routledge, 1988.
Schieffelin, Edward L. "Performance and the Cultural Construction of Reality." *American Ethnologist* 12, no. 4 (November 1, 1985): 707–24.
Scott, James C. *Seeing Like a State: How Certain Schemes to Improve the Human Condition Have Failed*. New Haven, CT: Yale University Press, 1998.
Shaglanova, O. A. "Kul't 'Mongol-Burkhanov' v Sovremennom Predstavlenii Buriat-Ekhiritov." In *Drevnie Kochevniki Tssentralhoi Azii*, edited by S. V. Danilov, 154–7. Izdatelstvo BNTs SO RAN, 2005.
Shah, A. "The Dark Side of Indigeneity?: Indigenous People, Rights and Development in India." *History Compass* 5, no. 6 (2007): 1806–32.
Sharakshinova, N. O. *Buriatskogo Narodnoe Poeticheskoe Tvorchestvo*. Irkutsk: Irkutskii Gosudarstvennyi Universitet, 1975.
Shoolbraid, G. M. H. *The Oral Epic of Siberia and Central Asia*. Vol. 111. Bloomington: Indiana University Press, 1975.
Shryock, Andrew. *Off Stage / On Display: Intimacy and Ethnography in the Age of Public Culture*. Stanford, CA: Stanford University Press, 2004.

Silverstein, M. "Shifters, Linguistic Categories, and Cultural Description. In *Meaning in Anthropology*, edited by K. H. Basso and H. A. Selby, 11–55. Santa Fe: University of New Mexico Press, 1976.

Singer, Milton. *When a Great Tradition Modernizes: An Anthropological Approach to Indian Civilization*. Chicago: University of Chicago Press, 1972.

Skrynnikova, T. D., D. B. Batoeva, G. R. Galdanova, and D. A. Nikolaeva. *Obriady v Traditsionnoi Kul'ture Buriat*. Moscow: Vostochnaia Literatura RAN, 2002.

Smith, G. "The Soviet State and Nationalities Policy." In *The Nationalities Question in the Post-Soviet States*, 2nd ed., edited by G. Smith, 2–22.

Smith, Graham, ed. *The Nationalities Question in the Post-Soviet States*. London: Longman, 1996.

Smith, Jeremy. *The Bolsheviks and the National Question, 1917–23*. Basingstoke, England: MacMillan in association with the School of Slavonic and East European Studies, University of London, 1999.

Smith, W. Robertson. *Lectures on the Religion of the Semites*. Vol. 1888–89. Edinburgh: Black, 1889.

Sneath, David. *The Headless State: Aristocratic Orders, Kinship Society, & Misrepresentations of Nomadic Inner Asia*. New York: Columbia University Press, 2007.

———. "Transacting and Enacting: Corruption, Obligation and the Use of Monies in Mongolia." *Ethnos* 71, no. 1 (March 2006): 89–112.

Stalin, Joseph. "Marxism and the National Question." In *Marxism and the National and Colonial Question: A Collection of Articles and Speeches*, 3–61. London: Lawrence & Wishart, 1936.

Strathern, Marilyn. *The Gender of the Gift: Problems with Women and Problems with Society in Melanesia*. Berkeley: University of California Press, 1990.

Stroganova, E. A. *Buriatskoe Natsional'no-Kul'turnoe Vozrozhdenie : Konets 80-Kh–Seredina 90-Kh Godov XX Veka, Respublika Buriatiia*. Irkutsk: Natalis, 2001.

Tambiah, Stanley J. "A Performative Approach to Ritual." *Proceedings of the British Academy* LXV (1979).

Tarmakhanov, E. E., L. M. Dameshek, and T. E. Sanzhieva. *Istoria Ust'-Ordynskogo Buriatskogo Avtonomogo Okruga: Uchebnoe Pocobie Dlia Obshscheobrazovatelnykh Uchebnykh Zavedenii*. Ulan-Ude: Buriatskii Gosudarstvennyi Universitet, 2003.

Tishanin, A.G., V. G. Maleev, V.K. Kruglov, and I.P. Morokhoeva. "Ob Obrazovanii Novogo Sub'ekta Rossiskoi Federatsii." *Panorama Okruga* (October 14, 2005): 1.

Torode, N. "National Cultural Autonomy in the Russian Federation: Implementation and Impact." *International Journal on Minority and Group Rights* 15 (2008): 179–93.

Tugutov. "The Tailagan as the Principal Shamanistic Ritual of the Buriats." In *Shamanism in Siberia*, edited by V. Diószegi and M. Hoppál. Budapest: Akadēmiai Kiadó, 1978.

Turner, Victor Witter. "Are There Universals of Performance in Myth, Ritual, and Drama?" In *By Means of Performance: Intercultural Studies of Theatre and Ritual*, edited by Schechner, R. and Appel, W., 8–18. Cambridge University Press, 1990.

———. *From Ritual to Theatre: The Human Seriousness of Play*. New York: Performing Arts Journal Press, 1982.

———. *The Ritual Process: Structure and Anti-Structure*. Transaction Publishers, 1995.

Ubeev, I. M., ed. *Buriatskoi avtonomii: byt' ili ne byt'*? Ulan-Ude: Kongress Buriatskogo Naroda, 2007.

Urmaeva, M. D. "Zastolhye Pesni Ekhirit-Bulagatskikh Buriat." In *Traditsii i Sovremennye Protsessy v Fol'klore i Literature: Materialy Nauchnoi Konferentsii*, edited by B. V. Bazarov, 145–48. Ulan-Ude: Izdatel'stvo BNTs SO RAN, 2006.

Vereshchagina, S. "Pesni Rodnoi Zemli." In *Razbuzhenniia Step'*, edited by V. N. Volovich, 172–88. Irkutsk: Vostochno Sibirskoe Knizhnoe Izdatel'stvo, 1987.

Vitebsky, Piers. "The Northern Minorities." In *The Nationalities Question in the Post-Soviet States*, edited by G. Smith, 94–112. London: Longman 1996.

———. *Reindeer People: Living with Animals and Spirits in Siberia*. London: HarperCollins, 2005.

Weiner, Annette B. *Inalienable Possessions: The Paradox of Keeping-While Giving*. Berkeley: University of California Press, 1992.

Widlok, Thomas. "Sharing: Allowing Others to Take What Is Valued." *HAU: Journal of Ethnographic Theory* 3, no. 2 (2013): 11–31.

Willerslev, Rane. *Soul Hunters: Hunting, Animism, and Personhood among the Siberian Yukaghirs*. Berkeley: University of California Press, 2007.

Williams, Drid. *Anthropology and the Dance: Ten Lectures*. Urbana: University of Illinois Press, 2004.

Zhambalova, S. G. *Profannyi i Sakral'nyi Miry Ol'khonskikh Buriat (XIX-XX Vv.)*. Novosibirsk: "Nauka," Sibirskaia izdatel'skaia firma RAN, 2000.

Zhukovskaia, N. L. "Buriatskii Shamanizm Segodnia: Vozrozhdenie Ili Evolutsiia?" In *Materialy Mezhdunar. Kongr. "Shamizm i Inye Tradutsionnye Verovaniia i Praktiki" Mokva: Rossiia, 7–12 Iulia 1999 g.*, 3:162–76. Moskva, 2000.

Zhukovskaya, N. L. "Neo-Shamanism in the Context of the Contemporary Ethno-Cultural Situation in the Republic of Buryatia." *Inner Asia* 2, no. 1 (2000).

———. "Religion and Ethnicity in Eastern Russia, Republic of Buryatia: A Panorama of the 1990s." *Central Asian Survey* 14, no. 1 (1995): 25–42.

———. "The Shaman in the Context of Rural History and Mythology (Tory Village, Tunka District, Buryat Republic)." *Inner Asia: Occasional Papers of the Mongolia and Inner Asia Studies Unit* 2, no. 1 (1997): 90–107.

INDEX

Abasheev, D. A., 120
Adyk, 49. *See also* Novonikolaevsk
aesthetics, 181–94, 239
Aga Buryat Autonomous Okrug, 7, 40, 131, 140, 152, 159, 163, 201. *See also* Buryat Autonomous Okrugs
ail, 58–59, 109
Akhin, 59, 107
Alar, 45
alcohol (vodka/*tarisun*), 2, 11, 15, 16, 17, 29, 35, 36, 67, 68, 70–71, 72, 73, 74, 76–77, 79, 80, 81–82, 92, 93, 94, 95–96, 97–99, 102, 103, 111, 113, 142, 183, 196, 197–98, 206, 208–9, 210, 211, 227, 233; alcoholism, 74, 120. *See also* offerings (for spirits)
Aleksei, 35–36, 46, 62, 63, 74, 88, 89–90, 109, 215–16, 222–23, 225, 226, 228, 229, 233, 234, 241, 242–43
All-Buryat Association for the Development of Culture (VARK), 131–34, 137, 154, 157–58, 166, 246
Altai, 220, 224, 242
Altargana festival, 44, 137, 142, 166, 174, 175
ancestors (and spirits), 11, 17, 29, 78, 87–88, 92, 97, 101, 106–7, 111–12, 176, 178, 196–99, 206, 217, 224, 234, 246–47; clan founders, 38, 59, 87–88, 172, 245. *See also individual names*; genealogy
Anderson, David, 85, 141, 165, 230
Andrei, 44, 194, 196, 199, 207, 209, 212, 217
Angara River, 42, 156, 203
Angarsk, 29, 43, 53, 63, 92, 140–41, 160, 164, 167, 225
Arzyutov, D. V., 165
Ashabagat clan, 109, 222, 223
Atkinson, Jane, 212–13
Austin, J. L., 18–19
Ayanga ensemble, 140, 142, 186–87, 189

Badluev, Dandar, 172, 182
Baiandai; Raion, 45, 55; settlement, 196
Baikal ensemble, 128, 172, 182
Baikal (Lake), 1, 3, 7, 37, 40, 127, 204, 207–8, 233, 242
Baikal region, 11, 38, 41–45, 88, 122, 136, 141, 153, 174, 218, 232, 242
Bair, 170, 180
Baitag, 87, 91–92, 96, 101, 203, 204, 213
Baldaev, S. P., 177–78
Baldaeva, Alla, 134

Balzer, Marjorie, 141, 250
Barlukova, I. V., 120
bar'sa (offering site), 74–75, 78, 79, 110, 194, 222, 244
Bateson, Gregory, 19
Bauer, Otto, 121
Bayan Tala ensemble, 139, 146, 175, 182
Bazarov, Boris, 201, 214
Belarus, 130, 152
belonging, 6, 8, 16–17, 23–26, 85–113, 117, 145–48, 170–90, 199–200, 218, 236; aesthetics of, 31, 184, 189–90, 194, 239–40; civic, 8, 21, 25, 86, 145–48, 176–77, 189–90, 236; idioms of, 85–86, 110, 145; national, 8, 21, 24–25, 124, 141–42, 147–48, 180, 188. See also communitas; kinship; placemaking
Bernstein, Anya, 232
Birobidjan Jewish Autonomous Oblast, 152
Bokhan, 45
Boldonov, Ia. A. and N. C., 119
Bolsheviks, 9, 39, 121–22, 124; Revolution, 39, 120
Böö Murgel shamans association, 201, 206–7, 215
Bourdieu, Pierre, 17, 110, 112, 183, 239
Bromlei, Iulian, 165
Bubaev, Semien, 243
Bubain Toodei, 243–44
Buddhism, 9, 39, 132–33, 140, 193, 206, 212; calendar, 136; deities, 68; lamas and monks, 126–27, 129, 160, 206, 214, 245; missionaries, 39; temples, 127, 245
Bukha Noyon, 38, 172, 245
Bulagat: ancestor, 38; clan, 38, 46, 109, 173, 203, 222, 245
Bulen, 203, 205
Bura clan, 59, 87–88, 203
Burnatskom (Buryat National Committee), 39, 120

Burovskii local administration, 55, 59. See also Bura clan
Buryat Autonomous Okrugs; history, 40; in 1993 constitution, 153; unification with larger regions, 41, 162–63. See also Aga Buryat Autonomous Okrug; Ust'-Orda Buryat Autonomous Okrug
Buryat-Mongolian People's Party, 131–32
Buryat national culture, 8–10, 20–22, 25, 44, 64, 116–26, 129–45, 147–48, 167; cultural-national construction, 4, 5, 9, 13, 24, 30, 40, 116–17, 121–23, 125, 127–29; exclusion/inclusion of shamanism, 21–22, 32, 116, 126–27, 202, 212, 214, 218–20, 240, 242; performing arts as part of, 2, 20–21, 64, 125, 172, 176, 189, 214, 244, 248; renaissance of, 1, 31, 130–31, 133–35, 140, 145, 147, 167, 172, 238. See also dance; music; performance; theater (genre)
Buryat republic / Buryatia, 29, 31, 41, 44, 127, 128–30, 132, 134, 135–36, 140, 172, 186, 250; Buryat-Mongolian Autonomous Soviet Socialist Republic, 39–40, 122; Republic of Buryatia (1991–present), 7, 11, 21, 29, 32, 42–43, 44, 54, 130, 132, 152, 154, 157, 188, 192, 200, 245
Buryat State University, 226, 246, 252
Butler, Judith, 18
byt, 117–19

Center for Buryat Culture (Irkutsk), 43, 140, 146, 159–60, 165, 181, 186, 241, 250, 252
Center for the Preservation and Development of the Buryat Ethnos (Irkutsk), 165, 207, 209, 214, 217
China, 7, 42, 137
Chinggis Khan, 47, 137

INDEX

Chita: city, 120; Oblast, 7, 71, 152, 159, 163
Christianity, 27, 39, 42, 231; Russian Orthodox church/faith, 39, 42, 44, 79, 80, 247
Cisbaikalia, 1, 6, 22, 24, 29, 32, 38–41, 42, 44, 48, 58, 60, 61, 69, 70, 71, 80, 83, 86, 88, 89, 101, 107, 110, 113, 118, 119, 127, 129–37, 140–41, 145–48, 151–68, 171, 174, 183, 185, 188, 192–94, 199, 200, 202, 203–7, 208, 212, 213, 215–17, 219–20, 225, 230, 234–35, 236, 239, 240, 241, 245–46, 247–48
clans, 72, 81–82, 86, 87–88, 91, 97, 100–101, 105–6; theories and definitions, 38, 57–60, 99–100, 106–9. *See also* ancestors (and spirits); belonging; genealogy; kinship
cleansing (within rites), 76, 92, 93, 143, 196, 227
clothes, 172, 200, 210; as gifts, 71, 81, 82; required for rites and rituals, 80, 100. See also *khadag* (scarf)
collectivization, 12, 24, 29, 31, 48, 125
commensality, 17, 67, 70, 86, 97–98, 101, 108, 109, 181, 218, 227
communion, 5, 6, 13, 15, 17, 21, 25, 30, 96–101, 102–3, 108, 109, 112, 145, 148, 184, 189, 205, 218, 239, 240, 249
communitas, 13, 17, 30, 31, 103, 108, 123, 181, 184, 188, 198, 218. *See also* Turner, Victor
costume: in dance, 21, 171, 173, 176; in folklore performance, 20, 138, 142, 143; headdress, 138, 171, 208, 209, 211; national costume, 20, 155; in rituals, 89, 213; shamans, 22, 200, 203, 206, 208, 209–10, 213, 244–45; traditional, 1, 21, 244. *See also degel; khadag* (scarf)
Curtin, Jeremiah, 222–23

dance, 4–5, 170–90; choreography, 2, 123, 170–72, 179; history, 123, 128, 171; theories of, 179–81, 183. *See also* Buryat national culture; *yokhor*
Dangina ensemble, 139
Daur Mongols, 90, 213
degel, 20, 138, 142, 151, 208, 244
Dmitri (Dima), 53–54, 61, 62, 76, 77, 78–79, 81–82, 86, 87–88, 91, 92, 94, 96, 97, 104–5, 107, 110, 213
Dombrowski, Kirk, 27
dom kul'tura. *See* houses of culture
Donahoe, Brian, 232
donations: to purchase animals for ritual, 91, 111; to shamans association, 200. *See also* homeland associations (*zemliachestvo*)
Dugarov, D. S., 178
Durkheim, Emile, 17, 103, 112

Eastern Siberian State Academy of Culture and the Arts, 45, 135, 142, 171
Ekhirit: clan, 38, 46, 59, 87, 91, 109, 196, 203; ancestor, 38
Ekhirit-Bulagat: dialect, 38, 68; Raion, 25, 29, 45, 46, 49, 55–68, 78, 81, 89, 93, 95, 98, 99, 139, 143, 147, 217, 228
Emneg Toodei, 245–46, 248
Erbanov, M. N., 122, 125, 126
Ërde, 242
Erdem Theatre, 1, 2, 9, 171
Erzhena, 53–54, 61, 62, 77, 78–79, 81–82, 96, 102, 105, 107, 110, 139, 143, 145, 146
ethnos theory, 165, 251
Evans-Pritchard, Edward, 106
Evenki, 37, 85, 141, 174, 241–42
ezhen. *See under* spirits

federalism, 4, 24–25, 122, 152–55
fire, 17, 35, 68, 72, 76–77, 79, 81, 92–93, 95, 96, 99, 101, 103, 111, 143, 144, 160, 183, 196, 198, 227. *See also* hearth

folklore, 61–62, 64, 117–19, 177, 186, 242; definition, 30, 119; ensembles, 20–21, 25, 50, 53–54, 72, 134–35, 136, 137–39, 140, 166, 172–73, 174–75, 186, 213, 244; preservation of, 172
framing, 18–23, 25, 116–48, 185, 186, 218–20, 240, 248, 250; public framing (in news media), 124, 161, 167, 190, 214, 219, 244, 245; theatrical frame, 19–23, 123, 143–45

Gakhan, 50, 55, 146, 228
Geertz, Clifford, 18, 112
gender, 18–19, 58, 89, 100–101, 112; in genealogy, 106–7, 197, 246; in performance, 138, 143, 172; restrictions, 80, 91, 100; in ritual, 68, 71, 72, 76–77, 79, 80, 91, 100–101, 195–98. See also *toodei* (grandmother spirit)
genealogy, 17, 61, 63, 94, 106, 107–8, 193, 225, 231; broken, 58, 61, 106–7, 199; lineage group, 58, 193; practice of counting joints, 106; shamanic assistance with, 212. See also kinship
Geser Khan, 45, 194; epic poem, 128
Goffman, Erving, 3, 18–20, 116, 123, 143
Graber, Kathryn, 230

habitualization/habitus, 31, 111, 183, 239
Hamayon, Roberte, 97, 174, 178
Handelman, Don, 14, 104, 112
hearth, 6, 16, 17–18, 24, 29, 30, 32, 53, 68, 70, 75–76, 81, 91, 99, 101, 108, 110–11, 112, 142, 144, 193–94, 199, 213, 229
hierarchy, 14, 111, 188; of belonging, 188, 231; within clans, 72, 92, 103, 236; of rituals, 204. See also precedence
Hobart, Angela, 183
homeland, 7, 22, 36, 37–41, 79, 121–22, 126–27, 164, 176, 187–89; ancestral, 30, 68, 78, 85–86, 109, 168, 199, 202, 239; *malaia rodina*, 75, 110, 199, 222; national, 43, 233, 236; *nyutag*, 75
homeland associations (*zemliachestvo*), 105, 134
hospitality, 15, 16, 29, 30, 50, 54, 61, 67–84, 98, 101–2, 111, 113, 119, 142, 151, 183, 231, 234; analogues in collective rites, 101, 111, 188, 234; critiques of, 83; hosting, 71–72, 74, 81–82, 102, 187–88; idioms of, 101, 187–88, 234; in relation to indigeneity, 188, 234
Hoton Babai, 211, 217
houses of culture, 1, 9, 50, 54, 125, 137–39, 142, 171; *klub*, 125, 139, 145
Humphrey, Caroline, 6, 10, 15, 57–58, 73, 81, 90, 99, 104, 107, 109, 146, 192, 213, 218
Hundley, Helen, 60

indigeneity, 23, 26–29, 32–33, 188, 229–32, 249–50; Buryats as indigenous population, 4, 7, 28, 32–33, 39, 44, 187–89, 227–28, 230–31, 232, 249–50; critiques of, 28, 230–31; global discourses, 26–29, 231, 240, 242–43, 250; indigenous relationships to place, 4, 23, 28–29, 32, 109–10, 187–88, 227–28, 232–33, 235; in Russia, 3–4, 7, 9, 27–29, 39, 60, 122, 229–30, 232–33, 235, 240, 241, 242, 252; theories and definitions, 32–33, 109–10, 141–42, 230–32. See also *korenizatsiia*; placemaking; shamanism
infrastructure, 1, 110, 124–26, 241, 251; link with cultural development, 31, 124–25, 148, 189; as state topography, 128–29, 189, 235–36; in unification campaign, 157, 241
Ingold, Tim, 110
Inner Asia, 8, 10–11, 39, 45, 47, 59, 68, 75, 93, 97, 106, 108, 192

intelligentsia: Buryat, 4, 39, 119–21, 130, 133–34, 154, 157, 165, 186; purges, 40, 126–27
inward-facing forms, 6, 15, 18, 21–22, 25, 30, 31–32, 64, 112, 117, 123, 144, 183, 190, 205, 219, 239–40, 245. *See also* Janus-like forms; outward-facing forms
Irkut River, 42, 203, 247
Irkutsk, 1, 29, 31, 41–45, 46, 51–53, 54, 63, 75, 92, 105, 136–37, 140–41, 142, 146, 148, 155–56, 159–61, 163, 165–68, 181, 185, 187–89, 194, 203, 209, 217, 219–20, 223, 226, 228, 232, 241–42, 244, 247, 249; Airport, 203; Governorate, 38, 39; history of, 41–42; market, 51, 54, 105; Museum of Art, 224; Palace of Sport, 160; Stadium of Labor, 204; State Linguistic University, 166; State Technical University, 43, 156, 226; State University, 43; teachers' seminary, 119–20
Irkutsk Oblast, 4, 7, 21, 22, 25, 27, 31, 40–41, 57, 141, 151–52, 153–54, 155, 162–63, 167, 188, 194, 219, 225, 228, 240, 241, 251; Center for the Preservation of Heritage, 135
Ivolginskii Raion, 245

Jackson, Michael, 183
Janus-like forms, 6, 22, 25, 32, 190, 219, 240, 250

Kapferer, Bruce, 182
Kapsal, 87, 244
Keane, Webb, 19
Khabarovsk, 48, 50, 55, 56, 139. *See also* Shikhi
khadag (scarf), 45, 71, 81, 143, 151, 188, 248
Khagdaev, Valentin, 160, 232, 242
Khalkha: language, 38, 47; Mongols, 38
Khamutaev, Vladimir, 131, 133, 154

Khangalov, Matvei, 119–20, 177, 179, 181, 208, 214
Khara-Nur, 48, 55, 56, 206
Kharazargai, 59, 88, 222
Khertoi: ancestor, 59, 87, 91; clan, 59, 72, 78, 79–80, 81, 88, 90, 91–92, 94, 104–5, 106–7, 110, 196, 215; *ulus* settlement, 48, 54, 55, 56, 76, 78–79, 80, 87, 92, 96, 105, 110, 213
Khongodor clan, 38
Khori: clan, 38, 68, 137; dialect, 38; origin myth, 171–72
Khoroshikh, Pavel, 224
khoziain: as head of household or host, 70–72, 91, 188; as master spirit, 87, 101, 231, 234
khubi (portion), 70–71, 91, 94–96, 98–100, 101, 102
Khudian Gol ensemble, 139
Khuty, 44, 46–47, 48, 50–54, 55, 56, 58–59, 61, 68–69, 71–74, 75–76, 80, 85–86, 87, 88, 90, 101, 105, 107, 108, 110, 117, 118, 146, 206, 217; brigade, 51; *tailgan* to dedicate a serge, 193–200, 203, 212
kinship, 8, 24, 57–61, 85–113; anthropological studies, 17, 58, 59–61, 85, 106–9; defining vs. constituting, 8, 57–61, 86, 106–9; emplaced kinship, 24, 109–10, 112; lineages, 8, 38, 58–59, 87, 97, 101, 106, 112, 142, 193, 195, 196–98, 199, 212, 239; malleability of, 57–58, 107–8; networks, 44, 104–5, 146; patriliny, 8, 30, 58–59, 79, 86, 101, 106–7, 108; practical, 107; ritual, 17, 116. *See also* belonging; genealogy; ritual
knowledge, 2, 63, 234, 250; anxiety regarding, 63, 199; of genealogy, 61, 106–7, 109, 199; of language, 90; of rituals, 61, 63, 80–81, 89–90, 109, 112, 203, 214; of shamanic practice, 90, 201, 207, 212, 214, 215, 217

kolkhozy, 48
Komsomol, 125, 128, 176
korenizatsiia, 39, 122, 123, 126–29
Krader, Lawrence, 59
Kuda: Buryats, 45; Native Administration, 46; River, 36, 222; Valley, 87, 88, 119, 139, 222, 225, 227, 229, 244
kul'tura, 117–19
Kuper, Adam, 230

land, 23–29, 37–41, 124–27, 166–68, 229, 234–36; conservation, 232–33; indigenous relations with, 23–29, 32–33, 85, 109–10, 187–88, 230–32, 234–36; mining, oil, and quarrying, 23, 28, 32, 42, 223, 225, 232, 233, 235. See also placemaking; shamanist topography
Langer, Suzanne, 182
Lenin, Vladimir, 128–29, 176
liminality, 13–14, 30, 94, 103–4, 111
lineage. *See under* genealogy; kinship

Magtaal ensemble, 134–35
magtaal praise song, 128, 172
Makhutov, Edward, 206
Malan Noyon, 223
Maleev, Valeri, 151, 153–54, 160, 163
Mankhai, 23, 26, 28, 32, 35–36, 87–88, 222–36, 241, 245, 250
Manzhigeev, I. A., 178
master spirits. *See under* spirits
Mauss, Marcel, 17, 83, 112, 183
media, 15, 20–21, 22, 25, 27, 64, 124, 151, 159, 200, 204–5, 214, 215, 219, 228, 246, 251, 252; propaganda, 126, 159; social media, 252. See also unification of Irkutsk Oblast and Ust'-Orda Bruyat Autonomous Okrug
menstruation, 80, 100
Metzo, Katherine, 232

migration, 55–57, 136, 222, 230; countryside to city, 24, 29, 55–57, 104, 134, 218, 246; forced relocation, 27, 55; historic migration, 37
Mikhailov, V. A., 119–20
milk, 16, 24, 51, 54, 105; as offering, 35, 68, 76–77, 79, 93–94, 97, 172, 197, 206, 227, 233
Misha, 2, 5, 8, 25, 46, 135, 170, 244
mongol spirit. *See under* spirits
Mongolia, 38, 39, 47, 68, 126, 131, 136–37, 201; language, 38, 47, 120, 193
Moscow, 3, 128, 252; government, 120, 122, 125–26
Muromtsovka, 48, 50, 51, 52, 55, 56, 59, 63, 69, 73, 206
music, 8, 22, 122, 128, 140, 171–72, 186. See also *magtaal* praise song; table songs
Muskom, 122

Nastia, 142
Natalya, 171, 180–81
National Cultural Autonomy, 4, 25, 28, 31, 33, 121–22, 151–68, 235, 240, 250
national self-determination, 121
Negedel (Movement for National Unity), 131–32
Nikolaeva, Baira, 187–88
Nikolai, 35, 46, 50, 52, 53, 87, 102, 137, 193, 223, 224–25, 226, 230, 242–43, 244
Novonikolaevsk, 46–56, 59, 61–62, 69, 72–73, 78–79, 85, 90–92, 96, 104–5, 107, 135, 139, 145–46, 176, 181, 204, 207. *See also* Adyk
Novosibirsk University, 224
Nukutsk, 45, 119

obo, 38, 93, 183, 193, 235
offerings (for spirits), 29–30, 35–36, 62–63, 68, 70–71, 75–81, 87–88, 89, 101, 196–98, 203, 210, 226–27;

annual household rituals, 29, 76–79; feeding the *mongol*, 29, 77–78, 109; restrictions/proscriptions, 79–80, 98; at the roadside, 11, 29, 67–68, 74–75, 79, 99, 222, 244; theatricalized representation, 143, 173. *See also* ritual; *tailgan*
Okladnikov, Alexey, 224
okrugs. *See* Aga Buryat Autonomous Okrug; Buryat Autonomous Okrugs; National Cultural Autonomy; Ust'-Orda Buryat Autonomous Okrug
Ol'khon: Island, 40, 201, 207, 209, 213, 215, 232, 233; Raion, 40, 127, 160, 163, 232, 242; Shaman Rock, 209, 232
Onon, Urgunge, 90, 213
outward-facing forms, 6, 15, 18, 21–22, 25, 30, 32, 64, 123, 144, 148, 188–89, 190, 219, 239–40. *See also* inward-facing forms; Janus-like forms

patriliny. *See under* kinship
performance, 5, 6–7, 13–15, 17–23, 116–17, 123–24, 128, 134–35, 137–39, 140, 142–45, 170, 182–83, 185–89, 212–15, 239–40, 249; of indigeneity, 26–27, 250; performativity, 15, 18–19, 144, 212–14, 240, 244, 249; performing arts, 3–4, 5, 14, 116–17, 123–24, 128, 147–48, 182, 239–40. *See also* Buryat national culture; framing
Petrovich, Ivan (Khertoi elder), 72, 91, 107
Pierce, Charles, 179
placemaking, 25, 30, 32, 109–10, 189, 199, 222–36. *See also* shamanist topography
po-solntsu. *See* sunwise direction
Povinelli, Elizabeth, 27
pragmatic meanings, 22, 185–89, 240

prayers, 13, 17, 77, 78, 79, 87–88, 89–93, 95–96, 97, 99, 100, 103, 107, 111, 112, 143, 160, 196, 197, 205, 206, 213, 227
precedence, 222–36; in relation to indigeneity, 188, 231; and rites, 70–72, 91, 188, 203, 204. *See also* hierarchy
Pribaikal National Park, 232
Putin, Vladimir, 153, 155, 157, 219, 233, 240, 247–48, 251–52, 253

Quijada, Justine, 199

Radlov, Vasily, 120
reciprocity, 16, 29–30, 67–84, 99, 101–2, 104, 113–14, 192, 223, 232, 239; between clans, 81–82; within communities, 61, 71, 72–74, 105; critiques of term, 29, 82–84; with kin, 24, 63, 86, 105, 107–8, 147; with spirits, 26, 28, 32, 73, 75, 86, 88, 108, 218, 220, 225, 231–32, 233–34, 240, 249. *See also* hospitality
Renner, Karl, 121–22, 164
Republic of Sakha (Yakutia), 47, 242
ritual, 13–23, 67–113, 141–45, 192–220, 233–35; ritualization, 13–21, 29, 67, 83, 96–97, 99, 104, 110–13, 212–13. *For particular practices, see also* offerings (for spirits); *serge* (tethering post); shamanism; *tailgan*
rod, 38, 58, 59. *See also* clans
Russia, 26, 33, 38, 42, 119, 121–22, 132–33, 139, 152–55, 163–64, 230, 251–53; Russian Empire, 26; Russian Federation, 7, 41, 130, 133, 152–55, 162–63, 230, 251; Russian Soviet Federative Socialist Republic, 39, 152
Russian Academy of Science, 45
Russian Geographical Society, 120

sacrifice, 12, 30, 72, 91–92, 96–99, 196, 197–98, 204, 206, 211. *See also* offerings (for spirits); *tailgan*

Sagaalgan (Lunar New Year), 43, 132, 136, 138, 140, 151, 159, 160, 161, 168, 174, 185, 214
Sahlins, Marshall, 82–83
Sakhilgaan shamans association, 22, 23, 32, 200, 202–5, 207, 208, 219, 235, 240, 242, 244–46, 248, 249, 250
salamat, 77–79, 93
Saltikov, I. G., 120
Sanditov, D. S., 154
Sapir, Edward, 9, 117
Schechner, Richard, 3, 14
serge (tethering post), 32, 136, 193–200, 235, 244; dancing around, 143–44, 179, 183; dedication of, 193, 196, 203, 212, 244; history, 193–94; as national symbol, 136, 194, 235
shamanism, 10–12, 21–22, 32–33, 39, 89–91, 192–220; commercialization of, 215–18; in hunting vs. pastoral societies, 96–97; initiation of shamans, 11, 89–91, 201–2, 206–7; institutionalized shamanism and shamans associations, 21–23, 32, 64, 192–93, 200–2, 216–17, 218–20, 249; local practice in Cisbaikalia, 22, 32, 63, 80, 148, 202–5, 215, 217, 218–20; local shamans / ritual practitioners, 88–91, 192, 216; neoshamanism, 200–202, 215, 220; purges, 11, 89, 126–27; theories and definitions, 10–11, 192–93. *See also individual associations*; ritual; shamanist topography; *tailgan*
shamanist topography, 24, 32, 110, 193–200, 204, 217, 219, 229, 235, 244, 246, 249
sheree, 93–94, 98, 101, 111
Shertoi, 48, 50
Shikhi, 48. *See also* Khabarovsk
Shireterov, Budazhab, 208–10
Shirokogoroff, S. M., 165
Shternberg, Lev, 120

Siberia, 2–3, 5, 7, 11, 26, 33, 37, 42, 68, 92, 117, 119, 141, 192, 214, 230, 231, 241, 251
Singer, Milton, 13
Skrynnikova, T., 176, 178–79, 180
Smith, William Robertson, 97
Sneath, David, 59–60, 106, 108
Soviet nationality policy, 121–22
Soviet Union. *See* USSR
sovkhoz, 47, 48–52, 55, 63, 104–5, 107, 145–47
Speransky, Mikhail, 60
spirits, 2, 10–12, 16, 24, 67–68, 70, 73, 75, 83–84, 86–88, 93, 95–96, 96–97, 101, 108, 109–10, 112–13, 201–2, 203, 208, 210–12, 217–18, 224–25, 231–32, 234–35; master spirits (*ezhen*), 11, 35, 75, 87, 96, 101, 202, 203, 209, 211, 217, 223, 225, 234; *mongol* spirit, 68, 77–78; pantheon of, 11, 201–2, 211, 217; possession by, 208, 211; *tengeri* spirits, 11, 202, theatrical representations, 143, 172–73. *See also individual spirit names*; ancestors (and spirits); *khoziain*; offerings (for spirits); shamanism; *toodei* (grandmother spirit)
sprinkling. *See* offerings (for spirits)
Stalin, Joseph, 40, 89, 121–22, 126–27, 128
Stepanov, Leonid, 195–97, 200, 202, 203, 205, 214, 217
Stepanova, Nadia, 201, 215
Stepnye Napevy ensemble, 1–2, 46, 135, 139, 160, 170, 172, 241
Strathern, Marilyn, 184
Stroganova, Elena, 132–33
sunwise direction, 16, 21, 70–71, 76, 93, 95, 101, 111, 174, 175, 183, 184
Sur-kharban traditional sports competition, 72, 128, 138–39, 140, 143, 145–46, 166, 174, 214
swan maidens, 38, 172, 173

table, 2, 15, 16, 68, 69–71, 81, 82, 92, 100, 101, 111, 209. See also *sheree*
table songs, 69–70
tagsha buryashad, 89. See also shamanism
Tahoe-Baikal Institute, 233, 243
tailgan, 2–3, 11–12, 17, 30, 59, 86–88, 91–100, 109, 111–13, 193, 196–200, 201, 203–5, 207–14, 215, 218, 222–23, 243–44, 245–46. See also donations; *khubi* (portion); sacrifice
tarisun. See alcohol (vodka/*tarisun*)
tea: drinking, 67, 68, 69, 208; as offering, 7, 11, 15, 67, 68, 111, 209
tengeri. See under spirits
Tengeri shamans association, 32, 201, 206–14, 217–20, 242, 245
theater (genre): in contemporary Buryat culture, 45, 142; early Buryat plays, 120, 123; as part of Buryat National Culture, 123, 128, 129
theatricalization (of rites, customs), 21, 141–45, 167, 172, 213, 215
Tishanin, Alexander, 151, 153, 154, 155, 160, 163, 166, 167
tobacco: as gift, 82, 142; as offering, 74–75, 142; use of, 74
toodei (grandmother spirit), 88, 101, 243, 245
trance, 89, 178, 201, 207, 208, 211, 213, 245
Transbaikalia, 176, 193, 232; Governorate, 38, 39; Krai, 159, 163
travel and transport: bus, 2, 46; *motorola*, 69; petrol, 52, 61, 73, 104, 146; private minibus, 46, 54, 194; tractors, 52, 56, 92, 104. See also offerings (for spirits); reciprocity
TsSRBE. See Center for the Preservation and Development of the Buryat Ethnos (Irkutsk)
Tsydynzhapov, Gombo, 123, 171
Tsydypov, Viktor, 207, 208

Tsyrendorzhevich, Bayar, 211
Tungusic-speaking peoples, 37, 68, 174
Tunka Valley, 232, 245
türge, 92, 93, 95
Turkic-speaking peoples, 37, 174, 193, 224; terminology in common, 47, 68
Turner, Victor, 3, 13–14, 17, 30, 103, 238

Ukir, 222
Ukraine, 130, 152, 157, 251, 252
Ulaalzai, 140, 142, 186, 188
Ulanbaatar, 137
Ulan-Ude, 29, 43, 44–45, 52, 54, 57, 63, 80, 92, 105, 107, 118, 129, 130, 132, 134–36, 140, 142, 157–58, 174, 230, 246–48; Anti-Religious Museum, 127; Buryat Theatre of Opera and Ballet, 45; Music and Drama Theater of Buryatia, 128; shamans associations in, 192–93, 200–201, 206, 215, 217–20, 245–46 (see also Böö Mürgel shamans association; Tengeri shamans association). See also Verkhneudinsk
uliger, 128, 172
ulus, 24, 29, 30, 51, 54, 55, 58, 75–76, 86, 87–88, 91, 92, 110, 178, 193, 194, 206, 222, 235, 239; meanings and history, 47–49, 59–61, 106–9
unification of Irkutsk Oblast and Ust'-Orda Bruyat Autonomous Okrug, 151–68; campaign, 27, 141, 152, 155–59, 165–66; opposition, 157–58, 162; referendum, 21, 25, 31, 41, 154–55, 161–62, 167. See also media
Urmaeva, M. D., 69
USSR, 4, 24, 26, 39–40, 48–50, 89, 118, 121–22, 126, 128, 130–31, 135, 152–53, 176, 230, 232, 238–39
Ust'-Orda Buryat Autonomous Okrug, 1, 4, 7, 12, 21, 22, 25, 27, 29, 31, 32, 40, 41, 43, 45, 57, 127, 129–30, 131, 133–36, 140, 141, 143, 151, 152, 153–54, 157, 158,

160, 162, 167, 172, 186, 194, 200, 202, 220, 223, 225, 235, 240 (*see also* Buryat Autonomous Okrugs); Center for Cultural Heritage, 226; Committee for Culture, 140; State National Museum, 136
Ust'-Orda settlement, 1, 35, 45–46, 53, 62, 88, 105, 133, 137, 138, 139, 142, 151, 157, 167, 171, 204, 223
utkha, 89–90, 243

Van Gennep, Arnold, 13
VARK. *See* All-Buryat Association for the Development of Culture (VARK)
Verkhneudinsk, 44, 123. *See also* Ulan-Ude
Vitia, Diadia (Vitali), 46, 52–53, 55, 58, 61, 69–70, 71, 73, 118; family role, 105, 107, 108, 110, 193–96; role as shaman, 62–63, 75–77, 79–81, 90–91, 213, 216–17
vodka. *See* alcohol (vodka/*tarisun*)

weddings, 74, 81–82, 104–5, 130; dancing at, 21, 177–78, 179, 180, 184, 186; gifts, 29, 81–82, 102; hosting, 81–82, 105; theatricalization, 142
Williams, Drid, 179

Yabloko (political party), 157
yahan (bone), 58, 106
Yeltsin, Boris, 57, 153
yokhor, 21, 31, 173–90; description, 174–75; experience of dancing, 181–84, 188; generational significance, 186–87, 188, 189; historical significance, 174, 176–78, 180, 189; symbolism and interpretation, 178–81. *See also* Buryat national culture; dance; framing

zemliachestvo. *See* homeland associations (*zemliachestvo*)
Zhamsarano, Tsyben, 77, 119–20, 126
Zhukovskaya, Natalia, 200, 202

JOSEPH J. LONG, PHD, is a social anthropologist based in Scotland. He is currently a director at the charity Scottish Autism, where he leads a program of applied research.

For Indiana University Press

Tony Brewer, Artist and Book Designer
Gary Dunham, Acquisitions Editor and Director
Anna Garnai, Production Coordinator
Sophia Hebert, Assistant Acquisitions Editor
Samantha Heffner, Marketing and Publicity Manager
Katie Huggins, Production Manager
Dave Hulsey, Associate Director and Director of Sales and Marketing
Nancy Lightfoot, Project Manager/Editor
Bethany Mowry, Acquisitions Editor
Dan Pyle, Online Publishing Manager
Michael Regoli, Director of Publishing Operations
Stephen Williams, Assistant Director of Marketing
Jennifer Witzke, Senior Artist and Book Designer